INVESTING
for
PASSIVE INCOME

*Get Up to 10% Dividends Each Year
and Make Money for Retirement
with Dividend Growth Stocks,
MLPs and REITs*

BY FREEMAN PUBLICATIONS

TABLE OF CONTENTS

DIVIDEND GROWTH INVE$TING

GET A STEADY 8% PER YEAR
Even in
A ZERO INTEREST RATE WORLD

FEATURING THE 13 BEST HIGH YIELD STOCKS, REITS, MLPS AND CEFS FOR RETIREMENT INCOME

HOW TO GET THE MOST OUT OF THIS BOOK

To help you along your investing journey, we've created a free bonus companion course that includes spreadsheets, bonus video content, and additional resources that will help you get the best possible results. We highly recommend you sign up now to get the most out of this book. You can do that by going to the link below or scanning the QR code with your cell phone

https://freemanpublications.com/bonus

Or text the word BONUS to 844-968-4152 (US only)

Free bonus #1: Company Valuation 101 video course ($97 value)

In this 8 part video course, you'll discover our process for accurately valuing a company. This will help you determine if a stock is overvalued, correctly valued, or a bargain. Giving you an indicator of whether to buy or not.

Free bonus #2: Guru Portfolios Analyzed ($37 value)

In these videos, we analyze the stock portfolios of Billionaire investors like Warren Buffett. As well as top entrepreneurs like Bill Gates.

Free bonus #3: Crypto 101 ($47 value)

When you have a paradigm-shifting technology like cryptocurrency and blockchain ... there are multiple ways to profit from it.

But before you rush out and buy every altcoin under the sun... there is a smarter way of doing this.

The ways used by hedge funds and Billionaire investors to make massive profits from the price of Bitcoin and other cryptocurrencies.

And you don't need anything more than a regular brokerage account to do so.

We covered exactly how to do this in a private call for our premium members recently and you'll get access to this video for free.

Free bonus #4: 2 Stocks to Sell Right Now ($17 value)

These 2 stocks are in danger of plummeting in the next 12 months. They're both popular with retail investors, and one is even in the top 5 most held stocks on Robinhood. Believe us; you don't want to be holding these going into 2021 and beyond.

Free bonus #5: AI Disruptor - The $4 Stock Poised to be the Next Big Thing in Computing ($17 value)

This under the radar company, which less than 1% of investors have heard of, is at the forefront of a breakthrough technology that will change our lives as we know them. Soon this technology will be in every smartphone, tablet, and laptop on the planet.

Free bonus #6: Options 101 ($17 Value)

Options don't have to be risky. In fact, they were invented to re*uce risk. It's no wonder that smart investors like Warren Buffett regularly use options to supplement their long-term portfolio. In this quick start guide, we show you how options work and why they are tools to be utilized rather than feared.

Free bonus #7: The 1 Dividend Stock to Buy and Hold for the Rest of Your Life ($17 Value)

Dividends are the lifeblood of any income investor, and this stock is a cornerstone of any dividend strategy. A true dividend aristocrat with consistent payouts for over 50 years which you'll want to add to your portfolio for sure.

 **Free bonus #8: Top 3 Growth Stocks for 2021 ($17 Value)**

Our 2020 selections outperformed the S&P 500 by 154%. Now we've released our 3 top picks for 2021.

Free Bonus #9: All the images inside this book in color ($17 Value)

As much as we'd like to print these books in full color, the printing costs prohibit us from doing so. So on our website, you can get all the images from the book in full color.

All of these bonuses are 100% free, with no strings attached. You don't need to enter any details except your email address.

To get your bonuses go to

https://freemanpublications.com/bonus

Or text the word BONUS to 844-968-4152 (US only)

INTRODUCTION

Two thousand five hundred years ago, The Greek Philosopher Heraclitus uttered some of the most profound words in human history.

"The only constant in life is change."

These words ring true in investing as they do in any other field. Back in 1990, you could have retired comfortably with a nest egg of $500,000. All you had to do was invest that money into a Treasury Bill, and you would have earned a steady eight percent every year. That's $40,000 every year from what most experts would consider the world's most stable investment.

These days, if you invest $500,000 into the same Treasury Bill, you won't be getting 8% per year, nowhere near that. In 2020, a Treasury Bill paid just 1.25% every year or $6,250 annually. Six thousand odd dollars barely covers the cost of your utility bills and groceries for the year. Compared to this, $40,000 per year is a princely sum indeed.

The American economy has changed massively over the past 30 years, and the stock market has changed with it. Back in the 90s, the buzzword was growth. The internet was going mainstream, and there were a number of companies that were ready to hit the big time. All that talk of growth fueled the dotcom crash of the early 2000s. Many of the darling names of the late 90s, such as Pets.com, 360Networks and eToys went bankrupt. Many individual investors saw their portfolios wiped out and were left scarred for life by the repercussions of this crash. However, the companies that survived the crash turned themselves into billion- and even trillion-dollar corporations, making their investors wealthy in the process. Meaning all that positivity wasn't totally misplaced.

These days, the talk around the stock market is more subdued. Many people ascertain that asset prices are being fueled by cheap debt, yet cheap debt is necessary because there seems to be no other way to jumpstart economic growth. The previous decade (2010-2019) witnessed the longest ever bull run in the stock market's history, but it's debatable whether economic growth kept up with it. The Coronavirus pandemic brought everyone's fears about another economic crash back to the surface, and the government responded by cutting interest rates even further.

This era is unprecedented. Never in history have governments printed money at such a rate to prop up assets, and never have they slashed interest rates as low as they currently are. This low interest rate environment has hit those who need income from their investments the hardest.

This low interest rate phenomenon is so strong that it has even moved from the real world to the virtual world. The fictional Bank of Nook in Nintendo's best selling video game *Animal Crossing: New Horizons* slashed interest rates from 0.5% to 0.05%, in an attempt to stimulate players spending on in-game items.

Back in the real world, this low interest rate environment has sparked fears of all manner of scenarios, ranging from deflation to hyperinflation. Which has led to alternative assets such as gold and cryptocurrencies witnessing huge jumps in value. While these assets make the financial headlines, none of this helps an income seeker since these alternative assets don't have any yields in the form of dividends or interest payments.

Speaking of dividends, while government bond yields have plummeted in the past 30 years, stock dividends have largely followed the same path. Figure 1 below illustrates how the dividend yield of the S&P 500 has varied since 1880.

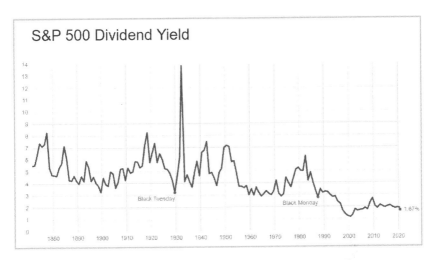

Figure 1: The average ivi en yiel of an S&P 500 stock

While the general trend of the graph has been downward, notice the massive dip after 1990. While spikes and volatility characterize the large portion of the graph, things have become quite stable recently. Yields have been low, fluctuating between 1 and 3 percent, and it looks like they plan on staying there.

In light of these facts, what should you do if you plan to live off the income from your investments?

Searching for Yields

Most investors have had one of two reactions to declining yields. The first has been to withdraw their initial investment (known as the principal) from the markets and stick the money in a savings account. The reasoning is that if the stock market doesn't provide yields, then it makes no sense to expose money to market risk. The problem is that the average savings or money market account doesn't pay investors anything.

17

As of this writing in October 2020, Wells Fargo's Way2Save account pays a pitiful 0.01% interest. That's not a typo. It really is 1/100th of 1 percent. They ought to call it Way2Deplete for all the good that interest rate does. Investors who choose this option avoid stock market risk, but they lose money once you take inflation into account.

The second reaction has been to sell stocks to generate income. For example, if you were earning five percent yields on your portfolio but are now earning just one percent, you could sell enough stock to generate the equivalent of that missing four percent yield.

There's only one problem with this approach. If the stock market falls, you'll have to sell more stock to cover that yield gap. When the stock market is high, you won't need to sell as much, however you'll have less to sell in the first place.

This seems to be a Catch-22 for income investors. Fortunately, that's where we come in. Our objective in this book is to help you spot those investment opportunities that can bring you a high yield without the additional risk that accompanies most high yield stocks and funds.

There are still great income-generating stocks out there. Our view is you need to think outside the box a little bit to spot them. The media and Wall Street are focused completely on the likes of Facebook and Amazon. They have all but ignored the companies we're going to highlight in this book. It's not as if these income-generating companies are small either. Many of the companies we're about to highlight have market caps greater than 30 billion dollars.

This is where the opportunity lies for you. There are companies out there that are steadily paying their shareholders monthly and quarterly paychecks, with yields greater than five percent, and in some cases as much as 10 percent annually. In today's zero interest rate environment, a yield of five percent and above is high. Combined with capital gains, you're looking at returns above eight percent per year from the stocks we will discuss.

The first part of this book will focus on how we've arrived in such a low interest rate environment. Then we'll move to the factors we focus on for profitable long term income investing. Finally we'll spotlight specific stocks, REITs, MLPs, ETFs and funds which satisfy our income investing criteria.

It doesn't matter what the size of your portfolio is now. You don't need a special investing account either, all you need is a standard brokerage account or a retirement account. The companies and strategies we're going to highlight will help you generate a full time passive income and supercharge your retirement. We'll also show you how you can grow a small account to a much larger one thanks to the power of compounding and dividend reinvestment.

All it takes for you to realize this potential is a little work and dedication. Put in the work today, and you and your family will benefit tomorrow.

Chapter 1

WHAT HAPPENED TO SAVINGS ACCOUNTS AND BOND YIELDS?

"You use, to have income an, safety. To,ay, with treasury yiel,s at 0%, you have income or safety."

- Howard Marks, Co-Founder, Oaktree Capital Management.

Before we dive into the best income generation opportunities in the stock market, it's important to understand the economic conditions which led us to this point. After all, bank savings accounts and certificates of deposit (CDs) used to be the norm in everyone's savings plan. These days, they don't provide value, as much as take it away from you when you factor in inflation. So what happened to the savings account, and why do we find ourselves in this position today?

Back in 1981, the average three-month CD paid investors 18.3%. Don't get too excited; the interest rate was this high because inflation was equally high. As time wore on, inflation decreased, and so did bank interest rates. In the 2000s, the interest rate on a CD was between three and five percent, which was still two percentage points higher than inflation. Then came the real estate and stock market crash of 2007-2009. As bad as the stock market crash of 1930 was, it isn't far-fetched to say that the global financial crisis of 2007-2009 had a similar generational impact in the following decade.

This is because the global financial crisis was the first time that one of the pillars of the American economy, real estate, had crashed. Before 2008, real estate had gone just one way, up. No one could have imagined an America where real estate would be worth less tomorrow than it was worth today. Real estate accounted for a large portion of American wealth, and once it dropped, people's savings and access to credit dropped as well.

As a result, the economy suffered, and the government had to figure out ways to solve the crisis. One option was to let everything fall following the principles of the free market. This option would mean assets (stocks and real estate) would drop to record low levels, and after that, market forces would figure out the way forward. In real world terms, this would be equivalent to digging a hole and continuing to dig until you reached the other side.

Most economists agreed that letting assets plummet to rock bottom prices was a terrible idea, with uncertain recovery times and further negative consequences beyond just a bad economy. The specter of the Great Depression also hung heavy on the government's head. The prospect of mass unemployment was unbearable, and as a result, the government chose a second option.

Monetary Band-Aids

The Band-Aid that the government applied was modest at first. In 2008, the US Treasury Department, led by former Goldman Sachs CEO Henry Paulson, announced that the government would guarantee bad assets in the most troubled banks. This was to avoid an all-out collapse of the financial system. This program slowly expanded to securing assets even at good banks. Followed by selectively stepping in to rescue banks close to the government's heart, while letting the others die (*Why the Fe# save# AIG an# not Lehman*, 2008).

Banks borrowed $700 billion from a government program named the Troubled Asset Relief Program (TARP), headed by former Goldman Sachs VP Neel Kashkari. With the governments now guaranteeing the bank's bad assets, these banks soon returned to making a profit.

However, a larger problem brewed. All these newly guaranteed assets needed to be paid for. So now the question was, just *who* was going to pay for all of this? Enter the Federal Reserve bank, headed by Ben Bernanke. The Fed began buying these terrible assets en masse.

So how did the Fed pay for this? It's simple, they started "printing money". Not literally, that's the US Treasury's job, but by purchasing Government securities the Fed adds money to its own balance sheet and newly created dollars to the balance sheets of banks such as Wells Fargo and Goldman Sachs.

Banks then get more money in reserve to lend to consumers, while avoiding a potential run on the bank from people wanting to withdraw their money. In return, the Fed takes ownership of assets, primarily Government bonds.

Economists greeted this level of money printing with great alarm. It wasn't the first time a central bank had tried this strategy. The Weimar Republic of Germany had tried it in the mid 1920s. Their policies led to massive hyperinflation, which threw the country into economic and social turmoil, ultimately leading to the political rise of Adolf Hitler. So to say the Weimar experiment didn't work is like saying the Hindenburg flight didn't go to plan or that Abraham Lincoln didn't enjoy his evening at the theater.

However, cloaked by the fancy name of "Quantitative Easing" (QE), Bernanke's Fed printed so much money that it became the norm to do so. The UK followed, as did the European Central Bank. The Swiss followed shortly thereafter. Meanwhile, the Japanese merely laughed and said that they had been doing this on and off since the 90s and were masters at it, despite the results showing otherwise. (*Japan's Expansionist Policies Have Brought Unexpecte▪ Results*, 2019).

Imbalances

While QE may have benefitted banks and larger institutions, there wasn't much of a trickle down effect for the middle or working class. Small businesses rushed to the bank when they learned big companies were being bailed out, only to find that they had to fulfill ridiculous terms such as having a million dollars in revenue and ten years' worth of profitable account statements. In short, the businesses who could borrow money were the ones who arguably needed it the least.

In the name of reducing asset risk and non-performing loans on their books, banks denied money to the engine room of the economy. Small businesses went bust and wages reduced. Economic reports didn't highlight this because unemployment wasn't increasing. Wage decreases are different from unemployment. Former investment bankers became bank tellers, former business owners worked hourly jobs, and former skilled technicians began waiting tables. So strictly speaking, people were still employed, even if they were in much lower paid positions than before.

The stock market, which is composed of huge companies, did very well with QE. The government purchased bonds from commercial banks, mainly in the form of US treasury notes. This led to bond yields plummeting and stock prices becoming more attractive in comparison to bonds. This led to a flood of money going into the stock market, which is why we see companies like Apple and Amazon now with a market cap of over 1 trillion dollars.

This is the essence of the "K" shaped recovery that economists have been talking about recently (Chen, 2020). The K economy has been highlighted recently as a reaction to the Coronavirus pandemic, but it is part of a larger phenomenon that started after the global financial crisis. From June 2008 to October 2020 (the time of writing), the Fed added almost $4 trillion into the money supply through QE.

A roaring stock market has the bonus side effect of being a political bargaining tool. It's easier to point to rising stock prices and claim to be a genius. But that doesn't change the fact that to print money cheaply, interest rates need to be cut.

This is why rates are at rock bottom today. Because of this low interest rate policy, we have seen rates on Savings and CD accounts plummet to below inflation. Whether the approach is misguided or not is debatable. However, there's no denying the aftereffects of it.

Negative Mortgages and Other Financial Quirks

It's easy to sit back and rail against the government for bad monetary policy. It's equally easy to frame an "us versus them" style argument and say that the rich are greedy, immoral, and so on. The fact is that a lot of the thinking behind QE was backed by solid economic theses. The primary thesis behind low interest rates and flushing the economy with cash is to get people spending money.

The thought process runs like this. With cash readily available for banks, they increase lending to ordinary folks. These people then use the money to buy goods and services that benefit small businesses. As small business prospects grow, so too does the economy and eventually, the government can stop printing money.

The problem is that everything went pear-shaped somewhere along the way. Banks didn't lend money to the people that needed it the most because they had to satisfy the government's strict leverage rules and set aside additional money for potential losses. The government's intention with this rule was to avoid a repeat of the credit crisis where the banks needed bailing out. As a result, cash didn't trickle to the underprivileged players quickly enough while the financial institutions gobbled it up in hoards.

This meant governments around the world printed even more money, then needed creative solutions to get people to spend more. One method was to then cut interest rates to a level where there was zero incentive to save. This is not just an American phenomenon either, The UK's rates currently sit at 0.1%. Switzerland and Denmark are at -0.75% and -0.6% respectively. Japan, who pioneered QE, sits at -0.1%.

The negative signs aren't a misprint. The government in these countries will charge borrowers money for holding onto their cash. This is why the Swiss giant UBS decided to charge people who held more than 500,000 EUR in savings accounts. Denmark even offers negative interest rate mortgages, which have decreasing payments over time. The effects of these creative policies are still unknown. However, in the States, we can make some ready observations for what QE's economic effects have been thus far.

First, the predicted economic boom from increased spending never came. People lost far too much to begin spending money once again immediately. After all, financial crises don't just bring monetary hardship, they also affect our psyche.

If you're reading this book, you likely have a parent or grandparent who grew up in the aftermath of the Great Depression. This was an entire generation brought up lacking faith in both economic institutions and their own future. This led to characteristics such as frugality with money, and a penchant for savings versus spending. It was only after World War 2, 16 years after the Great Depression when Americans really started spending again.

We're seeing similar effects now as a result of the Global Financial Crisis. At the beginning of 2010, Americans had around $4.8 trillion in total savings across all institutions. In August 2020 that number was $11.5 trillion. If you look at the data since 1975, savings rates have roughly doubled every ten years, regardless of the interest rate environment, but in the last ten years, they have nearly tripled.

Second, one of the underlying economic theories that supported QE was an old friend of any undergrad Economics student, the Phillips Curve. The Phillips Curve theory states that as economic spending increases, inflation increases. As this happens, the economy grows and more job opportunities are available. This leads to lower unemployment. However, between 2008 and 2020, this didn't happen. Inflation remained low, and many people just exchanged higher-paying jobs for lower-paying ones.

This year, the Fed's current Chairman, Jerome Powell, finally said out loud what everyone was thinking all the time. The Phillips Curve was dead. He was correct, but around 60 years too late in saying it. In fact if you look at the data, <u>inflation and unemployment haven't been correlated at all at any point since the 1960s.</u>

The early 1960s was a low unemployment, low inflation environment. The late 1960s was a low unemployment, high inflation environment. The 1970s was a high unemployment, high inflation environment. Between 2008 and 2013 we had high unemployment, low inflation and between 2013 and 2018 we experienced a low unemployment, low inflation environment.

In 2020, we are in an environment where inflation could potentially increase, and unemployment would increase because of it. After all, as more money is printed, the greater the spending amongst those who can access it. This drives prices up. Meanwhile, nationwide shutdowns are forcing more businesses to either lay off staff or permanently close their doors, which leads to an increase in unemployment. Welcome to the K-shaped world.

Meanwhile in the Stock Market...

Nowhere is the evidence of the K-shaped world more stark than with the stock and real estate markets. There aren't any real-time trackers of real estate prices, so media interest has been subdued there. However, America is experiencing a real estate boom (D. Williams, 2020). Many real estate experts are scratching their heads at the way the market is behaving. How does one explain record-high house prices against high unemployment numbers?

The stock market has been even more nonsensical. It began from the bottom of 2009 when QE fueled its growth. Until 2015 or 2016, everyone was under the impression that QE was working and that the economy was recovering. However, with the passing of five years since the crisis, it became increasingly obvious that QE wasn't having its intended effect.

Famed Value investor and hedge fund manager extraordinaire Seth Klarman wrote to his investors in 2015 that the stock market was about to enter a bear market (*2015 Letter - Klarman tells investors he is looking for bargains ami* "*stealth bear market,*" 2015). Klarman's analysis was correct. Things stopped making sense. However, even an investor of his caliber misjudged the effect of the K-shaped recovery.

Klarman's prediction was correct when looking at the broad market. Since 2015-2016, the Russell 2000 index, which tracks small cap companies, has been flat, with periods of intense volatility. In contrast, the S&P 500 has risen like a phoenix, conquering one all-time high after another and scarcely losing breath. What's going on here?

It turns out that the more privileged of the privileged few have used QE to astonishing effect. The S&P 500 is heavily weighted towards the so-called FAANG-M stocks. These companies are Facebook, Amazon, Apple, Netflix, Google, and Microsoft. You see, as QE was unfolding and as everyone was coming to grips with the 2008 financial crisis, the internet finally stepped up and delivered what it had promised back in the late 90s.

Increasing technological advances by these companies, coupled with cheap money, meant growth was inevitable. As these companies grew, their weight in the S&P 500 grew as well. The index has historically sought to maintain equal weighting between all 500 components. Today, FAANG-M accounts for an astonishing 25% of the index, and drives the majority of the growth. (*Tra*•*e Signals - FANG Stocks Up 400%,*

S&P 500 In•ex ex-FANGs up 35%, S&P 500 In•ex up 45% (2015-Present),
2020).

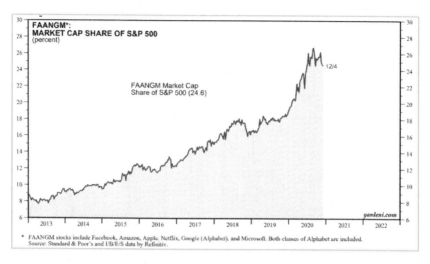

Figure 2: *Market cap of the top six companies as a total share of the S&P 500*

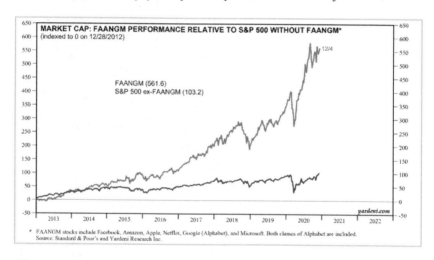

Figure 3: *The relative performance of the S&P 500 if you remove the FAANG-M stocks*

This means if you buy an ETF that tracks the S&P 500 (like SPY or
VOO), you're essentially buying exposure towards FAANG-M. This
is great if you're chasing capital gains. However, an income investor
is left out in the cold. Of these six stocks, just Apple and Microsoft

pay dividends. Even then, Apple had to be cajoled and threatened by activist investors before it agreed to pay. These companies operate in rapidly changing industries, and it's unfair to expect them to pay stable dividends.

The performance of the stock market in 2020 further highlights how heavily weighted the market is towards these companies. Here is the performance of these stocks as of November 26th 2020 (YTD):

◇ Facebook: 34%

◇ Apple: 58%

◇ Amazon: 72%

◇ Netflix: 50%

◇ Alphabet (Google): 32%

◇ Microsoft: 35%

While these six companies have soared, if you subtract them from the index, the rest of the S&P 500 has remained relatively flat. Right now, the stock market is in a weird place. Everyone acknowledges that there is something resembling a bubble going on. However, no one thinks that a pop is justified. After all, these huge tech companies are performing incredibly.

In fact, they're doing so well that any company with even a whiff of tech about it gets sent to dizzying heights, which is another indicator of a bubble. For example, Tesla is now the 7th largest company in the world by market capitalization, passing Warren Buffett's Berkshire Hathaway. Elon Musk's company joined the S&P 500 on December 21st 2020, which will likely see the index growth concentrated in even fewer stocks.

The Tesla halo has passed to companies such as Nikola and other unproven, zero-revenue (yes revenue, not income) companies such as Hyllion, which have hit billion-dollar valuations.

Other companies such as Zoom and Peloton are still selling for absurd earnings multiples, but there's seemingly no end in sight. The pandemic was supposed to erase these gains and pop the bubble, but the market roared right back within a couple of months. To say that the market is in a weird space right now understates what's going on. No one can make any sense of things, and perhaps this is a good thing for an income investor like you.

Then Versus Now

The primary takeaway from this economic lesson/horror story is that change happens all the time, and there isn't anything you can do to predict it. It's easy to connect the dots in hindsight, but when you're in the thick of a situation, it's close to impossible.

Instead of focusing on what you could have or should have done, it's best to reorient your focus towards what you can do. The second half of this book will cover principles and give you examples of companies that can generate both income and capital gains for your portfolio.

To illustrate how much the world has changed, let's look at how your income streams look now versus in the past. First, let's take the case of a standard savings account with $100,000 deposited into it. Here are some of the other assumptions we've made:

◇ Inflation is set at three percent per year over a 20-year period

◇ Column 1 is the year

◇ Columns 2 and 3 contrast growth in an account that pays one percent interest (more representative of the current landscape) with an account that pays five percent interest (more representative of the 1980s/1990s)

◇ The value in each column is what your money is worth after accounting for inflation.

Year	1%	5%
1	$97,115.38	$100,961.54
2	$94,313.98	$101,932.32
3	$91,593.38	$102,912.44
4	$88,951.27	$103,901.98
5	$86,385.36	$104,901.04
6	$83,893.48	$105,909.71
7	$81,473.48	$106,928.07
8	$79,123.28	$107,956.22
9	$76,840.88	$108,994.26
10	$74,624.31	$110,042.28
11	$72,471.69	$111,100.38
12	$70,381.16	$112,168.66
13	$68,350.93	$113,247.20
14	$66,379.27	$114,336.12
15	$64,464.48	$115,435.50
16	$62,604.93	$116,545.46
17	$60,799.02	$117,666.09
18	$59,045.20	$118,797.49
19	$57,341.98	$119,939.78
20	$55,687.88	$121,093.04

You can see the effect that the one percent "depletion" account has. Because of inflation, you're steadily losing money as the years go by.

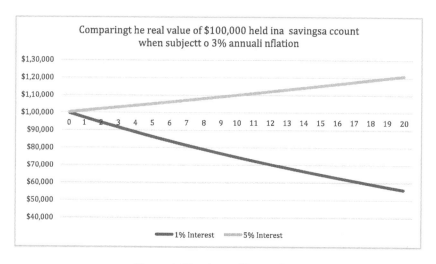

Figure 4: *The above table visualize*

In real terms, you'll end up with half of your original principal after 20 years. Meanwhile, your five percent interest bearing account increases the value of your money and creates true wealth.

Let's now look at how bond returns change depending on the coupon you're paid. Here are the assumptions we've made when creating the table below:

◇ Your initial investment principal is $500,000

◇ The withdrawal rate is four percent. This is how much you'll withdraw every year to pay for expenses.

◇ We've contrasted the returns between a bond that pays 3.5% and another that pays 0.01%.

◇ The second column lists the principal left over after withdrawal when the bond pays 3.5%. The last column lists the leftover principal when the bond pays 0.01%.

◇ You will withdraw four percent of the number that is listed under the "3.5%" and "0.01%" columns every year.

◇ To keep things simple, in this example, we have listed the nominal values, which are not adjusted for inflation

Year	Principal	3.50%	0.01%	Principal
1	$500,000.00	$517,500.00	$500,050.00	$500,000.00
2	$497,596.15	$515,012.02	$480,865.39	$480,817.31
3	$495,203.86	$512,536.00	$462,416.80	$462,370.57
4	$492,823.08	$510,071.88	$444,676.01	$444,631.54
5	$490,453.74	$507,619.62	$427,615.84	$427,573.08
6	$488,095.78	$505,179.14	$411,210.19	$411,169.08
7	$485,749.17	$502,750.39	$395,433.96	$395,394.42
8	$483,413.84	$500,333.32	$380,262.98	$380,224.96
9	$481,089.73	$497,927.87	$365,674.04	$365,637.48
10	$478,776.80	$495,533.99	$351,644.82	$351,609.66
11	$476,474.99	$493,151.61	$338,153.83	$338,120.02
12	$474,184.24	$490,780.69	$325,180.43	$325,147.91
13	$471,904.51	$488,421.17	$312,704.76	$312,673.49
14	$469,635.74	$486,072.99	$300,707.72	$300,677.65
15	$467,377.88	$483,736.10	$289,170.95	$289,142.04
16	$465,130.87	$481,410.45	$278,076.80	$278,048.99
17	$462,894.66	$479,095.97	$267,408.27	$267,381.53
18	$460,669.21	$476,792.63	$257,149.05	$257,123.34
19	$458,454.45	$474,500.36	$247,283.43	$247,258.70
20	$456,250.34	$472,219.10	$237,796.31	$237,772.53

As you can see, a four percent withdrawal rate reduces your principal in both cases. This is understandable since you're withdrawing more than what you earn in interest. However, when you earn 3.5% your principal reduces to $456,250 compared to $237,772 in the 0.01% interest case.

Another way of interpreting these results is to say that you'll lose more than half your money to withdrawals over 20 years in the latter case, whereas you'll lose less than 10% in the former scenario.

This highlights the importance of focusing on the returns your investments are making if you plan to withdraw part of the principal to live off. Remember that this table doesn't even account for inflation, so in real terms your money is worth even less in the 0.01% scenario.

You will always have to combat inflation, and your portfolio needs to overcome these drags on performance.

Which is why from now on, we will emphasize finding investment opportunities that give you a combination of capital gains and dividends. It isn't enough to focus on just one of them since this will lead to your principal being depleted and lowering the amount you can withdraw, as the above two tables show.

It's not just enough to consider inflation, though. We also need to consider the costs associated with investing. Which is precisely what we'll do in the next chapter.

FREEMAN INCOME INVESTING RULE #1

AN IDEAL DIVIDEND PORTFOLIO STRIKES A BALANCE BETWEEN INCOME AND CAPITAL GAINS

Chapter 2

ONE PERCENT MATTERS – WHY YOUR FINANCIAL ADVISOR MAY BE KILLING YOUR RETIREMENT

The first place most prospective retirees head to when they have issues with their portfolio is a financial advisor or a financial advisory company. Like most individual investors, financial advisors have been battered since the 2008 crisis. This is because of how the financial advisory industry is set up. Most managers distinguish themselves on the basis of outperformance. The greater someone outperforms the broad market, the more sought-after they are.

This might sound a lot like how hedge funds work, but there's a crucial difference. Hedge funds have the freedom to invest in whichever assets they like and use any strategy that they please. It's entirely between the fund manager and the investors. If the fund manager decides to use astrology to predict markets, the manager is free to do so if investors like the idea.

Financial advisors don't have near as much leeway when advising clients. They need to deal with largely unsophisticated clients who need to be guided away from risky investments. The advisor has to prioritize capital preservation above all else, which means they can't take risks like hedge fund managers do. Furthermore, they need to make clients money without putting it at risk of a drawdown since this will lead to their clients walking out on them.

35

A drawdown is defined as a loss in account equity. Let's say you invested $100,000 in the market, and the value of your portfolio decreased to $50,000. That's a 50% drawdown. If you decide to sell the stocks in your portfolio, it becomes a realized loss. If you hang onto it, it's unrealized and isn't a cash loss. The problem for financial advisors is that most clients are impatient and this impatience turns unrealized losses into fully realized ones. This damages the reputation of the advisor, and as a result, they stick to promoting staple investment sources.

However, this brings another issue with it. The recommendations that they hand out and the strategies they ask their clients to follow come across as being plain vanilla. If your advisor is telling you to buy the same thing that a popular financial magazine is, what's the need to pay the high advisor fees? The financial advice industry has come up with a creative way to sidestep this issue.

Fund Recommendations and Commissions

Visit many financial advisors, and the first thing many of them will tell you is to divide your portfolio into a 60/40 split between stocks and bonds. If you're an income-seeking investor, the split will be the other way around, with 60 percent allocated to bonds and 40 percent to stocks. Some advisors still recommend subtracting your age from 100 and using that allocation for stocks. So if you're 60 years old, you'll allocate 40% to stocks and the rest to bonds.

This method of portfolio allocation makes no sense. It was originally proposed as a shortcut and an excellent way to get started thinking about portfolio allocation as you grow older. It wasn't meant to become a rule. Proper portfolio allocation is all about your goals and the level of risk you're willing to bear.

Financial advisors will then recommend specific mutual funds and other investment products to you. Herein lies another problem because if your advisor works for or is affiliated with a large investment firm, they'll almost certainly push one brand of mutual fund and investment choices to you. This is because in addition to charging you advisory fees, the advisor earns commissions from those mutual fund houses. This isn't to say that they're pushing bad mutual funds at you. It's just that you're only given a choice of a tiny subset of all the investment products that are out there.

Most people go to advisors because they are intimidated or overwhelmed by the variety of choices, so they blindly accept what their advisor tells them. By pushing seemingly specialized mutual funds, advisors sidestep the question of why their strategies seem pretty basic. They'll respond that most basic strategies tend to be poorly executed and that the fund they're recommending executes it the best.

They're not wrong in saying that it can be tough to execute basic strategies in the market. However, the notion that one mutual fund does it better than another is extremely hard to prove. When you buy a mutual fund, you're buying a specific set of investment objectives. These objectives can either be growth or income-oriented. There are many subdivisions to these categories depending on the types of instruments the fund invests in.

No matter the strategy, the average mutual fund aims for outperformance. They measure their performance against a market-relevant benchmark. For example, a mutual fund that aims to generate tax-free income will invest in municipal bonds, private tax-free bond issues, and treasury inflation protected securities (TIPS). They'll measure their performance against the muni bond index. If the index rises by five percent and the fund rises by six percent, that's outperformance. Similarly, fund managers will choose appropriate indexes when investing in stocks. If they're investing in European small cap companies, they'll benchmark themselves against the European small cap index.

There are two issues with this approach. Let's take a look at them.

Issue One - Concentration and Di"Worse"ification

The first issue from concentrating on particular asset classes is that fund managers hamstring themselves. They don't do this by choice, of course. Many complicated laws are surrounding how a mutual fund manager should structure their funds. Most of them set up their funds with the aim of gaining pension fund money. Pension funds have hundreds of billions of assets under management and need to allocate that money somewhere.

They do this by splitting that giant hoard of cash across different asset classes. The specific asset classes will vary from one fund to another, but the average pension fund manager will never stick all of their money into a single asset class. If that asset class fails or underperforms, it'll result in billions of dollars of unrealized losses. Besides, pension fund managers have their own benchmarks to worry about.

From a mutual fund manager's perspective, the best way of increasing the assets they manage is to hyper specialize in an asset class. This is why certain mutual funds invest solely in European small cap healthcare stocks and nothing else. If they receive allocations from pension funds, it's a windfall for the fund house and the fund manager.

The problem occurs when your financial advisor recommends funds like these to you. They'll push these funds to you in the name of diversification. However, you likely don't have billions of dollars in your portfolio. If you invest in European small cap healthcare companies, your portfolio is extremely concentrated. You need to invest in European large cap stocks as well. What about bonds? Well, invest in European bonds as well. All of these are foreign holdings, you'll need American exposure as well. You'll buy American large cap, small cap , and mid cap mutual funds. You'll buy bond funds, real estate funds, and who knows what else. By the time you're done diversifying your portfolio, you'll hold around seven to eight mutual funds and will have spread your money so thin that none of these instruments will have any effect on your portfolio.

This is what the famous mutual fund manager Peter Lynch described as di"worse"ification (Lynch & Rothchild, 2000). Lynch helmed Fidelity's Magellan fund from 1977 to 1990 and earned an average annual return of 29.2% for his investors. It's safe to say he knows what he's talking about.

At the end of the year, the fund manager and your financial advisor will point to their benchmarks and note that they outperformed the market. This justifies their collection of fees from you. We'll get to fees shortly and highlight their effect on your portfolio. After you pay fees, your portfolio that's spread too thin will be in a worse position than what it started the year with. Since no single instrument in your portfolio will affect the total portfolio's value, you'll end up going backward after fees and inflation.

Issue Two – The Problem of Outperformance

Performance in a mutual fund is measured against a benchmark, not the overall market. Unless the fund aims to invest in the entire market, you're unlikely to find it benchmarking itself against the S&P 500 or other major market indexes. By being too broad in their investment approach, they can't attract pension fund money.

We mentioned that by hyper specializing, fund managers hamstring themselves. The reason is that it's hard to make money when your investment options are limited. Consider the case of our European small cap healthcare fund. How many companies can it possibly invest in? There aren't many profitable small cap companies to invest in, to begin with, let alone profitable small caps situated solely in Europe. Once you add the healthcare requirement, your world of opportunities shrinks massively.

There's also the problem of portfolio concentration. This issue was highlighted first by Peter Lynch in his book *One Up on Wall Street*. Let's say a fund manager is running a portfolio where three companies are doing well, and three aren't doing so well. There are no other companies in their portfolio. As the three companies' market value rises, and the value of the three underperformers falls, the weight of the high achievers increases in the portfolio. Much like how FAANG-M has taken over the S&P 500, these three will dominate the fund manager's portfolio.

If the mutual fund manager was an individual investor, the logical step would be to dump the three underperformers and invest more money into the outperformers. However, we're dealing with the money management industry here, so nothing is logical. The fund manager will be rapped on the knuckles by their pension fund investor, who'll ask them about their increasing concentration risk. As a result, the mutual fund manager will sell their profitable holdings and buy more underperformers to redistribute portfolio weights.

This creates a ton of trading activity since rebalancing is a daily task for a mutual fund. This generates trading commissions from the fund's prime broker, and those fees are passed on to you. At the end of the year, the fund outperforms its benchmark, and everyone pats themselves on the back.

Except, who's to say that the benchmark is a valid measure of outperformance? What if the S&P 500 gains 30% and the European small cap healthcare index gains just 10%? That's gross underperformance. Even if the fund gained 15%, on the year, it underperformed the broad market by 50%! That's not anyone's idea of success.

Most mutual funds fail to outperform the broad market (Pisani, 2019). Instead of specializing deeply in obscure healthcare stocks, the manager would have made more money by merely buying everything in the S&P 500 and sitting tight. However, that's too simple, and they won't earn fees by doing that. Neither can your financial advisor justify their fees by recommending such a simple strategy.

This is why most mutual funds are a dud when it comes to investing for growth or for income. Last year, the S&P found that after ten years, 85% of large-cap funds underperformed the S&P 500, and after fifteen years, nearly 92% trailed the index.

The fund benchmarks make no sense, and they aren't even targeted to benefit small investors. They're targeted at big pension funds that have to distribute their assets across multiple classes to achieve an adequate level of diversification. If you replicate their asset allocations, you'll spread your money too thin and will end up trailing the market.

Fees

All of the previous issues occur before we even get to the biggest problem with mutual funds. The fees are exorbitant. The numbers themselves don't seem too high, but when you account for them against the average performance you can expect, things don't look rosy. Mutual funds (except index funds) charge 1 to 1.5% in annual fees. That's 1.5% of your principal, not gains. If you invested $100,000 in a fund, you'll pay $1,500 every year no matter what the market does.

There are other fees as well. The most notorious of them all is the load fee. Loading is the process by which a mutual fund incorporates your money into the rest of its portfolio. A fund will charge fixed loading fees. If you're charged fees on deposit, it's called a front loading fee. If you're charged on withdrawals, that's a back loading or withdrawal or redemption fee. Whatever the name is, you'll have to pay to access your money.

Then there are 12B-1 fees that go towards paying for the advertising and marketing expenses. In essence, you're paying the manager to advertise the fund to even more pension fund managers and pay for any additional office space or bonuses they might need.

These days, mutual fund managers are conscious of how unfair their fee structures can be and have reduced fees by a large amount. There are no-load funds and funds that don't charge 12-B1 fees. However, some funds offset this by charging a greater percentage of assets as performance fees. At the very least, no mutual fund will ever decrease its performance fee.

Let's run some numbers now and look at how just a performance fee of one percent affects your profitability on an initial investment of $100,000.

We'll compare this to a broad market ETF like the Vanguard 500 Index Fund ETF (VOO) that charges just 0.03% of principal as fees. We'll assume that both funds return seven percent every year and that inflation is two percent.

Year	1% Performance Fee	0.03% Performance Fee
1	$103,883.50	$104,871.12
2	$107,917.81	$109,979.51
3	$112,108.79	$115,336.74
4	$116,462.53	$120,954.93
5	$120,985.34	$126,846.78
6	$125,683.80	$133,025.64
7	$130,564.73	$139,505.47
8	$135,635.20	$146,300.94
9	$140,902.59	$153,427.43
10	$146,374.54	$160,901.06
11	$152,058.98	$168,738.74
12	$157,964.19	$176,958.20
13	$164,098.72	$185,578.04
14	$170,471.48	$194,617.76
15	$177,091.74	$204,097.82
16	$183,969.08	$214,039.66
17	$191,113.52	$224,465.78
18	$198,535.40	$235,399.77
19	$206,245.51	$246,866.37
20	$214,255.05	$258,891.52

At the end of 20 years, you'll have $214,255 after accounting for inflation and one percent portfolio management fees. This is a 3.88% compounded annual growth rate (CAGR). On the other hand, you'll have $258,891 after 20 years if you pay just 0.03% performance fees.

That's a CAGR of 4.87%. In absolute terms, you'll make 20% more over 20 years. Fees alone account for this difference since everything else was the same.

Where can you find investment funds that charge you just 0.03% per year? Well, that's what index funds and index ETFs are for. Funds issued by Vanguard charge just 0.03% management fees every year. What's more, index funds are more likely to earn the seven percent return that we assumed in this calculator. This is because they simply track the S&P 500, which usually returns this much over the long run. In fact, the index has returned an average of 8% per year since 1957 (Maverick, 2019), and as we've already seen, most mutual funds underperform the index.

This level of underperformance doesn't matter to your financial advisor. They'll get paid no matter what. What's more, they'll even earn money based on the number of funds they can push to clients. Fund houses pay them handsome commissions, and this puts many financial advisors in conflict with your best interests.

This isn't to say that all financial advisors are bad. Many of them are fantastic and truly have their clients' best interests at heart. It's just that you need to be aware of what the investment advisory industry is like and act accordingly. You are more than capable of constructing a portfolio that generates steady income all by yourself. As we'll show you in this book, it isn't as hard as you think it is.

FREEMAN INCOME INVESTING RULE #2

ALWAYS UNDERSTAND THE FEE STRUCTURE BEFORE WORKING WITH A FINANCIAL ADVISOR

A Quick Word on Annuities

As times have turned more uncertain, many investors have been pushed towards annuities by their financial advisors. Annuities are an insurance product, and they can get pretty complicated once you begin to dive into them. The basic premise of every annuity is the same. You invest a certain amount of cash with a life insurance company or annuity provider. Then tell them when you wish to start receiving monthly payments. From that date they'll pay you that fixed sum every month until you pass.

Unlike mutual funds, there's much good to be said about annuities. They provide guaranteed cash flow, and this is what many investors are seeking in retirement. However, the biggest knock against them is that they don't account for inflation. Your fixed payments will be eaten up over time if inflation rises. For example, if you want to earn $10,000 per month for the rest of your life, starting ten years from today, you'll have to invest roughly $2.3 million.

Assuming you live for another 25-30 years, a monthly guaranteed income of $10,000 is going to help you live a good life even if inflation rises by two to three percent every year. However, the catch is that you need $2.3 million in the first place, and this is a pretty large sum that not everyone will have.

Our objective in this section is to help you understand how annuities need to be evaluated. The reason is that many financial advisors will push them to you as a wonderful investment tool. They do this because they earn a ton of commissions by selling them. On average, insurance companies pay advisors three to four percent of the invested amount as commission.

On top of this, some features of an annuity can work against you if you're not careful.

Term

There are two aspects to an annuity's term that you should be aware of. The first is the date from which you wish to start receiving monthly payments. For example, the further in the future this date is, the higher your monthly payment will be. It's also tied to your age. The older you are when payments begin, the higher the payments will be.

The second aspect of the term of the annuity term is how long you want your payments to last. You can opt for a fixed term (say ten years), as well as payments until the end of your life, or payments till the end of your spouse's life. Once the term ends, the remaining principal may or may not be refunded, depending on your choice.

If you choose to have the remaining principal refunded, you'll receive a lower monthly payment. There are also many other moving parts to an annuity than the term, so it's best to consult a life insurance specialist to determine how much you can expect to receive. Also, your chosen location and residence matters.

Inflation

Inflation is the biggest negative of opting for an annuity. Since your monthly payments are fixed, you'll receive less cash in real terms as time goes on. This doesn't always have to be a negative. If you've provided enough for your dependents and opt for payments beginning when you're 70 or older, you won't necessarily have to worry about inflation. At that age, income generation matters the most, and an annuity can give you that security.

However, if you're younger, an annuity will put the brakes on capital growth and will actually lose you money. It's equivalent to letting cash sit in the bank instead of putting it to work. This is why an annuity isn't a sure-shot solution to income generation issues. The closer you are to the conceivable end of your life, the more an annuity makes sense. You also need to consider how much you would like to leave your heirs after your passing. If maximizing their inheritance is your highest priority, then an annuity won't do you much good.

Company Risk

Annuities are products of insurance companies, and as with every insurance contract, counterparty risk is real. For example, you can take the right step and insure your home for flood insurance. However, if the insurer (your counterparty) cannot pay, your insurance contract is worthless. This is pretty much what happened during the financial crisis in 2008. Many banks had insurance contracts on their portfolio of bad assets. However, the insurers weren't able to pay and, as a result, a few banks went under.

There is a possibility that the insurance company responsible for your annuity might go bust. Insurance companies go out of business all the time. You can mitigate this risk by opting for a large insurer, but the risk remains.

Although many states in the U.S. have Departments of Insurance that regulate against this, if an insurer goes bankrupt, the annuity contracts are assigned to other carriers, effectively guaranteeing the contract. It's important to know if that is the case in your state of Residence.

Annuities aren't fully FDIC-insured. You might be able to recover a few pennies on the dollar of your investment, but there's no way you will ever be adequately compensated. We're not saying annuities are unsafe. It's just that trusting your entire nest egg to an annuity is not a good move. It leaves you exposed to counterparty risk, no matter how large the counterparty is.

Remember that there are deep mechanisms that govern which product is recommended to you. Complexity is never a sign of competence.

Now we've covered what to watch out for, let's focus on something more positive, how you can implement a profitable income investing strategy.

FREEMAN INCOME INVESTING RULE #3

THE ONLY "GUARANTEE" WITH ANNUITIES IS THAT THEY WILL EVENTUALLY SUCCUMB TO INFLATION.

Chapter 3

THE IDEAL INCOME INVESTING STRATEGY

If the investment advisory business isn't going to do you any favors, what kind of investment strategy should you follow? The answer to this question isn't as hard as it seems. The financial markets provide you with comprehensive tools and instruments to design a portfolio that generates your desired income level. Before we get into the portfolio, though, it's important to take some time to look at the overall strategy you need to adopt.

Successful investing isn't a question of merely picking the right stocks and then letting the income roll in. Many investors fail to fully take advantage of market conditions because they aren't temperamentally suited to maintaining a long-term income-generating portfolio. They aren't entirely to blame for this because surprisingly little investment advice caters to long-term wealth generation.

Even respected magazines and media outlets parrot a few lines about investing for the long term but turn resolutely back to focusing on short-term market forces. They report daily market movements as if they have a significant impact on your portfolio. This tricks investors into thinking that they need to jump in and out of the market to take advantage of every tick up and avoid every tick down. While this sounds good in theory, it's impossible to pull it off in practice.

This is just one of the many behavioral changes you need to make. Your investment strategy isn't so much about picking the right stocks as much as it's about helping you get out of your way when it comes to making money.

48

Invest for the Long Term

Your investment timeline is the best place to begin. How long do you think you need to remain invested to generate profitable returns? Let's look at an example. Let's assume you had the chance to invest in a company; let's call it General Widgets Corp (GWC).

GWC rises by 3,000% over the next two years, but it seems to be overheated. Let's say you sell it and capture a 3,000% gain. Over the next two years, your decision appears vindicated because GWC loses more than 90% of its previous gains. Your decision to time your entry and exit made you an increase of 3,000% in this stock over four years. That's an excellent performance no matter which way you slice it.

However, there's an issue with this approach. You see, this isn't a made-up example that we've highlighted. GWC is Amazon, and between 1997 and 1999, the company's stock rose 3,000% and then lost 90% between 1999 and 2001.

If you mapped the performance of Amazon's stock from 1997 to 2017, the stock has risen by more than 30,000%. What if you had simply bought Amazon and held it, without bothering about what the market was going to do over the short term? You would have netted a 30,000% gain by this time. Suddenly, earning 3,000% over four years doesn't seem too attractive, does it?

Long-term investment is what works best in the markets. Curiously, most long-term investing is defined by a *lack* of activity. On a portfolio level, long-term investors might be active. For example, Warren Buffett isn't a passive investor by any means. He constantly looks at Berkshire Hathaway's portfolio and buys new companies or sells existing holdings.

However, at a position level, he's pretty much inactive. This is why he's held Coca-Cola since 1988 (and made 1,750% in the process, combined with more than $7 Billion in dividend payments). Plus, Buffett has maintained many of his insurance holdings since the 1970s.

Good things take time to grow, and it makes no sense for him or you to attempt timing the market's short-term fluctuations. Predicting the short term is tough, and this is where many investors go wrong.

Short-Term Market Moves

The trouble with figuring out and anticipating short-term market moves is that there's no sensible and repeatable way to predict them. There's no telling what might move the markets on a day-to-day basis. What's more, your margin of error when predicting short-term market moves is a lot less. You need to be more precise with your predictions since there isn't much room for you to be wrong. For example, if you've bought a stock for $100 and plan on selling it within a year, your expected profit isn't going to be too large.

Assuming it moves in step with the market's long-term growth rate, you can expect it to increase by 10%. This equals a final price of $110. If you sell it for $105, which is just $5 away from the maximum price of $110, you've given up 50% of your potential profit. What if the price dips to $90 before it reaches $110? You're planning on holding onto it for just a year, so how can you be sure that the price will rise to that level again within your time frame?

Stock prices rise by a lot more over the long term, giving you the luxury of being less accurate and still profiting by a large amount. Looking at the example of Amazon that we highlighted, a short-term investor who bought the stock in 1997 and sold it in 2000 would have seen most of their gains erased. A long-term investor who bought it in 1997 and simply held on for 20 years would have earned far more. If Amazon stock fell by a few points in a short-term bear move in 2017, it would hardly impact their 30,000% gain.

Long-Term Market Moves

The great thing about long-term market moves is that they always track fundamental factors. For example, if you had the chance to buy Disney stock in 1995, would you have bought it? A cursory glance at the company would have told you that it had valuable intellectual property, a licensing business like no other, and a strong brand that everyone was familiar with. There are very few people on earth who haven't heard of Mickey Mouse, Donald Duck, or Elsa from Frozen. It was a good bet that the company would be around for many years to come.

We're not saying that investment analysis should be reduced to a few lines such as this. However, as far as starting points go, this is a pretty good place to begin. You are investing in a strong company that has many things going for it, is more likely to work out than an investment in a small company that no one has heard of. Disney has weathered more storms and has seen more ups and downs.

Similarly, what if you had the chance to invest in Coca-Cola back in 1983? You would have probably jumped on it without hesitation. Here is the point we're trying to make. Coca-Cola's stock sank after the 1987 market crash, and Disney underwent major restructuring to address its falling stock in 2003 and 2004. Short-term investors would have bailed on the stock during these lows and would have tried to jump back in once things became good once again. However, how does one know when things have turned good?

In the long term, a business's stock price will reflect its earnings growth. Amazon's stock rose and fell many times during its meteoric rise. However, when viewed from 1997 to today, its stock price has grown in proportion to the company's fortunes. It's far easier to invest for the long term since you'll have to deal with real numbers and business prospects.

You don't have to worry about what the economy does or what the monthly jobs report number looks like. You simply buy and hold on until your investment thesis is no longer valid. You sell only when your original reason for investing isn't valid anymore or if you want to use the cash. You'll sleep better at night and won't have to worry about what tomorrow will bring.

Another advantage of long-term investing is that you don't need too many great ideas to succeed. If you had withdrawn your money from Amazon after the 3,000% gain in 1999, you would have had to reinvest it somewhere. Finding investment opportunities isn't an easy task. It's not as if great ideas grow on trees. They don't come by very often, and if you're someone who has a full-time job, it's going to be pretty tough to find new opportunities.

With long-term investing, all you need are a handful of good ideas, and you're set for life. After all, you aren't looking to sell your holdings anytime soon, and your money grows by itself without you having to do anything with it. It's easier to come up with two or three great investment ideas over the course of a decade than it is to come up with them every three months.

What To Ignore

Focusing on long-term investing means you ignore short-term market moves as well as the media hysteria that accompanies them. The financial media exists to sell views and clicks, and the sophistication with which they present data is a veneer. The media's job is to gain enough eyeballs so that advertisers can pay them more. Don't mistake round the clock news coverage for intelligent analysis.

It's a lot like a person who responds to work emails at three in the morning. Very few good decisions get made at that time of the day, and odds are that nothing real or informative is achieved by responding to work emails at that hour. The media often trots out experts who recommend stocks. There are even shows dedicated to buying and selling stocks with literal bells and whistles to drive the point home (we're looking at you, Jim Cramer).

All that these shows do is emphasize the need to trade over the short term. In this sense, the financial media is a lot like the nightly local news. How many times have you heard headlines like "A deadly killer in your area... tonight at nine"? More often than not, these headlines are just baiting you into watching the news. Do you remember what the local news reported a year ago? Probably not. Treat the financial media with the same degree of importance.

Brokers and certain media houses give priority to covering Wall Street analyst reports. These reports are useful if you want to learn the broad brushstrokes of a company's business. If you need to know in-depth information about a company's various business units and how its departments operate, an analyst's report is a good resource.

However, Wall Street, by its very nature, is a short-term beast. When these reports talk about buy/sell ratings and earnings projections, they focus on quarterly performance. The concept of figuring out what a business will be worth in ten years is alien to these people. This is because the majority of Wall Street clientele are hedge funds and pension funds. Hedge funds mostly love trading over the short term, and pension funds need these reports to determine whether there's any asset allocation risk to their portfolios over the short term.

Every Wall Street analyst knows who they're creating reports for. If they started focusing on long-term projections, their employers would lose the millions in fees that hedge funds and pension funds pay them. The average retail investor, such as yourself, cannot pay this amount of money to justify such coverage. This is why you need to take analyst coverage with large heaps of salt. Use the reports to gain high level knowledge of companies, but don't use them to figure out valuations or even sentiment.

This is why we recommend that you remain invested for a period of at least five years, with ten or fifteen years being ideal. Focus on the business's quality, not just on the dividends it pays or how fast its stock rises. The quality of the company comes first. This is what creates wealth. Stock markets don't rise linearly, so ignore short-term market moves. This includes any pandemic-induced bear markets or election-related volatility.

Minimizing Risk

What is risk when it comes to investing? The simple definition is that risk is the probability of you losing your entire investment. The less you know about what you're investing in, the more you risk losing your investment.

Many Wall Street analysts like to equate risk with return, but this is a fallacy. Common investment advice suggests that high risk equals high returns. However, this isn't true. Risky assets often appear to yield high returns because this is what convinces people to invest in them. For example, if someone asked you to invest in a gold mine in a war-torn country, your first instinct would be to ask for something that would make this risk worthwhile. Typically, this compensation is a high rate of return.

However, does the high rate of return reduce your risk? Not really. Your chances of losing money are just as high no matter what the return is. It isn't as if some rebel warlord is going to look at your high rate of return and call off a coup. Divorce risk from return, and you'll begin to evaluate risk in much better ways.

This is especially true in today's low-yield environment. Many assets are being pushed to investors, such as yourself, with the promise of generating high returns. The returns that these assets generate are not correlated to their risk profiles. If it were that easy to evaluate risk, everyone would construct mathematically precise portfolios all the time.

54

The best way to get a handle on risk is to ask yourself an acceptable level of personal risk. Everyone views risk differently. You might look at that gold mine and run away from it, but someone else might be willing to stomach the loss of the money invested in it. As an income investor, your definition of risk is pretty easy to narrow down. You're looking for assets that will generate cash flow regularly. This means these assets should be predictable, or as predictable as possible.

Volatility

In the stock market, there's a word for measuring predictability. It's called volatility. The more an asset price jumps around, the more volatile it is. Think of it this way. Let's say you're running a business and employ two people. Both of them are excellent workers and deliver outstanding results. However, they have different personalities.

The first person is a steady and reliable worker. He arrives on time, every time, and diligently carries out all of the tasks he is assigned. If you were to grade his work on a scale from 1 to 10, his output would be a 7, a highly predictable 7. It's good enough for you to make money in the business, even if it lacks the brilliance of a genius.

The second employee has the potential to give you results that are 10 out of 10. She has a real talent for her work and possesses a streak of brilliance that the other employee doesn't have. However, she is more "erratic." You never know *when* she will deliver said results, even if the results may be brilliant when you get them. Imposing hard deadlines doesn't work with her, and she might not even show up to work for a few days. Despite all this, when she does deliver her work, it's always exceptional.

Clearly, the second employee is going to give you more sleepless nights. Thanks to her brilliance, she could take your business far, but it's going to be bumpy. She might even let you down a few times, even if she manages to pull something out of a hat in the end. The first person is a relatively dull but steady earner. Your business isn't going to make the headlines for creativity, but you'll chug along at a good pace. The

55

question is: Which person should you choose to keep if you had to keep just one?

Clearly, this depends on your outlook and goals for your business. If you're someone who wants to achieve the highest growth possible and produce the best possible products, the second employee is the one for the job regardless of the potential struggles. If stability is your goal and you don't mind missing out on your business's highest goals, the first is the person for the job. Is this analogy sinking in yet?

The first employee represents a steady company that produces predictable cash flow and doesn't throw too many surprises in investing. The second company is a hot growth stock that is always in the news, has a ton of attention, and is expensive to buy. It jumps around all the time and is volatile. However, it could give huge capital gains by the time it grows. Tesla is an example of such a company, while Coca-Cola is an example of the former.

From an income investor's perspective, stability is all-important. This means you need to minimize volatility. You need an asset that is going to show up to work at nine every day, is going to give you a predictable work output, and is going to behave in ways you can handle. Above all else, it should not possess any artistic streak that may or may not go anywhere. You can hold such stocks in your portfolio, but their weight needs to be minimized.

Beta

The easiest way to measure the volatility of a stock is beta (β). Beta is a measure of volatility, and it's often substituted as a measure of risk. We'd like to reiterate that volatility does not equal risk. It equals risk only for someone looking for steady income without significant drawdowns.

The overall market index is pegged with a value of one. A beta value greater than one indicates a stock that is more volatile than the market average. A beta value that is less than this indicates a stock that is less volatile than the market. If steady income without a massive upside is your main goal, low beta stocks are the kind you should prioritize owning. Your goals should be to earn decent gains (not the highest) with as much stability as possible.

To demonstrate this, here are some five year Beta values for a handful of popular companies as of November 26th 2020 (source: Yahoo Finance)

◇ Nio – 2.61

◇ Tesla – 1.97

◇ Apple – 1.35

◇ Amazon – 1.3

◇ Chevron – 1.26

◇ Kinder Morgan – 0.93

◇ AbbVie – 0.69

◇ AT&T – 0.67

◇ Pfizer – 0.64

◇ Coca-Cola – 0.55

◇ Wal-Mart – 0.52

As you can see, the hot growth stocks which don't pay dividends tend to have higher beta values, whereas the steady income generators have lower beta values.

Seek To Live Off Gains, Not Withdrawals

A popular piece of retirement advice is the four percent withdrawal rule. If you've read anything about retirement planning, you've probably heard of this. The idea is to withdraw four percent of your nest egg every year to have money to pay for expenses. There's a lot of misinformation about this, so let's explore it in more detail.

William Bengen is the person we have to thank for this rule. Bengen is a retired financial advisor who proposed that a withdrawal rate of four percent is a good rule of thumb to begin figuring out how much a person needs to withdraw to ensure their portfolio provides for them in retirement.

Bengen's conclusion was based on data gathered between 1926 and 1976. During these periods, a million dollar portfolio composed of 50% stocks and bonds would not have depleted in less than 33 years if four percent of it was withdrawn every year. This means you could have withdrawn $40,000 every year safely. Bengen intended to begin a discussion on safe withdrawal rates, but it turned into something else entirely. Instead of being the beginning, it became the end of all conversations regarding withdrawal rates.

There are many problems with assuming a four percent withdrawal rate. The first is that if the market crashes early on, the amount of money equivalent to four percent will be very low. Living expenses don't fluctuate with the market, and people will end up selling more of their portfolio to pay for their living costs. This is exactly what happened to people who retired in 2007 and saw their portfolios crash within 12 months.

By withdrawing too much (in percentage terms), they took money off the table precisely when they ought to have been loading up even more. As a result, they couldn't fully partake in the bull market that occurred over the following decade.

Another point to note is that retirement spending isn't flat. The early years of your retirement will account for larger expenses. This is often due to people still providing for their children and supporting them financially. Data from the Bureau of Labor Statistics supports this. According to its Consumer Expenditure Survey, the mean spending for households headed by 55 to 64-year-olds was $65,000 in 2017. Spending dropped to $55,000 between ages 65 and 74, and after age 74, it fell to $42,000. Housing costs remained steady for older people, and health care expenses increased, but nearly every other category, including transportation, entertainment, clothing, food and drink, declined sharply.

This is why reducing your withdrawal to a fixed amount every year, and limiting yourself isn't a good idea. It's also why we mentioned previously that it's best to seek income and capital gains in some proportion. If your portfolio earned an average of eight percent every year, and if your portfolio was worth one million dollars, you could safely withdraw $80,000 without touching the principal.

This method isn't foolproof, of course, since no one can predict how the markets will behave. However, it's better than adopting the four percent rule. That rule works if your nest egg is large and if your living expenses are comparably low. It isn't a solution that works for everybody.

FREEMAN INCOME INVESTING RULE #4

THE 4% RULE IS A GUIDELINE, NOT A LAW

Cut Out the Middlemen

The investment advisory industry lives off commissions. Everyone has the best investing strategies that they'll charge you an arm and a leg for. Once you're done paying commissions, your gains are typically worse than the market average. Get off this treadmill if you want to make real money.

Commissions are a big reason for this. We've already illustrated a scenario where commissions and fees eat into the majority of your gains. These days, brokerage commissions are zero or pretty close to it, whether you choose an app-based broker or a regular one. One step above this is the fees that fund managers charge. Minimize this with low cost ETFs and index funds instead of opting for fancy mutual funds that rarely outperform the market.

To make our point even more precise, paying one percent of your assets as fees is unjustified. Instead, stick to funds that charge less than 1% every year. The only exceptions are the closed end bond funds (CEFs) we'll be discussing later in this book. Minimize your trading activity and choose discount brokers who charge zero commissions. The easiest way to make money is to stop losing it. Think of the following example when you evaluate prospective fund investments.

Let's say you're filling a bucket with water, but this bucket has a large hole at the bottom. The amount of water you'll need to pour into the bucket needs to overcome the water that drains at the bottom. That hole at the bottom is how fees behave when it comes to investment performance. You can't eliminate the hole when investing in funds, so it's important to minimize it as much as possible.

Chapter 4

DIVIDENDS 101

D ividends are a staple of every income investor's portfolio. Many novice investors chase dividends and yields but very few actually understand what dividends are and how they work. This chapter aims to help clarify many of the myths and poor investment practices that dividends have created amongst investors. Many of them succumb to greed and end up investing in the wrong companies.

The dividends we're talking about here refer to cash dividends, not stock dividends. Stock dividends or bonus shares are great, but they don't produce income for you. Investors often view a cash dividend as the surest sign of a company's stability. However, it's not as simple as this.

The presence of a dividend is an excellent thing, but basing your entire investment thesis on it is not the smart thing to do. After all, even a failing company can pay a dividend to cloak poor performance. Sadly, many investors fall for this trick regularly. Instead of looking at the dividend, you need to look at the quality of the business first and foremost because the better a business is, the more sustainable its dividend.

Remember that your aim is to earn steady returns (capital gains and income) over a period of at least ten years. This is why it's imperative for you to look at the business and the quality of its cash flows instead of merely the dividend it pays you. With this point being made, let's look at why it's a good idea to invest in dividend-paying assets.

61

Why Dividends Are a Good Investment Indicator

Let's say you have two companies, A and B. Both companies earn a steady 12% on equity every year and post similar revenue growth. The difference is that A pays 20% of its earnings as dividends to its shareholders while B doesn't. What can we infer from this example?

For starters, we can quickly surmise that A offers its shareholders more benefits. Not only is it giving its shareholders capital gains (unrealized), it's also providing its investors with realized gains in the form of a dividend. The 20% of its earnings that it pays its shareholders are real gains investors earn in their portfolios.

Stability

If A pays dividends, it means that its management has enough cash set aside to take care of business for the next year at the very least. They have enough money to cover their current liabilities and other expenses. What's more, they've also budgeted for capital expenditures and have reinvested enough money to ensure the business is competitive.

This probably means that the environment they're facing isn't all that competitive. If you knew tough times were ahead, or if you knew that you lived in a dangerous environment, would you ever distribute your resources to others? You'd probably hang onto them no matter what. Cash is a company's most important resource. If there are dark clouds on the horizon, a company isn't going to distribute its cash.

Business is always competitive, and if a company is sure that it can withstand challenges, it often means that it has a dominant share of the market. The bigger and more entrenched a company is, the more it can afford to distribute to its shareholders and still maintain its competitive edge.

Sharing company profits with shareholders is also an indicator of a management team recognizing how best to utilize cash. Holding onto cash for no reason is wasteful. After all, if the company can't use it to enhance its competitiveness or acquire other companies, the cash is better off in their shareholders' hands. The cash distribution also creates an expectation in the minds of the shareholders. The market begins to expect the company to maintain its stability and its dividend.

This means management needs to plan ahead of time and maintain a business's competitive edge. There is a disadvantage here in that a company cannot take huge risks or gambles. If their business targets disruption, they might not react quickly enough to address new challenges. However, generally speaking, dividends force management to think deeply about investing capital and bringing returns to shareholders.

All of this means company A is a much better investment than B from an income-generation perspective. B has a few advantages because it can reinvest more of its cash to ward off any disruptive threats. Take the example of Amazon and Google. Despite being huge in their industries, both of these companies regularly face threats to their business models. If a person sitting in his or her garage invents a better search engine algorithm than Google's existing algorithm, Google's entire business is threatened. They need cash in the bank to buy their competition and protect their business.

Similarly, Amazon's eCommerce business model is based on offering the lowest prices. The company underprices its products to kill competition and gain market share wherever it goes. It needs cash to maintain profitability and to fund its acquisitions. Both of these companies could land in hot water if they went around distributing cash to their shareholders.

The only tech giants that pay dividends are Microsoft and Apple. Even these companies pay a very small portion of their earnings to shareholders. Apple currently pays 24% of its income while Microsoft pays 35% (Sparks, 2020). Both are on the lower end of the scale when it comes to dividend-paying stocks. Technology is an inherently unstable line of business where disruption is a constant threat.

As an income investor, your priority is to seek stability. Dividends point to this factor in a business quite reliably.

Performance

Stable companies that pay dividends don't appreciate as much as non-dividend-paying companies do. The very fact that these companies pay a portion of their profits out to investors means their ultimate growth is capped. However, a more significant reason is that most of these companies are simply too big to grow larger. Take the case of Coca-Cola or PepsiCo, two competitors which both happen to be stellar dividend-paying companies.

How much larger can they grow? Unless Elon Musk delivers on his promise to colonize Mars by next year, it's hard to envision these companies growing their businesses by even ten percent every year. However, this lack of growth doesn't mean their stocks don't perform well. This is because dividend-paying stocks become a safe haven during both bull and bear markets. They tend to fall less than their non-dividend-paying counterparts. The presence of a dividend acts as an assurance that things aren't as bad with these companies as they could potentially be with others.

JP Morgan Asset Management (JPMAM) conducted a study in 2013 that looked at US dividend-paying stocks' investment performance versus those that don't pay dividends (US *ivi*en*s for the long term, 2013). The study tracked companies from 1972 to 2010 (38 years) through all the ups and downs during that time. JPMAM found that companies that paid and raised their dividend payouts returned an average of 9.5% per year over this time period. In contrast, non-dividend-paying companies returned just 1.6% over the same time.

We must point out that increasing dividend payments was a large factor in the 9.5% yearly performance. An increasing dividend means company profits were probably growing over this time period. However, don't confuse a dividend increase with revenue increases. Often, companies will maintain their dividend to preserve stock price levels.

A good case of this was Boeing in 2020. The company has had a terrible decade and faces lawsuits worldwide thanks to faults in its 737 Max jet. On top of this, its 747 airliner finally became obsolete and was retired without a clear replacement. These events, along with declining defense industry contracts, led to a CEO's resignation and a huge turnaround plan being initiated. Then came COVID-19.

With plane orders hitting rock bottom, Boeing declared a loss for the year 2019 and projects to make a loss in 2020 as well. However, its dividend is stable. Management figured preserving the dividend would help the stock price remain at decent levels. Withdrawing a dividend is often viewed as heretical by the institutional money management industry. As a result, many managers maintain dividends, even when the company is losing money.

This is why it's crucial to assess a business's quality instead of merely looking at its dividend. In Boeing's case, the company is large and dominant enough to plausibly bounce back. It has just one competitor in the commercial airplane manufacturing industry because of the considerable competitive advantage (also known as a "moat", as popularized by Warren Buffett) caused by the immense amount of capital needed to manufacture planes. Boeing management's decisions to preserve the dividend might prove to be a good one in the long run. Our point isn't to say that you should buy Boeing. It's just that you need to take all factors into account. A business is much more than its dividend.

As the JPMAM study shows, the presence of a growing dividend is a good starting point from which you can narrow down good candidates that will provide you with a steady cash flow for the long term.

Yields and Payout Ratios

Two metrics that are often quoted when looking at dividends are the yield and payout ratio. The **yield** is calculated by dividing the annual dividend amount by the current price. If a company paid two dollars in dividends and is selling for $100, it's yielding two percent. The tricky thing with yield is that it is always based on the previous year's payout amount.

For example, let's say a company paid two dollars the previous year, but its stock price is currently selling for $10, having fallen from $100. It hasn't paid a dividend this year, so its yield will be 20%. Many new dividend-focused investors chase high yields thinking they're sustainable when in fact, they aren't. A falling stock price usually creates a high yield.

The key to successful dividend investing is finding a company with a high yielding stock but pays out a sustainable portion of its income. That's what the **payout ratio** measures. It's calculated by dividing the dividend payment by the net income and is expressed as a percentage. In the previous section, we highlighted how Apple pays just 24% of its net income to shareholders. This means Apple's payout ratio is 24%. Low payout ratios combined with high yields are an investor's dream. However, the market typically ensures that such combinations don't remain in place for very long. As more people notice the situation, investors jump into the stock, and the price rises, which causes yields to fall.

At the time of writing (late 2020), the average S&P 500 dividend yield is less than two percent. Anything above five percent is considered high yield for an individual stock. REITs or real estate investment trusts yield higher than five percent regularly, but that's because of the way they're structured. They're legally obliged to pay 90% of their profits back to shareholders, which automatically boosts their dividend payments. We'll examine REITs in more detail later in the book.

When looking at payout ratios, it's essential that you pay attention to the ratio between the dividend payment and free cash flow as well. Free cash flow is calculated by subtracting capital expenditures from the cash flow from operations. Both of these numbers are present on a company's cash flow statement. If there's a wide divergence between this and the payout ratio, you'll need to investigate why this is.

Divergence isn't always a bad thing. It depends on what causes the divergence. If the company has understated its net income, creating a high payout ratio, but still maintains stable cash flow, this is a good situation. However, if cash flow is far less than net income, this is a bad situation. Typically, companies that incur high capital expenditures (such as airlines, oil refining and telecoms) will have much lower free cash flow than net income. This is because capital expenses are not included in the calculation of net income.

Our point here is to tell you that payout ratios and yields are not a quick-fix way of figuring out a business or its dividend quality. A high yield or a low yield isn't "good" or "bad" by itself. You must consider the broader scope of the company and the industry it's in.

Dividend Dates

Dates are all-important when it comes to dividends. The most important date to keep in mind is the ex-dividend date. This is the date you need to be a shareholder in the company to earn a dividend check. Then we have the payment date, which refers to when the dividend will be deposited in your brokerage account and is typically two to three weeks after the ex-dividend date. The date when a company announces a dividend payment is called the announcement date.

For example, at the time of writing, Starbucks' latest ex-dividend date was August 6th, 2020. If you held shares before this date and continued to hold through August 6th, you would receive the dividend. The quarterly dividend was paid on August 21st at a rate of $0.41 per share ($1.64 per share annually, a yield of approximately 1.74%), so if you held 100 shares, you would have received $41. The next ex-dividend date is November 12th, 2020, and the payout date is December 4.

Many short-term traders try to time their stock purchases to collect a dividend payment. We recommend against investing in this manner. It's a good theory on paper, but it almost always fails in real life.

Here's the theory. If you can buy a stock before it goes ex-dividend, and sell it after this date, you can theoretically earn capital gains on the stock's appreciation as well as the dividend. Let's say the dividend yield on the stock is currently five percent. By buying the stock and capturing the dividend, you're capturing at least a five percent gain. This is a huge windfall if you're a short-term trader. A gain of five percent over a few days is well over 200% per year.

However, things are not so simple. Before the ex-dividend date, the price of the stock usually rises to account for the dividend payment. In this case, it will increase by five percent before going ex-dividend. This means short-term traders will buy it for an inflated value.

Once the ex-dividend date passes, the stock declines in value by the same amount. Anyone who bought the stock will therefore suffer a capital loss by selling it at this point. The dividend payment compensates them for it and thus nullifies any gain you can make. It's not impossible to earn a profit doing this. However, you'll also incur higher trading commissions and taxes.

Due to all of these disadvantages, we highly discourage you from adopting such trading tactics. Stick to long-term investing, and you'll make more than enough money to retire comfortably.

Dividend Reinvestment

Dividends are powerful for another reason. They allow you to reinvest them and to capture the power of compounding. Every stock or asset that pays a dividend will enable you to reinvest the proceeds through a Dividend Reinvestment Program or DRIP. DRIPs are instituted by the companies you invest in, and are managed through your broker.

Briefly, here's how they work. Let's say you receive a dividend payment of $5 from your investment. If you elect to participate in a DRIP with your broker, they will automatically buy $5 worth of stock in the company for you at no charge. Even brokers who charge you commissions will typically offer this for free because the company is the one that automatically issues equivalent shares of itself to you. All the broker does is record the transaction in your portfolio. You should check with your broker whether they'll charge you fees for this. For example, both Vanguard and TDAmeritrade have free DRIP programs.

Your new shares will be purchased at whatever the stock price is on the payment date. DRIPs are a great way to automate your investing over the long term. You can take advantage of compounding in an entirely passive manner.

There are other advantages of DRIPs as well. Let's say you have $5 but wish to buy shares of a company that's selling for $100 per share. You cannot buy any shares of the company on many broker platforms because you don't have enough money.

Mutual funds allow you to purchase fractional units, but this often isn't possible with common stocks. However, you can buy fractional shares through a DRIP. Some companies even offer special benefits when purchasing through DRIPs. For example, Enterprise Products Partners (EPD), one of our favorite dividend stocks, offers up to a five percent discount on its units for DRIP participants. You can think of this as a five percent built-in gain the moment you buy your new shares.

The younger you are, the more DRIPs make sense. The closer you are to requiring income from your investments, the more it makes sense to withdraw your dividend payouts instead of reinvesting them. You should also check which stocks your broker allows you to DRIP into.

For example, most UK brokers don't allow you to reinvest dividends into US companies automatically. There are also currency restrictions to take into account. European brokers typically allow you to DRIP into stocks denominated in local currencies but not in foreign ones.

Despite these restrictions, DRIPs allow you to automate compounding into your portfolio, and they make a massive difference over the long run. We can illustrate how powerful they are using a simple example.

Let's assume you invest $100,000 by buying an ETF that tracks the S&P 500 and remain invested for 20 years, electing to DRIP your dividends back into the ETF.

We'll use the current average figures and use a steady two percent yield, with the ETF appreciating at an average rate of eight percent per year. How will this investment compare to another where you choose not to reinvest your dividends?

Year	With DRIP	Without DRIP
1	$110,160.00	$108,000.00
2	$121,352.26	$116,640.00
3	$133,681.65	$125,971.20
4	$147,263.70	$136,048.90
5	$162,225.69	$146,932.81
6	$178,707.82	$158,687.43
7	$196,864.54	$171,382.43
8	$216,865.97	$185,093.02
9	$238,899.56	$199,900.46
10	$263,171.75	$215,892.50
11	$289,910.00	$233,163.90
12	$319,364.86	$251,817.01
13	$351,812.33	$271,962.37
14	$387,556.46	$293,719.36
15	$426,932.20	$317,216.91
16	$470,308.51	$342,594.26
17	$518,091.85	$370,001.81
18	$570,729.99	$399,601.95
19	$628,716.15	$431,570.11
20	$692,593.71	$466,095.71

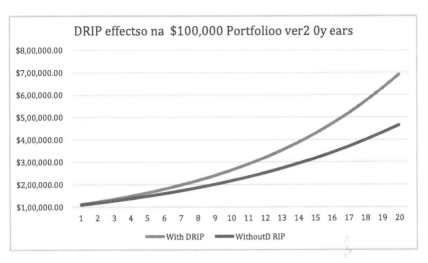

Figure 5: The above table visualize

As you can see, there's a vast difference in the final value of the investment. You'll earn 48% more by reinvesting your dividends over 20 years. We must point out that we've made some assumptions when constructing this table, so you probably won't see these exact numbers. Perhaps our biggest assumption is that the ETF will rise by eight percent every year. This won't happen in real life because there will be years when it will fall, and some years will rise by a greater percentage.

However, over the long run, an 8 percent return is a reasonable expectation. If you elect to DRIP throughout this period, you'll end up buying more units of the ETF when the index is low and less when it's high. This way, your gains will be potentially larger once the index moves back upwards. By looking at things this way, you can begin to understand the power of investing an additional two percent for free every year compared to withdrawing it. You'll build a larger nest egg at the end of your investment period by choosing to reinvest dividends.

Chapter 5

AVOIDING YIELD TRAPS

As we mentioned earlier, a considerable problem when investing in dividend-paying assets is that people often confuse high yields with good investment opportunities. Stocks and funds that pay high yields but don't offer any prospect of capital gains are referred to as **yield traps**. You need to avoid them at all costs if you want to be successful. Yield traps are abundant in bear markets since it's during these times that stock prices fall dramatically.

The typical manner in which investors unearth these traps is to set a fixed yield percentage on a stock screener and invest in whatever comes up. For example, you could head over to the FinViz.com stock screener and search for companies that currently have dividend yields greater than five percent.

However, many of these companies are horrible choices for a smart income investor. For example, one particular instrument that has routinely been showing up over the past few years is the Credit Suisse X-Links Crude Oil Shares Covered Call ETN. Assuming you can digest its name, you'll then need to figure out what it does. If you can't, allow us to explain.

ETN stands for Exchange Traded Note and is a type of ETF. The specifics of why this fund is structured as an ETN and not an ETF aren't relevant, but the point is that it behaves like an ETF. You'll notice the term crude oil in its name, and this points to what the fund tracks. This ETN tracks crude oil prices through a relevant index. You'll also notice the term covered call in the ETN's name. This points to what its strategy is.

Covered calls are an options trading strategy. An investor can buy underlying shares of a stock and sell call options on the same stock at higher prices to generate income from it. This is a popular income strategy when executed correctly and the subject of one of our other books, *Covere Calls for Beginners*.

However, while covered calls are a profitable investment strategy, they aren't foolproof. This ETN pays dividends on the profits it makes by implementing the covered call strategy on oil indexes. Its dividend yield is a spectacular 18% and is listed as 26% in some outlets. This discrepancy in itself is an indication that not everything is right with this ETN.

It means it isn't traded often enough and that its prices fluctuate wildly. After all, if dividend payouts remain the same, the only other factor that accounts for different yields is the price. If stock prices can produce yields as far away as six percent from one another, this means prices are jumping all over the place. This is a sure sign of massive volatility, and is the enemy of an income investor.

Why are yields this high anyway? Well, this is because share prices have declined by a whopping 79% over the past year. Not only have prices fallen, but dividend payouts have also reduced as well. The dividend growth over the past three years is -12.27%. This means the most recent payout of $0.45 per share is unlikely to be sustained.

This ETN can be summed up pretty easily. The positives are that it has a great name that you can throw around at cocktail parties and draw impressive nods. The cons are pretty much everything else. It boasts high yields, but the constant capital losses will quickly destroy any yields you'll earn by owning it.

Safety and Value Traps

A big reason investors go chasing yields over five percent is that they were conditioned to expect such yields from safe investments in the past. For example, savings accounts used to pay four to five percent, with CDs yielding slightly higher amounts. As the yields on these investment options crashed, many investors began searching for the same level of yields without understanding that the safety aspect was gone.

Instead, it's far riskier to invest in instruments that yield such high interest rates. Does this mean it's impossible to find safety in such yields? Hardly. In further chapters, we'll explain how you can screen and install processes to uncover such companies. However, it's equally important for you to understand what an unsafe investment opportunity looks like.

You've just read an example of a dividend trap. A close cousin of the dividend trap is a **value trap**. Value traps are popular in the quantitative value investment community. These investors adhere to the original principles of value investing, as proposed by Benjamin Graham. Graham, who first proposed the system in the late 1930s, sought to identify companies selling for less than the value of their net current assets (NCAV). This value is calculated by subtracting the current liabilities from the current assets.

Graham would then buy companies selling for two-thirds of the price of the NCAV, and buy a lot of them. This gave his portfolio a decent margin of safety. If the company went bust, he wouldn't lose too much money since he bought it at a steep discount. If it did well, he'd net at least a 35% gain since he bought it at 65 cents on the dollar (two-thirds discount.) This investing method is also referred to as "cigar butt investing" and it's a method that Warren Buffett, Graham's most famous student, used to make his first million.

Value Traps

As Buffett discovered, the problem was that such quantitative bargains were harder to come by as time went on. As more people began investing in stocks, good companies were harder to find as the market itself began rising higher. Most of these NCAV stocks were poor companies whose businesses were on a downward spiral. Investors would have to wait until they were liquidated to receive any return on their money.

In many cases, these companies would do nothing. Their share prices would neither rise nor fall, which meant anyone who invested money into these companies would incur massive opportunity costs. Perhaps the most famous cigar butt that Buffett ever invested in was Berkshire Hathaway, which began life as a textile mill on the rocks before transforming into the holding company it is today. That experience, along with Charlie Munger's advice, was more than enough to turn him away from looking for such companies.

Value traps these days are easier than ever to find because they usually pay high dividends. As a result, they yield a high percentage, but the problem is their stock prices either go nowhere or go down. Your money remains stuck in such stocks while the amount of money you'll receive will gradually decrease.

You might be wondering how such companies can pay high dividend amounts? This happens because they typically have a lot of cash on their books. Don't mistake this for a company that generates loads of free cash flow. A value trap company has cash lying dormant on its books. Their primary business is being wound down, and there's nowhere to invest that cash. All the company can do is return it back to investors.

An even worse value trap is the business that is trying to turn itself around but is simply operating in an industry that is going extinct. Japan's stock market famously contained many of these zombie companies in the past 20 years. An investor could have invested in companies with loads of cash on their books thanks to cheap debt, but these companies were operating in head-scratching industries.

Some companies made CDs, and CD players but were pivoting to real estate. There were scaffolding companies who were turning to real estate and making pipes. Electronics companies were pivoting to, you guessed it, real estate. These companies' stock prices rose thanks to prevailing bullish conditions in Japan's stock market, but none of them were making money. You could have earned dividends and capital gains for a few years before everything came crashing down.

This is the most significant risk with value traps. By investing in them, you'll likely earn decent returns initially due to high yields, but the minute the tide turns, you'll see the share price come crashing down, and your gains will be erased. The high dividend yields you earned will not be enough to overcome your capital losses. We'll explain shortly why capital losses (or gains) are more important for you to focus on instead of yields.

Given prevailing market conditions, there will be many of these zombie companies available for you to purchase. They'll have loads of cash on their books, fueled by cheap debt. They will have businesses disrupted thanks to automation, AI or the pandemic and will start paying cash back to investors. They'll cut their dividends at some point, which will send their stock prices crashing, leaving investors with capital losses and extremely low dividend payments. Their yields will remain high though!

Kinder-Morgan

A good example of a company that previously burned its investors is Kinder-Morgan. This wasn't a value trap in the classic sense, but it had all the characteristics of one. Let's begin by looking at what this stock has done since 2014.

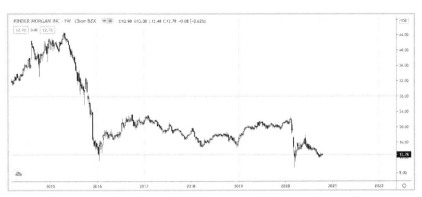

Figure 6 - *Weekly Chart of KMI from 2014-2020 (Source: TraｄingView)*

In Figure 6, note the precipitous drop in share price in early 2015. This is because the board of Kinder-Morgan announced a dividend cut at that time. The dividend yield prior to this cut was eight percent. After the announcement, the effective yield was just two percent. The drop highlights an important point about value and dividend traps.

The stock prices of such companies are routinely inflated, well beyond what their businesses are worth. In the case of Kinder Morgan, every investor was in it for the high yield. Notice that the stock has traded sideways since 2016. COVID-19-induced panic selling did not affect the stock. It merely bounced to a previous low and has half-heartedly stayed there ever since.

Kinder Morgan isn't the only company that has behaved in this manner. Figure 7 illustrates another case.

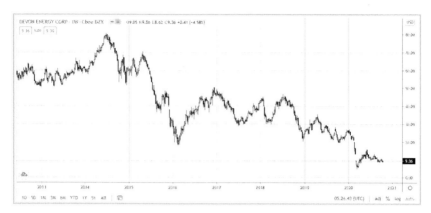

Figure 7: Devon Energy Weekly Chart from 2013-2020 (Source: TradingView)

Figure 7 illustrates the behavior of Devon Energy (DVN). Up until 2016, it paid a handsome 26 cents per share dividend. However, you can see that the stock price was falling well before that. This drove yields up massively. Notice the bounce the company experienced in 2016. This was purely because its yield was massive. It was so massive that even a dividend cut to eight cents per share kept its yields high. Prior to 2016, its yield was around two percent.

The stock price rose because of the yield and not due to anything special in Devon's business. Since then, Devon has meandered sideways before moving downwards. Utility stocks such as Devon attract a lot of attention from income investors because they're viewed as a safe haven. This is because utilities are highly regulated, and have high barriers to entry. This leads to steady dividend payments. However, it isn't as simple as that, as the case of Devon Energy illustrates. The stock is down more than 67% from its peak, a loss that will wipe out any gains from dividends.

To drive the point home, let's look at another example and a famous one. Warren Buffett made a huge splash when he bought Heinz in 2015 and then invested more money to merge Kraft Foods with Heinz to create The Kraft Heinz Company. Two venerable food brands combining to create one of the largest conglomerates in history. What could go wrong? Apparently, a lot. Buffett still owns a stake as of this writing but has publicly admitted to overpaying for the company.

Figure 8 illustrates what he has had to go through since investing in the company.

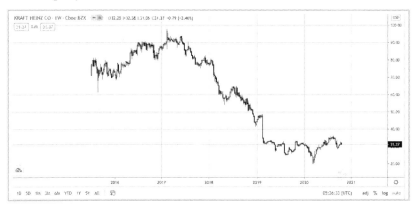

Figure 8: KHC Weekly Chart from 2015-2020 (Source: TradingView)

Notice the peak in 2017? It so happens that towards the end of 2017, the directors of KHC announced they'd have to slash dividends by almost 50% the following year. This led to the stock gradually falling. The company has repeatedly restated its financial results, which indicates a lack of internal audit quality control. For a company of this size, earnings restatements are a huge issue, and the stock's performance has reflected this.

KHC currently pays around $1.10 per year in dividends and yields over five percent. This makes it a high yield stock. However, given its problems and its unwieldy size, clearly, this is a value trap.

Cash Flow and Debt

When looking at these high yield companies, it's best to pay attention to their free cash flows and debt levels. We've already discussed the logic behind looking at free cash flows. After all, without cash, a company can't pay dividends. Why should you pay attention to debt levels, though?

Many companies borrow money from their creditors to finance dividend payments. This is done to maintain a high dividend yield and keep the stock price at a certain level. Boeing has done this recently, as we mentioned previously. Note that there's a lot more to evaluating a company's business than merely looking at increasing debt and dividend payments. In Boeing's case, if the company manages to bounce back and pay dividends from profits, the decision to borrow money to pay dividends would have been a good one. It would have prevented the stock from experiencing volatility.

However, if the company cannot turn itself around, the decision will be painted as a bad one. A lot depends on how the company can execute its strategy. This is why it's critical to look at the business itself instead of merely looking at the numbers.

So now we've ascertained what metrics *on't* matter for dividend growth stocks, let's examine the two which do have an effect.

Chapter 6

THE 2 METRICS THAT MATTER FOR INCOME INVESTING — PAYOUT RATIOS AND DIVIDEND GROWTH

I f focusing on yields leads you right into a trap, what should you be looking at instead? We've mentioned that you should pay attention to the underlying business, but this is a nebulous criterion. In this chapter, we aim to provide more color on this statement. Specifically, we recommend looking at the dividend payout ratio and the history of dividend growth (or shrinkage.)

Why are these metrics so powerful? For one thing, it's hard to analyze a business with a high degree of accuracy. If you're anything like the average investor, you probably don't have tens of hours to sift through 100+ page annual reports. Dissecting a business fully requires a lot of time and expertise.

In place of that, we need to find suitable metrics that will help us get an accurate picture of a business. They might not provide as deep insight as a full business analysis will, but they will give you 80% of the story in 20% of the time. To expand on this, it's best to turn to what Benjamin Graham once said about figuring out a company's true worth.

These days, the universally accepted method of figuring out a company's true worth is to discount its future cash flows back to the present at an appropriate risk-free hurdle rate. Back in Graham's day though (in the decade after the Great Depression) this method wasn't widely practiced. Instead, Graham proposed that investors would be better off trying to figure out what something was roughly worth, instead of trying to land on an exact price (Graham & Dodd, 2009).

For example, you might not know what a melon is worth, down to the final cent. If you have the time, you can read weather reports and crop yield surveys and speak to farmers and analyze the quality of the soil. You'll be able to figure out a reasonable price with all this insider knowledge. Or, you can head down to the market and look at the prices. If someone offers you a melon for $100 per lb, you know this is way too much. On the flip side, if you're offered melons at one cent per pound, this seems too little.

Every one of us has a rough idea of what a melon is supposed to cost, given its size. We might not have a precise figure in mind, but we can get in the ballpark. Graham stated that as long as you're in the ballpark and apply an appropriate margin of safety to your purchases, you'll come out ahead in the long run. In his own investing, he had no idea whether the NCAV values he was looking at were legitimate or not. This is why he bought stocks for at least 35% off. That was his margin of safety.

When it comes to dividend stocks, the payout ratio and dividend growth profile get you into the ballpark and provide a decent margin of safety to your investment. You won't know the precise value of your investment by examining these metrics, but as Graham illustrated, you don't need to. This method isn't foolproof, but then again, nothing is. As long as the probability of accuracy is high, it's an excellent method to follow. By repeatedly investing in high probability situations, your likelihood of success will be high. That's how successful investors make money.

Payout Ratios

The payout ratio is the percentage of net income that is paid as dividends. For example, if a company earns $1.00 per share and pays $0.30 as dividends, its payout ratio is 30%. If it pays $2.00 per share, its payout ratio is 200%.

Payout ratios by themselves are tricky to evaluate. This is because you want to balance a good payout ratio and one that is sustainable. The definition of "good" varies from one company to another. What's good for one company or business might be bad for another. There's also the stage of the company to take into account.

A company that is growing quickly might not be able to sustain a 10% payout. This is because it needs cash to grow. A mature company might not be able to sustain a 90% payout. They might not need all the cash, but this hardly means they don't need any of it. As an income investor, high payout ratios are good for you since it means more income. However, you don't want it to be so high that it begins affecting the company's long-term health.

Ideal Ratios

So what is an ideal ratio? For mature companies, we recommend investing in companies that pay out between 15% and 65% of their net income. Mature companies are the ones that are behemoths in their industries, and that dominate their space. For example, Coca-Cola, Procter & Gamble, and Johnson & Johnson are mature companies. Typically, they have market caps over $100 billion, which makes them mega-cap stocks. The average payout ratio for a Dividend King stock (a company with a record of raising annual dividend payout amounts for at least 50 consecutive years) is 54%.

You can invest in companies that pay more than this, up to a ratio of 75%. For example, Coca-Cola pays out 73% of its net income to investors.

The problem with stable high payout ratio companies is that the market recognizes the value of these stocks and bids prices up. This means the dividend yield on these companies sinks. Coca-Cola is currently yielding 3.25%, which is a good yield, but this is because the pandemic has hit the stock. PepsiCo yields 2.9% but has also been hit by the pandemic, which has artificially inflated yields. Both of these companies usually yield around 1%.

This is why we recommend sticking to companies that pay less than 35% and avoid those that payout more than 55%. If they're bad companies, you'll lose money. If they're stable companies, you can earn higher yields elsewhere, with equally durable companies. The only exception to this rule is REITs, which are mandated to pay out 90% of their net income, so their yields will naturally be higher.

The pandemic has shifted the dividend yield and payout picture considerably. In the REIT sector, yields have gone through the roof, while payouts have also inflated due to lockdowns. Make sure that they're blips caused by the pandemic and aren't indicators of longer-term trends.

In the case of most mature companies, a high payout ratio often indicates a dividend cut is coming. A good example is the professional wrestling company WWE. In June 2011, the company paid 182% of its earnings as dividends while paying out $0.36 per share. The next quarter, they cut the dividend to just $0.12 per share in order to preserve cash. WWE's dividend has remained at that level for the past nine years.

The problem with high (greater than 75%) payout ratios is that they're unsustainable in downturns. Cash is the lifeblood of any business, and by letting it go, companies find themselves precariously perched when things go south. If the payout is unsustainable, the stock nosedives, and investors are left with large unrealized losses on their portfolio.

Dividend Growth

The second metric that we can use to evaluate a company's dividend stability is the rate at which payouts have been growing. It's true that when it comes to investing, we're more concerned with the future than the past. However, the past, in this case, can help us approximate the future. A company that has been paying dividends consistently and has also been increasing payouts is undoubtedly a healthy business to invest in.

There's also the fact that such businesses are a rarity, not just in America but in the entire world. By concentrating your money into these companies you can rest assured that you'll be investing in companies with stable businesses that have stood the test of time. This doesn't mean these companies will have posted profits during every single year of their existence. There will be periods where their payout ratios might have moved to unsustainable levels. However, the key is to look at how they rebounded from these tough times. Take the case of AT&T (T) as illustrated in Figure 9.

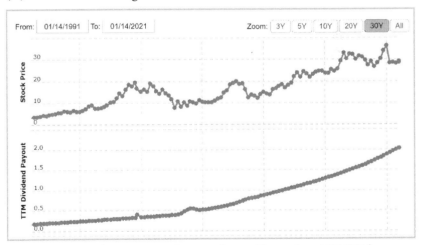

Figure 9: AT&T's Stock Price & Dividend Payout History from 1991-2021 (source: Macrotrends)

Clearly, there's a trend of increasing dividend payments, which is a good thing. The company is also an undoubtedly mature one in its space. However, its stock price has moved relatively sideways since 1996. This is because the company has regularly paid out a very high proportion of its earnings to shareholders. T's average payout ratio has always hovered over 55%. The board has justified paying such a huge amount because of the cash flow it generates.

Currently, AT&T yields 7.46% (annual dividend payout divided by the current stock price) which is almost equal to the average capital gains that the S&P 500 posts every year. The strong history of dividend payment increases means that the company can support a high payout ratio. Besides, research and development expenses aren't as critical in the telecoms sector. It's not as if AT&T has to develop 5G chips or completely revamp its mobile signal towers and cables to support new tech.

The downside is that you can't expect substantial capital gains in the stock. This is true of pretty much every high yielding dividend stock. However, our aim isn't to capture market leading capital gains. Instead, it's to search for a combination of capital gains and yields that will give us an above-average performance. For example, given AT&T's current yield, all we need is a percentage point increase in the stock price to provide us with a good gain for the year.

Some companies fall into various categories depending on how long they have increased their dividend payouts. Companies that have increased dividends consistently for over 50 years are known as **Dividend Kings**. Procter & Gamble, Coca-Cola, 3M Company, American States Water, and Cincinnati Financial are examples of Dividend Kings.

Those companies that have increased payouts for at least 25 years consecutively are termed **Dividend Aristocrats**. Realty Income, Kimberly-Clark, Clorox, McDonald's, and Genuine Parts Company are examples of such businesses.

Finally, those that have increased their payouts for at least ten years are termed **Dividend Achievers**. Microsoft, Visa, Nike, Best Buy, and Verizon are examples of such companies.

Keep in mind that yield is not a factor in preparing these lists. For example, American States Water yields just 1.74%. The average yield of these companies tends to be low since most people in the market recognize their value. The Achievers tend to yield higher, but this doesn't mean their absolute yield is high. For comparison purposes, the Vanguard Dividend Appreciation ETF (VIG), which tracks the Achievers, yields between 1.5 and 2 percent annually.

This is equal to the average stock yield. ETFs that track the Kings and Aristocrats post similar yields. Typically, capital gains tend to make up for the lack of a yield in such investments. Our point is that despite being stellar dividend providers, Dividend Kings, Aristocrats and Achievers aren't necessarily the best stocks for an income investor.

Instead, you need to focus on the combination of the payout ratio and the history of dividend appreciation. Evaluate both of these factors before deciding to invest. High yields aren't important, but you don't want to be stuck with low yields either. Having said that, investing in a company that has steadily increased dividends is a good way of ensuring your money will remain safe and that you'll earn steady returns.

The Danger of Monthly Payments

There has been an increasing trend in the markets recently of so-called "paycheck stocks." These companies pay their investors monthly dividends instead of quarterly or yearly. Many inexperienced income investors have rushed into these stocks, and their prices have risen as a result. Our advice is to stay away from these kinds of companies. This is because most of them are gimmicks.

A monthly dividend payment is a gimmick by itself. A company that conducts business in hundreds of millions or billions cannot afford to pay cash out every month. It would be impossible for its managers to predict what cash flow would look like over such a short time period. It's a bit like someone asking you how much you can pay them every hour of the day. You wouldn't mind paying a cent every hour, but over time it's going to be tough for you to continually devote resources to paying someone a penny all the time.

In the case of public companies, this burden is even larger. Companies need to announce dividend dates and rework their budgets as of the ex-dividend date. All of this takes time and costs them money. It's a lot easier to pay shareholders once every quarter or yearly, and concentrate on running the business instead.

The only companies who wouldn't mind putting up with all the fuss are those who are looking to inflate their stock prices for some reason. You can bet that these companies have insiders who are looking to get rid of their stock and are using the monthly dividend gimmick to get rid of their holdings for high prices.

Understand that a six percent yield remains the same whether the amount is paid monthly, quarterly, or yearly. You'll still receive six percent of what you invested when you bought the stock. Sure, it's great to receive a check every month, but this should never be your sole reason to invest in a company. The fundamentals matter the most, and you should be taking a look at them before making any investment decision.

We don't mean to say that every company that pays monthly dividends is a bad one. There are certainly a few good ones (one in particular, which we'll be discussing later on). It's just that the very nature of this gimmick attracts certain types of companies. The odds of finding a bad company is higher than finding a good one.

To illustrate this, we'll look at the returns of the Global X SuperDividend ETF (SDIV), the largest of the "Monthly payout" ETFs. In the company's own words, "The Global X SuperDividend® ETF (SDIV) invests in 100 of the highest dividend-yielding equity securities in the world."

The fund attracts many new income investors because of its 8% yield and monthly payouts. However, performance leaves a lot to be desired. The fund is down 34% in the past five years, before management fees. Meaning any potential income gains would have been negated by huge capital losses.

Chapter 7

HOW CAPITAL GAINS AND DIVIDENDS WORK IN UNISON

Many income investors don't fully grasp how important capital gains are for their portfolios. In their pursuit of income, they routinely capture less than ideal capital gains and end up leaving a lot of money on the table. Even worse, they might find themselves in dividend or value traps where they earn a steady income, which is then negated by huge capital losses.

It's important to understand that capital gains are just as important as any interest or dividend income you earn from your investments. An excellent example of the role of capital gains is to look at the world of junk bond investing.

Junk bonds are termed as such because they pay a high coupon (interest rate). Every bond is provided a rating by the investment rating agencies, and bonds with a rating below B are considered junk. Junk bonds are mostly issued by bad companies, but good companies issue them as well. Usually, good companies' junk bonds are either redeemed early or are converted to common stock before maturity.

Why are these bonds rated as junk in the first place? Simply put, companies either don't have the cash to pay interest until maturity, or these bonds are known as "junior debt", which means the company doesn't prioritize repaying them. Junior debt often gets converted to equity, which means you are better off buying the stock of the company instead of the junk debt.

To compensate investors for these risks, companies attach high coupon rates to junk debt. It's not uncommon to see coupons of 12-15% attached to junk bonds. This sounds like a great deal to uninformed investors.

You hear the word bond and think safety and see 15% coupons and see dollar signs. So you buy junk debt, and before you know it, the company defaults on payments, leaving you with nothing.

You see, with junk bonds, there is almost no hope of earning capital gains, but there is close to a 100% chance of earning a capital loss. Bond prices are quoted as percentages, so let's look at an example.

If a bond's price is $1,000 and the coupon rate is 15%. Your annual interest payment will be $150.

If that same bond is trading at 65 (65% of its value,) you're getting a lower price on an asset and thus your relative interest rate will be higher. So your $1,000 bond now costs $650 and your $150 annual payout is now at a rate of 23% ($150/$650).

However, once the company defaults, your bond is going to be worth zero. This means you'll earn a capital loss of 55%. How does an income gain of 23% compare against that? It hardly compensates you for the risk of losing 55%. You'll need to buy the bond for less than the coupon percentage to compensate you for the risk, and no company or investor is going to sell junk that low unless default is imminent.

As you can see, capital losses always overshadow income gains. There is also another reason we're highlighting junk bonds. In low interest rate environments like we are in now, junk bonds become more popular. Cash-strapped companies know that investors are hungry for income, and they begin issuing junk debt to capture whatever money they can quickly. The stock market equivalent for such behavior is to split stock when euphoria and blind optimism are at an all-time high. It costs companies nothing, and the euphoria or desire to earn more money drives interest.

Watch out for advertisements pushing junk bonds towards you over the next few years. They'll often be advertised as "high income" or "high yield" instruments but will more than generate less money for you in the long term when compared with a stock that offers a balance of capital gains and dividends.

Capital Gains in Stocks

While junk bonds have almost no hope of earning a capital gain, stocks can potentially earn them at all times.

In fact, when it comes to stocks, capital gains are the primary drivers of wealth. The stock market rises at an average of 8 to 10 percent every year, while the average dividend yield is around two percent. Clearly, a gain or loss of eight percent every year overrides income gains of two percent. Let's look at an example to see how this works. The table below illustrates the difference between a stock that gains 10% per year on average but pays just one percent in dividends, versus another stock that yields eight percent but gains only one percent every year. Our initial investment is $100,000.

Year	10% Gains/ 1% Yield	1% Gains/ 8% Yield
1	$111,000.00	$109,000.00
2	$123,210.00	$118,810.00
3	$136,763.10	$129,502.90
4	$151,807.04	$141,158.16
5	$168,505.82	$153,862.40
6	$187,041.46	$167,710.01
7	$207,616.02	$182,803.91
8	$230,453.78	$199,256.26
9	$255,803.69	$217,189.33
10	$283,942.10	$236,736.37
11	$315,175.73	$258,042.64
12	$349,845.06	$281,266.48

13	$388,328.02	$306,580.46
14	$431,044.10	$334,172.70
15	$478,458.95	$364,248.25
16	$531,089.43	$397,030.59
17	$589,509.27	$432,763.34
18	$654,355.29	$471,712.04
19	$726,334.37	$514,166.13
20	$806,231.15	$560,441.08

It's clear that there's a big difference between the two columns. Despite investing in a high yield stock, your portfolio grows to just $560,441 compared to $806,231. The question of where to invest your money isn't as straightforward, though. A lot depends on your priorities too. While the first choice makes you more money, you'll earn just one percent as cash flow.

This isn't enough for income investors under any circumstances. You'll earn a large check every year with the second choice, but your investment isn't growing as quickly. The ideal investment would combine the first option's capital gains and the yield of the second, but such investments are exceedingly rare.

The point of this example is to illustrate that capital gains are just as powerful as dividend yields. And yet, there's another issue with high yields. The real amount you'll earn from the second investment will be lower than what's indicated due to ordinary income taxes you'll pay on your investment. Your eight percent yield will be reduced to 6.4% after taxes. Capital gains aren't taxed until you sell your investment. This means you can compound your money freely. You can't compound your money to the same extent with dividends because you'll pay taxes every year. This happens even if you DRIP your payments back into the stock, which we've assumed in this example.

Chapter 8

THE 11 PRINCIPLES FOR FINDING GREAT DIVIDEND PAYING STOCKS

Now that you've learned what NOT to look at when searching for dividend-paying stocks, it's time to develop a process that will help you find the best dividend paying stocks in the market.

In our previous book *The 8 Step Beginner's Guide to Value Investing* we defined a rational process that helps you discover great stocks for the long term. We're going to stick to the same base formula when it comes to dividend investing.

This is because evaluating a good dividend-paying stock isn't that much different from evaluating a stock for long-term investing. In the latter case you'll be content with earning capital gains while in the former case you'll need the stock to pay you dividends. This means the bulk of our process is pretty much the same, except we need to add one additional criterion to find good dividend-paying stocks.

Let's go through all of these criteria one by one.

Principle One: The Warren Buffett Test

This principle runs extremely deep. There are many consequences of following this rule, and by itself it'll help you avoid many of the pitfalls that individual investors face. The rule itself is simple. Always treat your investments as if you're buying a business. You're not buying stock or buying shares but are grabbing a piece of a living, breathing business that has employees, profits, and office space. This means you need to act like a business owner and not as a speculator.

Speculation in this context refers to implementing money-making schemes that contain high risk with an uncertain reward. For example, buying a stock because it's about to go ex-dividend is a speculative practice. The same applies if you buy the stock just before an important interest rate announcement because you expect a rate hike to benefit its prospects over the next year.

As a rule of thumb, if your investment horizon is less than ten years long, you are more likely speculating rather than investing. We're not saying you need to hold onto your investment for that entire period. Instead we're saying you need to evaluate what the business will look like over the next decade at the very least. Since you can't predict macroeconomic factors very well over the next decade, the only solution is to turn to business fundamentals.

This is how smart business owners think of their enterprises. You are unlikely to find the owner of a company selling their stake in their company because they are facing a few macroeconomic headwinds. Neither do they plan to repurchase it on the cheap once it falls from a high sale price. This kind of owner won't have time to run everyday operations, producing earnings and revenues

Yet, many investors behave in this manner. At the mere hint of economic uncertainty, they run for the hills and the stock price crashes. Ask yourself this: If you bought a company for $100 per share and if the business fundamentals remain the same while the stock price crashes to $50, would you buy or sell? A business owner would always buy in this situation. If the business was a good buy at $100, it's an even better buy at $50. The company's fundamentals are the same, so what does it matter what the stock price is?

Buffett's mentor Benjamin Graham has an interesting way of describing the above situation. He envisioned a situation where the investor owned an important asset that they had bought for a price, say $100. Every day a person named Mr. Market would walk up to them and offer the investor a price for that asset. Mr. Market was a bit of a manic depressive and would one day offer $40 for the asset, and the next day would offer $1,000. There was never any rhyme or reason behind his prices.

This is how the stock market behaves. Buffett has also spoken of how people view real estate property prices compared to how we view stock prices. If you owned a piece of land, would you consider buying it today and selling it tomorrow, only to repurchase it on the third day? It's absurd! Neither would you check what the property is worth every single day.

Yet so many investors do this with stocks because they view them as mere numbers on a screen. By engaging in such short-term behavior, you increase your likelihood of making poor decisions. Market timing is also not as easy as it sounds on paper. No one, not even the best paid Wall Street pros who spend their entire lives painstakingly analyzing chart patterns and order flows, can time the top of a market or its bottom. If someone could do this with perfect accuracy just 2-3 times in a row, they'd likely be the richest person alive.

In reality, the richest person alive, Jeff Bezos, is a business owner who has held his favorite stock (Amazon) for more than 20 years. This is why it's best to stick to a company's fundamentals and treat it as an asset, not as a piece of paper.

Principle Two: Understand the Business Thoroughly

Businesses are complicated creatures. They aren't always what they seem on the surface. For example, McDonald's is seemingly a fast food company, but it's real business lies in real estate. Similarly, Starbucks is a coffee chain, but it's real business is a cheap source of entertainment and socializing, along with serving as a makeshift office and meeting room for people.

As a business owner, you need to drill deep into how a company makes money. The business environment that companies face is challenging, and over time almost all of them have to adapt, or they die out. Even a company that is in a seemingly simple business such as Coca-Cola has to adapt. In Coca-Cola's case, it's easy to think they could simply keep producing Coke and leave it at that. However, with people becoming increasingly conscious of the environmental impact of their choices and becoming more health-conscious, how much longer can Coca-Cola rely on sugary syrup?

This is why Coca-Cola owns more than 500 brands worldwide. It's also why PepsiCo long ago diversified its business by purchasing FritoLay, which is the world's largest producer of snacks. If a soft drink manufacturer faces such challenges, imagine the challenges that a more sophisticated business faces. As an investor, you don't need to figure out how companies should react to such environments, but you do need to know where the business makes its money.

For example, a PepsiCo shareholder who doesn't understand that their dividends come largely from the snack business doesn't understand how their company works. Why is it so vital for you to understand the business? After all, isn't that management's job? It's important for you as an investor to understand it too because this prevents you from selling or buying at inopportune moments.

For example, Coca-Cola's stock sank after the market crash of 1987. Millions of Coca-Cola shareholders sold their shares. Warren Buffett instead went out and bought as much of the company as he could lay his hands on. Today he owns close to 10% of the company, having paid $1.8 billion for his stake, as a result. Berkshire Hathaway earns $640 million in Coca-Cola dividends alone every year (*Here's How Much Warren Buffett Has Ma♦e on Coca-Cola*, 2019).

Berkshire has earned over seven billion dollars in dividends from its investment in Coca-Cola. That's just dividends. It doesn't include capital gains from the 1,750% rise in Coca-Cola's stock since 1989. What's the key behind such monstrous gains? Buffett understood how Coca-Cola makes money and the advantageous way it had structured its relationships with its bottlers.

To understand a business, you need to understand the sector it operates in and how the economics of that sector work. Some sectors are allergic to money. For example, with the exception of companies like Southwest Airlines, the commercial airline business has long been a terrible place to invest money.

However, commercial airplane manufacturers have always had profitable businesses, their current troubles notwithstanding. Similarly, cruise ship operators have always had to deal with tough business conditions. Cruise ship builders? Not so much.

A similar example is in the mobile phone industry. The tussle between Apple and Samsung has always grabbed headlines. However, the glass on both phones comes from the same company: Corning Inc (GLW), whose stock has doubled over the past five years while still paying around a 2.5-3% dividend.

Intelligent investors understand that great companies are still subject to their industries' economics. Sometimes it's better to invest in shovels than dig for gold yourself.

Principle Three: Understand The Relationship Between the Business & the Sector

A rising tide lifts all boats. Bull markets have always operated on these terms and have made even the most unintelligent speculators lots of money. However, once the tide goes out, we get to see who's well-positioned and who isn't. Sector growth often lifts every single company operating within it, irrespective of whether these companies make money or not.

In our previous book, we highlighted the case of 5G stocks, but since then, we've been presented with an even better example: the electric vehicle market. Nothing makes sense when it comes to EVs anymore. It began with Tesla, a company that for years existed solely on the promise of "what if", since it took 16 years to make a profit. The company was formed in 2003, and it posted its first profit in 2019. It's since posted consecutive quarterly profits, which is a great thing for investors, and will likely end 2020 with its first-ever annual profit.

The company's lifeblood is the subsidies it receives from the government for selling energy credits to other manufacturers. Without this subsidy, the company continues to lose money with every car it produces. However, at least Tesla has a good product, real customers, the best technology in the sector, and a visionary leader.

The same can't be said of other EV manufacturers. The events that recently engulfed alleged electric truck maker Nikola (NKLA) were a good example. The company made the headlines in the middle of 2020 after its stock price soared 3,000% in a matter of days. However, this was illustrative of how irrational markets can be in the short term, and the company's fortunes began unraveling from there.

On September 10th, 2020, a report compiled by Hindenburg Research showed that Nikola's products were nonexistent and that their Nikola One semi-truck was functional only if it was plugged into a wall outlet, amongst other lies. This resulted in GM pulling out of a deal to buy the company, and led to CEO and Founder Trevor Milton being forced to resign.

Other EV startups that have reached multi-billion-dollar valuations are Hyllion, Fisker, Karma, Workhorse, and Spartan. Fisker interestingly has been around since 2007, went bust in between, and has since made a comeback. Sounds like a great story, except, the comeback was primarily because of the huge surge of interest in EVs, prompting the founders to cash in on the boom and raise money. The company produced a car back in the day that rivaled Tesla's Roadster but was even more unreliable than its competitor.

These examples demonstrate that the EV sector is a perfect example of how unprofitable and fundamentally flawed companies benefit from generally favorable business conditions. You need to look underneath the hood to reveal which companies have staying power and which are built on thin air.

Principle Four: It's a Newer Company, The Founder Should Still be Involved

The time it takes these days for a company to go public has decreased significantly. Even as recently as the 1990s, companies had to prove a significant level of profits and revenues before considering listing themselves on exchanges. Over and above listing requirements, the Initial Public Offering (IPO) process was tough and required a ton of regulatory documentation. IPOs also cost a lot, and most companies couldn't afford them.

These days, thanks to reverse merger processes and Special Purpose Acquisition Companies (SPACs), the time it takes to go public is shorter than what it used to be. We're witnessing more companies go public in the earlier stages of their lives. As a result, the market has become more unstable since you have billion-dollar companies that are essentially startups.

In such environments with younger companies, it's imperative that you evaluate whether the founder is still on board. The founder's presence mitigates much of the risk that these companies pose to investors because the person with the grand vision is still on board. The founder is the one who has been there since the beginning and is the person most responsible for steering the company this far. They're also the true visionaries who can help guide the company through tough times.

Take the case of Apple and Steve Jobs. Around the turn of the millennium, Apple was a distant second to Microsoft, and closing the gap seemed hopeless. Only a founder such as Jobs could have turned the business around by changing the rules completely. He turned Apple from a computer company to a communications product manufacturing company. As a result, after dominating for several years in its field, Microsoft found itself playing the wrong sport entirely.

This pivot wasn't entirely original, unlike popular imagination suggests. Sony had been making phones, computers, and electronics for many years. However, it hadn't experienced anywhere close to Apple's eventual success. The reason was primarily that Apple had the advantage of being guided by its founder through a new market and developing unique philosophies and business processes that allowed it to thrive.

Technology companies face many hurdles, and it's essential that their founders remain close to the company. With many of the trailblazers now growing older, this is more important than ever. The fact that Bill Gates wasn't present to counter Jobs and the ascent of Google and Facebook hampered Microsoft for over a decade. To its credit, the firm has bounced back admirably thanks to its shift in focus to the cloud computing business. However, one wonders how much further ahead they might have been with Gates on board.

Principle Five: Intangible Asset Advantage

A company's balance sheet lists all of its assets and liabilities. The most interesting section, and the one most ripe for manipulation, is the intangible assets section. This is where the company lists the assets that don't have a specific monetary value attached to them. For example, Coca-Cola's brand name is an intangible asset. If you were to pour Coke into a bottle branded as "Bubba's Cola," it's unlikely to sell in the same volumes.

It isn't just the brand name but the colors, the script, the taste of the product, and 60+ years of feelings brought upon customers by global advertising that is an intangible asset. Coca-Cola also owns the patent on its formula as well as trademarks on its name and brand products. All of these are extremely valuable to the company. Without these intangible assets, Coca-Cola would likely be a pretty ordinary business.

So why are intangible assets so highly valued? Put simply, they signify competitive advantages that cannot be quickly eroded. It's easy to create a better formula than Coca-Cola's. Well, not easy, but it's certainly within the realm of possibility.

However, what constitutes better? More importantly, how does one go about overcoming how consumers feel when they look at the Coca-Cola brand and the red labeling? It's close to impossible to push a new brand as being more attractive.

Many pharmaceutical companies operate in this manner, as well. Despite the field relying heavily on disruptive inventions, few staple companies dominate the industry. Every now and then, one gains the upper hand over another, but in the long run, all of them remain roughly in position. This is because of the large hoard of intellectual property (IP) they own. Intellectual property is an intangible asset and includes patents, formulas, and designs. The patent libraries that these firms hold are enough to drive billion-dollar valuations by themselves.

The computing industry, or at least the companies which dominated the early internet era, are heading to a similar structure. The likes of Google, Apple, Amazon, Facebook, and Microsoft own vast patent libraries, and it's hard to see how these companies will ever be disrupted in the future. This illustrates how strong the effect of intangible assets is.

Principle Six: Upper Management is Bought In

If you ask a CEO of any public company if they are focused on the long term goals of the company, it's likely that at least 95% would say yes. However, in reality, actions speak louder than words. This is why we like to take a more quantitative look at management's goals. We do this by looking at how management is compensated to get a deeper insight into where their incentives lie.

For starters, you should look at companies that have a good amount of insider ownership. Insiders constitute a company's officers, directors and C-Level executives (and their families), who have access to key company information before the general public. If these people, who theoretically should know more about the company than anyone else, have enough confidence in the company to place their own money in the stock, then that's a positive sign.

In public companies, insider ownership (the total percentage of shares held by insiders) greater than 20% is considered extremely high.

To check what percentage of a company is owned by insiders, you can go to Yahoo Finance, select your company of choice and click on the Holding tab.

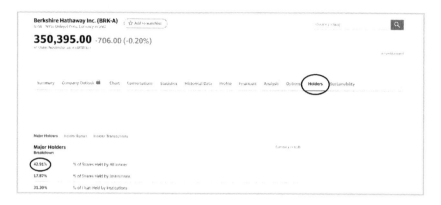

Figure 10: The insider ownership for Berkshire Hathaway (Source: Yahoo Finance)

High insider ownership far greater than 20% isn't always a good thing. When it's that high, it is difficult for shareholders to have any say over management and changes can be hard to implement. If the company with high insider ownership is being run inefficiently, then as a shareholder, you won't be able to do anything.

So always look for a good amount of insider ownership but not too much. Some institutional presence is positive unless the company is too small to be attractive to a large institution. However, too much institutional ownership makes the company subject to activist investors. This is where hedge funds with large ownership stakes will pressure the company's board of directors to make changes to increase short term profits.

Look at the management compensation structure as well. Companies explicitly list this out in their annual reports (10-K). A compensation structure that is primarily based on stock options is a good sign since this incentivizes executives to reward investors.

Just as with insider ownership, though, there's a possibility to go overboard with this. If executive compensation is tied directly to stock prices, executives are incentivized to maximize stock prices. The short term performance of a company's stock and its long run profitability are two different things. In the long run, they converge, but in the short term they don't. Management that is primarily focused on quarterly stock performance is not setting the company up for long-term success.

Look for stock options being awarded a few years down the line instead of being awarded over the short term. Another important factor to look for is the impact of issuing options on shareholders' equity. Typically options are expensed, and this amount needs to be a reasonable charge. If it significantly detracts from earnings, then it's probably excessive.

This isn't always possible to figure out, but take a look at the severance packages that are being offered to departing executives. Many CEOs collect tens of millions in compensation even after doing a bad job. You won't be able to get details on individual contracts, but if the company has a history of making poor deals with its executives, this means the Board of Directors isn't doing their jobs properly. Stay away from such companies.

Twenty years ago, to find real time information on insider ownership, you would have needed a Bloomberg terminal, or you would have had to wait weeks for your broker to send you the information in the mail. Fortunately for you, technology is a great equalizer, and now you can instantly access the same information for free.

The two best websites to find data on insider ownership for free are FinViz.com and GuruFocus.com – both of which track trades made by company insiders. If you see the company CEO buying stock, that's an excellent sign. After all, if a CEO is confident enough in the company's long term outlook to put their own money on it, that's a glowing recommendation.

We should note that while insider buying is usually a positive sign, insider selling is less of an indicator of the long-term prospects of a company. Insider sales are often made for reasons beyond the person's expectations for the company. It is often as simple as a board member wanting the cash to purchase a new home.

Principle Seven: The Company Has Strong Advertising, Marketing & Sales Operations

A company might have a great product or service, but all those pretty features are of no use if they cannot sell it, which means that sales and marketing are the lifeblood of every organization.

A sign of a company with strong sales and marketing is increasing revenues. While profits can be massaged, revenues are quite basic and cannot be fudged without doing something grossly illegal. If you see healthy growth in revenues year after year, and if these revenues are keeping up with net income increases, this is a good sign. Another positive indicator is low turnover within the upper management of the sales and marketing departments.

Since net income can be massaged to make it look better than it is, it's a good idea to look at free cash flow and compare that to increases in revenues. If revenue increases aren't resulting in higher free cash flows, either the company is reinvesting vast amounts of cash into capital expenses, or they're employing some creative accounting with regards to recognizing revenues. If you aren't sure where to find these numbers in a company's financial statements, make sure you grab a copy of our free video course *Company Valuation 101*, which shows you exactly where to find these numbers.

> You can get the course as part of your bonus resources by going to
> https://freemanpublications.com/bonus

To figure out marketing strategies, read a company's press releases and new product or service announcements. Sure, there will be a lot of fluff in these releases, but you'll get a good idea of how a company is positioning itself in the market.

Principle Eight: Management is Willing to Make Short-Term Sacrifices for Long-Term Results

As a long-term investor, your focus is going to last longer than ten years. It stands to reason that you want management that is equally focused over the long term. Company executives need to balance both the short and long-term demands of their businesses. An excellent example of this is happening with Disney right now.

In July 2020, Disney made a stunning announcement when it decided to forego paying its dividend. This saved the company $1.6 billion in cash. With its businesses being hit hard by the pandemic, any reasonable investor and business owner would have applauded this move. However, the market being what it is, rewarded Disney with a tumble in stock price. Naturally, long-term focused investors could have taken advantage of this opportunity to buy more.

This particular decision was made keeping in mind the medium-term effects on the company's profitability. With the majority of its business coming from parks and entertainment while facing uncertain reopening times, it stands to reason that Disney's executives would choose to hang on to cash to weather tough times.

However, an even bigger decision is looming ahead for Disney. The company has been robust enough to begin diversifying beyond its traditional parks and entertainment model. The launch of Disney+ was such a move. With streaming picking up the pace and with the vast inventory of IP that the company has, releasing entertainment directly onto streaming services makes a lot of sense. As the pandemic has ravaged other areas of Disney's business, Disney+ remains a bright spot and offers enormous potential.

It's so huge that prominent institutional investor and Disney shareholder Dan Loeb wants the company to forego its dividend entirely and devote more cash towards developing Disney+ (de Haas, 2020). If management follows through on this, they'll be explicitly prioritizing the long term and will hurt their short-term prospects.

A good management team will create a balance between the two while leaning towards the long term. Regardless of how the situation at Disney plays out, there is no doubt that the company has management that seeks to create value for the long term above all else. There aren't many managers who will willingly cut their dividend entirely and risk a tumbling stock.

One of the best metrics to look at the long-term orientation of a company's management is to look at the return on equity that the managers have generated. You calculate this by dividing earnings by the shareholders' equity as listed in the balance sheet. Long-term-oriented management continually reinvests profits to create better assets. The better their reinvestment decisions are, the better the assets that they create. This is what drives long-term earnings growth.

Stability in management is also an essential quality to look for. Many companies have long-standing CEOs, but the people around them come and go frequently. High executive turnover is a hallmark of a CEO who pushes blame onto his/her subordinates and doesn't accept it themselves. Instead of looking at how long the CEO has been there, look for low turnover in the company's upper echelons and whether the organization has a succession plan for when the current CEO leaves.

General Electric is a famous example of how future CEOs are groomed in the final years of the previous CEO's tenure. Steve Jobs also spent many of his last years at Apple preparing Tim Cook to step into the CEO role. A position that Cook himself now finds himself in as he enters his 10th year as the company's leader.

Developing a core management team is a sign of preparing for the long term. The founder won't always be around, so there has to be someone to pick up the slack. The stronger the team is, the stronger the organization is.

Principle Nine: The Company Has an Economic Moat

The concept of the economic moat was popularized by Warren Buffett and his business partner Charlie Munger. They preferred investing in companies that had some sort of unfair (but legal) advantage in the way they ran their business. Coca-Cola has an unfair advantage by being around for so long and having a fully recognizable brand name. See's Candies, a highly publicized Berkshire Hathaway investment, has a strong brand name as well. So does GEICO and other companies that they've invested in over the years.

A moat comes in many forms. Walmart's moat is the high economies of scale it achieves, enabling it to slash prices to levels that are unsustainable for smaller competitors. A local store cannot buy inventory in the volumes that Walmart does and cannot reduce prices to that extent. This naturally eliminates competition. Amazon enjoys similar advantages in the online retail space.

Google and Facebook enjoy another type of moat, which is increasingly relevant in the digital business era. This is referred to as the network effect. The more that people use a company's product, the better the product becomes. For example, compared to these days, Google's search algorithm was extremely rudimentary when it debuted. However, as more people used Google, the more data it could collect, the more its algorithm learned human speech patterns and search tendencies. For companies like Google, more users equal greater profits.

Similarly, Facebook derives most of its market value from its large user base. The more that users stay on the platform, the greater the quantity of data that Facebook collects. This insight allows Facebook to provide better targeting services for advertisers, which fuels ad spend on the platform.

For example, a Facebook advertiser can elect to show their ads only to female small business owners aged between 35-44, who live in Los Angeles. When you compare that level of specificity to TV or print advertising, it's easy to see why total advertising spend on Facebook has increased by 400% over the past five years.

The network effect is tough for competitors to overcome since they cannot merely improve on an existing product. They need to reinvent the entire business model.

Businesses that have economic moats survive tough times better than ones that don't. The opposite of a company that has a moat is one that sells a commodity product. A commodity product is one that differentiates itself solely on its price. For example, if you were in the market for a new mouse for your laptop, you're going to choose one that is ergonomic and effective but only up to a certain price. Another example is the pen you choose to write with.

On the face of it, Walmart has a commodity product. The only reason people shop there is that they offer the cheapest goods. However, there's a difference between selling products that are differentiated solely on price versus what Walmart does. Walmart consistently delivers the cheapest goods, no matter the broader economic conditions. There is no other business in America that can do this as efficiently as Walmart does. Thus, the moat it has doesn't have to do with price. It's more about how Walmart conducts its processes that ensure it can offer the lowest price all the time.

Other examples of moats are companies operating in non-sexy industries. Unattractive industries are great because companies receive less analyst attention, they are less prone to disruption, and the incumbents can often have a natural monopoly.

A great example of this is Waste Management. You don't have to be a genius to figure out which industry the company is in. Now imagine being an employee of Waste Management. If you met someone at a barbecue, would you introduce yourself as your job title "I work in marketing," or would you let them know you work for a company called Waste Management?

In addition, there aren't too many 20 somethings in Silicon Valley spending all night hyped up on caffeine and Adderall hypothesizing on how to disrupt the waste management industry. That is a big reason why the stock is up 400% in the past decade while simultaneously increasing its dividend payouts.

Another factor that can cause a moat is a company operating in a morally or ethically dubious industry. Tobacco, alcohol, and casino companies all fall under this category.

We should note that you should never compromise your moral or ethical views just to make money. The beauty of long term investing is that you can eliminate pretty much any industry you *on't* want to invest in but still make a killing in sectors that do fit within your views or beliefs.

Principle Ten: The Business Can Weather a Storm

Anyone can make money when times are good. However, it's a sign of strength when businesses can thrive during downturns. We don't mean to say that you should look at businesses that benefit from downturns, such as collection agencies or receivables financing companies. These industries benefit when things are bad but are depressed when conditions are good.

Instead, your task is to search for companies that do well when times are good and bad. Walmart is a good example of such a business. When times are good, it does decently since everyone needs cheap groceries and goods. When times are rough, it does even better. Compare them to the likes of The Fresh Market and other high-end grocers, and you'll see the difference. While the quality of food at the latter supermarkets is undoubtedly better, your concern as an investor is the business and its economics.

There are some key factors you can look at when figuring out how recession-proof a business is. Look at the number of suppliers and customers it has. Companies will disclose this in the introduction of their annual 10-K filings. If more than 90% of revenues derive from a single customer, this is a very bad sign. Remember, public companies on average sell hundreds of millions of dollars worth of products and services per year. If a single customer drives 90% of this revenue, what's going to happen if that customer hits a rough patch?

Similarly, having just one supplier is a risky move. In some industries, having a single supplier is a feature, not a bug. However, even in these businesses, managers typically have backup plans to mitigate the loss of a supplier. This is why the troubles that befell Intel over the past few years haven't affected their customers too much. They had backup suppliers ready to go.

Lastly, leverage is an especially relevant feature to consider. Leverage refers to the ratio of debt to equity on a company's balance sheet. In our current low interest rate environments, companies have taken on huge levels of debt since it's cheap. With the Fed indicating that they'll be maintaining low interest rates for the foreseeable future, this might lead to management taking things easy and underestimating the risk of overleveraging themselves.

The best way to think about leverage is to compare it to an investment you might routinely make. Let's take the case of a house you buy. If the home is worth $100,000 and you borrow $90,000 to finance it, you own just 10% of the property. If you rent the property out to pay for the monthly mortgage, this looks like a great decision. However, what happens when your tenant moves out and you can't find someone else? All those mortgage payments will come out of your pocket, and if you can't afford to make them, the house gets foreclosed.

This is pretty much what happens to companies as well. The tricky thing with companies is that they need to service debt from revenues. Due to the very nature of the business, revenues will move up and down. It's not as if companies can accurately predict what might happen tomorrow. Look at the number of bankruptcies and layoffs that occurred due to the pandemic-enforced lockdowns. This is a surefire indicator of how companies have overleveraged themselves to the point that two to three months' worth of lockdowns toppled them into the red.

It's a bit like a household not having enough emergency cash to pay for three months' worth of living expenses, which is extremely risky. As investors, we often pay special attention to the good times but neglect the bad. An intelligent investor always considers risk above reward. Eliminate how you could lose money, and you'll automatically start making money.

Principle Eleven: Implement The 10-10-10 Rule

The ten preceding criteria were presented in our book *The 8 Step Beginner's Guie to Value Investing*. For Dividend Growth investing, we can now present the 11th factor to help guide your investment process. This is the 10-10-10 rule.

The first factor to look for in a company is **paying dividends for the past ten years**. This is a minimum criterion, so the longer the dividend payment record is, the better.

Next, you want to look for companies that have **consistently grown their dividend payouts over the past ten years**. We're not talking about massive increases in yield but sustainable ones. A stable and slowly increasing payout points to a stable stock price and solid long term company prospects.

Lastly, you should look for companies that can conceivably **grow their stock prices for the next ten years**. It's no use getting healthy dividend payments if your capital is being eroded by a declining stock price. This is why it can be helpful to look for stocks that have had their prices beaten down recently. If it's a high quality company, its prospects of increasing in value over the next decade are much better.

With all of these principles in mind, we're now ready to present the best income investment candidates for your portfolio.

Chapter 9

THE 7 BEST DIVIDEND GROWTH STOCKS FOR 2021 AND BEYOND

Before we dive in, we'd like to start by saying certain sectors gravitate more towards a balance of dividends and capital gains. These are energy, financials, and pharmaceuticals. We'll also include REITs in there, but we'll discuss REITs in more detail in the next chapter.

Generally speaking, if a company isn't in one of these sectors, you should avoid dividend yields of greater than four percent. AT&T is the most famous exception to this, but many investors fall into yield traps when seeking income-producing stocks outside of these sectors.

The Best High Yield Stocks To Invest In

Of the non-penny stocks listed in the United States, 1,982 stocks currently pay a dividend of over one percent.

Change that to five percent, and the number goes down to 526. Of those 526, we want to identify stable companies whose earnings are growing. This is because we want to pick companies that can reliably pay high dividends for the foreseeable future while also offering capital gains potential. From that list of 526, we've selected seven stocks which meet these criteria.

Abbvie Inc. (NYSE:ABBV)

◇ Market Cap - $148 billion

◇ 52 week high/low - 101.28/62.55

◇ Current yield - 5.14%

◇ Beta - 0.69

◇ Number of years of dividend increases - 47

While AbbVie has only been operating as an independent company for seven years, it has long been a staple of the pharmaceutical industry. The company was spun off from its parent Abbott Labs in 2013. AbbVie has a long and profitable track record extending back to its days as a division of its larger parent company. Abbott Labs spun off its research-based pharmaceutical manufacturing business, and AbbVie was the result.

The company is best known for its Humira medication, which is used to treat rheumatoid arthritis, Crohn's disease, and ulcerative colitis. Humira is the biggest money spinner for the company and accounts for as much as 50% of the company's revenues. Going back to our principles in the previous chapter, this might seem like a huge risk. However, we still like AbbVie because the dependence on Humira is shrinking. In 2018, the percentage of revenues that Humira accounted for was 65%.

The pharma industry can present cyclical advantages for the firms operating in it due to the way patents work. The typical cycle runs something like this. A firm pours resources into developing a drug and, after lengthy trials, is granted permission to mass manufacture it. The patent on the drug lasts for around 20 years, giving the firm a monopoly in the developed world.

As the 20-year cycle ends, the firm usually has other drugs in development, and this starts another 20-year monopoly on the formulation. This doesn't mean the firm has a monopoly on how the disease is treated. Other firms can step in with their own formulations. However, the combination of treatment periods and side effects causes one drug to be favored over another. Sales and marketing also play an important role with sales reps routinely keeping tabs on what doctors are prescribing their patients.

Coming back to AbbVie, the patent on Humira expires in 2023, and this might be a cause for concern for a smaller firm. However, AbbVie has other drugs poised to take over the heavy lifting. The firm produces drugs such as Imbruvica and Venclexta that are used to treat blood cancer and are prescribed routinely. Other immunology drugs such as Rinvoq and Skyrizi are also poised to take over the space.

Moving away from the product specifics, the financials of the company are robust. It has reported positive cash flow for the past ten quarters and has no significant litigation expenses. This is a huge plus. In comparison, Johnson & Johnson spent $5.1 billion in lawsuit-related expenses in 2019. Since splitting from Abbott Labs, AbbVie's stock has grown by 160% and has maintained high dividend payouts.

Thanks to its association with its parent, AbbVie is already a Dividend Aristocrat and will soon become a Dividend King, assuming it maintains its record of increasing dividends. Its payout ratio is 47.5%, which is a great balance between sustainability and rewarding shareholders. The company pays $1.18 per share quarterly, which works out to a five percent yield annually. Investing $8,000 in AbbVie will net you just over $400 per year in cash flow ($100 per quarter.) Its beta is low as well, meaning the stock's volatility is less than the market average.

Given that Humira's 2023 patent expiration is already known, the event is priced into the stock by the market. In 2019, the firm acquired Irish pharmaceutical company Allergan for a reported $63 billion. Allergan is mostly famous for being the manufacturer of Botox. This diversifies AbbVie's product offerings.

In terms of future prospects, the company currently has over 120 clinical trials with more than 60 of these in the mid to late trial stage. AbbVie also holds several cannabis-related patents, including cannabinoids used to treat cancer, a treatment for juvenile idiopathic arthritis, and cannabis to treat skin disorders. A study by Data Bridge Market Research projects the Medical Marijuana market poised to be worth over $82 Billion by 2027. If AbbVie can capture just a fraction of the market share, this will mean great things for the company's outlook.

The next five years are being characterized as low growth for this company, but we're extremely positive on the long-term outlook with a solid 5.5% dividend in the meantime.

Chevron Corporation (NYSE:CVX)

◇ Market Cap - $137 billion

◇ 52 week high/low - 122.94/51.60

◇ Current yield - 6.3%

◇ Beta - 1.26

◇ Number of years of dividend increases - 34

Don't be fooled by the higher beta value of this stock. Chevron is a classic example of how Warren Buffett's recommendation of being greedy when others are fearful and fearful when others are greedy can make you money. The stock currently has a high beta because the oil industry and energy sector have been battered throughout 2020.

Oil prices have steadily declined, and with the current pandemic, the stock has fallen 30% this year. It has also reported a large quarterly loss in Q2 due to falling demand. However, your job isn't to think in quarters. It's to think in decades.

Rewind back to 2005, and we see that Chevron was the smallest of the U.S domestic oil producers. As of this writing, it's close to toppling ExxonMobil for the top spot. The energy sector hasn't been battered just in the markets. Public sentiment against oil producers has been turning negative as well. All around the world, governments, and people are waking up to the realities of climate change, and alternative energy use is on the rise.

However, this doesn't mean alternative energy sources are ready to replace oil. Within the next 50 years, we see oil becoming obsolete, but not within the next decade. The fundamentals of the sector remain the same. After all, it took 100 years for oil to replace coal. While the replacement process will occur quickly in the developed world, the developing world is another issue.

Even the likes of China, which is a fully developed economy, relies on oil heavily. This is also the case with other economies such as Brazil and India. As one of the world's top producers, Chevron is uniquely positioned to prosper over the next decade. The company's debt to equity ratio is just 0.25, which means it isn't heavily leveraged. It's a lean operation for an oil and gas company. The next best debt to equity ratio is Exxon with 0.38. This will stand Chevron in good stead as oil promises to be volatile for the upcoming decade.

One of the strongest points of this company is its management. They are committed to rewarding shareholders with dividends. On their Q2 earnings call, CFO Pierre Breber stated (*2Q20 Earnings Conference Call Eꞏiteꞏ Transcript, 2020*):

"All of our actions are ꞏesigneꞏ consistent with our financial priorities. The first is to sustain anꞏ grow the ꞏiviꞏenꞏ. We showeꞏ our stress test last quarter at $30 [cruꞏe oil prices] that I think was maꞏe very clear that we have the financial capability anꞏ the flexibility in our capital program, the ability to manage our costs to sustain that ꞏiviꞏenꞏ through what is a stress test."

Chevron's management has repeatedly shown remarkable capital management in a sector that is rife with overleveraging and excessive spending. Acquisitions are commonplace in the energy sector, and companies often acquire others to present themselves as having done something. However, Chevron's management was willing to walk away from a deal in 2019 because it was deemed too expensive. They then acquired oil and gas producer Noble Energy in 2019 for what was considered a relative bargain.

As you can see from Breber's comment above, the dividend is safe until mid 2021 and has been stress tested to withstand oil prices of $30 per barrel. As of this writing, oil prices are above $40 per barrel. Given its high yield of six percent and strong company fundamentals, it's hard to find a better energy prospect than Chevron.

IBM (NYSE:IBM)

◇ Market Cap - $99.94 billion

◇ 52 week high/low - 158.75/90.56

◇ Current yield - 5.14%

◇ Beta - 1.16

◇ Number of years of dividend increases - 25

IBM is another example of a company that has been beaten down recently. Once an innovator in the technology space, it is treated as a grandfather of the industry these days. It has a market cap of close to $100 billion, which looks like pocket change compared to Apple's $2.75 trillion. From 2015 onwards, IBM's core business was beset by declining revenues and a complex management structure.

Detractors even named it International Bureaucratic Monstrosity for its complex structure. These days, IBM has moved well away from its days as a mainframe supplier to providing cloud computing, data analytics, and AI services. In line with this vision, the new CEO Arvind Krishna hails from the cloud computing division. Microsoft made a similar pivot in 2014, and over the past six years has witnessed huge growth.

Krishna's first quarter in charge was a positive one, with earnings and revenue beating analyst estimates. Cloud revenue was up 30% in the previous quarter, which continues to reinforce IBM's desire to move into the cloud computing world. Its cloud computing division now makes up 33% of overall revenues. In the next quarter, it is expected to surpass technology services as the largest revenue division for the entire company. The overall cloud computing market is valued at $1.2

trillion, with almost half of that market being a potential fit for the company's business consulting division.

IBM's cloud services are sufficiently differentiated from Google, Microsoft, and Amazon offerings to make an impact. 60% of their contacts are on a recurring revenue stream. Recent customer wins include Adobe, Salesforce, SAP, Box, and Slack. All are using IBM's hybrid cloud platform to modernize mission-critical workloads.

The acquisition of Red Hat in 2019 put some strain on IBM's balance sheet. However, IBM has enough cash flow to cover the stress from it. In addition, IBM also acquired AI pioneer WDG Automation.

IBM has a proud history of increasing dividend payouts. The company kept growing dividends through the darkest days of the dotcom crash in 2000 and throughout the financial crisis of 2007-2009. We expect to see a similar story as we move forward, with a return to solid growth numbers in 2021.

We also like the makeup of the new management team, particularly with their preference for share ownership. Currently, the management team owns around 400,000 shares, which gives them a significant incentive to perform.

Another important metric is the value of share compensation relative to cash compensation. IBM's management team has share to cash compensation ratios between five and eleven, with anything over three considered significant from a "management buy-in" perspective.

Trading at just 11x forward earnings, it is a bargain when the rest of the S&P 500 is around 27x current earnings. The company has massive upside potential with its new direction. It can use its size and depth of experience to fully capitalize on future cloud computing opportunities while still offering healthy dividend payouts for income investors.

AT&T (NYSE:T)

◇ Market Cap - $194.65 billion

◇ 52 week high/low - 39.7/26.08

◇ Current yield - 7.07%

◇ Beta - 0.64

◇ Number of years of dividend increases - 35

We've highlighted the positives of AT&T previously in this book. With 170 million customers and revenues of $170 billion, it's the largest telecom operator in the world. The high yield is explained partly due to investors getting alarmed at the high levels of debt on the books and pushing the stock price lower. $152 billion is an alarming figure, but it isn't all that bad upon close inspection. This figure is 15% lower than its current book value and factors in debt following Time Warner's acquisition.

Free cash flow is projected at $23 billion, which is down from pre-pandemic levels of $29 billion. Dividend payments currently cost AT&T $14 billion annually. Assuming the company uses the remaining amount to pay down its debt at current rates, it could reduce its debt burden to $100 billion by 2025.

Buying a company with strong long-term cash flows during a time of trouble is a time-tested way to outperform. Of course, the current dividend yield is extremely enticing for investors. The financials show no indication of this being cut anytime soon.

The stock was also battered due to the company's perceived slowness to enter the streaming revolution. In fact, HBO Max was slated to release in 2018 but was delayed due to the failed DOJ suit that was brought against the company concerning its acquisition of TimeWarner. This allowed Apple and Disney to get the jump on the streaming game. However, with HBO Max now launched, we expect it to bring massive cash flow to its parent.

AT&T currently trades at just 9.3 times earnings even though the current year's earnings will be weaker due to the pandemic. We fully expect earnings to recover to their usual level as the world moves forward. The current earnings multiple is half of what it was 20 years ago. The stock is also a favorite with covered call writers, thanks to the relatively flat price movements. If you'd like to know more about covered call writing, we covered this income strategy in depth in our book *Covere* Calls for Beginners.

A low beta of 0.64 also means that it fluctuates 36% less than the rest of the market. All of this makes AT&T a great income-generating stock.

ExxonMobil (NYSE:XOM)

◇ Market Cap - $141 billion

◇ 52 week high/low - 73.12/30.11

◇ Current yield - 8.7%

◇ Beta - 1.31

◇ Number of years of dividend increases - 37

With the stock price down 40% this year, perhaps no other large cap stock has been beaten down more than Exxon. This fall culminated in the stock being removed from the Dow Jones Index after nearly 100 years. It's a spectacular fall from grace for the company, which was the largest in the world by market capitalization in 2007.

While being removed from the Dow is not a death sentence (Honeywell International, one of the largest industrial companies in the US, re-entered the index in 2020, 12 years after it was initially removed), conditions have changed. As of this writing, Tesla has a higher market capitalization than BP, Shell and Exxon combined.

The bad news doesn't end there. On a 20-year basis, Exxon stock is down 3.5%, compared to the S&P 500, which is up 130%. The COVID-19 pandemic created chaos in the oil and gas industry, with demand plummeting. This culminated in oil and gas futures going negative for the first time ever. So with all this bad news, why would we recommend

123

Exxon? Surely the company seems doomed at this point?

For starters, bankruptcy is not on the table. A debt to equity ratio of 0.38 is much lower than its peers. For example, BP is at 1.1. Secondly, as we already noted with Chevron, oil demand will recover. It's already back up to $40/barrel from the lows we saw in April/May. Besides, with emerging markets still relying heavily on oil and gas, we don't see demand for oil disappearing anytime soon over the next decade. This prediction is backed up by the International Energy Agency's long-term outlook despite carbon emission reductions being a global focus.

Exxon is doubling down on its core competency while its competitors like BP and Shell are moving towards a more renewable energy-focused business model. The important thing to remember is that energy shifts take decades rather than years. Oil will still be relevant for the next decade. The low stock price provides you with a great entry point.

What you may not know is that Exxon is an "integrated" oil company. It doesn't make all of its money from drilling operations. It also has refining and chemical divisions that generate cash. This sets it apart from most of its peers who primarily rely on drilling, which will have to be scaled back over the next few years.

In their Q2 earnings call, management reiterated their stance on supporting the dividend payouts while its competitors cut their payments. If its dividend payout remains rock-solid, it'll double shareholders' reinvested dividends in roughly eight years (Williams, 2020).

However, a dividend cut is possible because management also stated that it would not add more debt. This largely depends on which way oil prices go. The mass global shutdowns of March/April/May 2020 are unlikely to be repeated at such a scale, even if individual countries choose to once again go into lockdown.

Despite the perceived risks, Exxon remains a behemoth that is unlikely to go anywhere. We expect the company to provide its shareholders with steady dividend checks for the next decade at the very least.

Kinder Morgan (NYSE:KMI)

◇ Market Cap - $28 billion

◇ 52 week high/low - 22.58/9.42

◇ Current yield - 7.3%

◇ Beta - 0.93

◇ Number of years of dividend increases - 5

We're aware that we previously highlighted Kinder Morgan as an example of a dividend trap. However, bear with us because this a fantastic example of a company recognizing its own shortcomings.

Kinder Morgan is one of the largest energy infrastructure companies in North America. It owns or operates more than 83,000 miles of pipelines that transport oil, natural gas, refined petroleum products, and carbon dioxide. The company's stock was down 34% in 2020 due to lower oil and gas prices and fears that future demand for oil and gas will be less than today.

Kinder Morgan thinks this impact will only affect its 2020 earnings by about nine percent thanks to its reliance on long-term contracts (Foelber, 2020). This is because 68% of the company's earnings come from what is known as "take or pay" contracts, which are unaffected by natural gas prices.

The question of sustaining the dividend is a key one with KMI. Fortunately, smart capital management means that current levels are sustainable. The Q2 dividend payout was covered 1.7x by that quarter's earnings, showing a healthy balance sheet even amid uncertainty. During the Q2 earnings call, CEO Rich Kinder stated,

"We want adequate coverage of that dividend, and we want to make damn certain that once we do a dividend increase, that dividend increase is permanent and that we're not retracting that at some later date."

Unlike other stocks here, KMI has only increased its dividend for the past five years, after cutting it in 2015. Since then, significant management changes have been made, and in terms of dividends, the outlook has never been more positive than it is today. Although this was a short-term hit for income investors, it was the right move for long-term company sustainability, and that has been rewarded today with higher dividend yields.

2021's expansion budgets have been cut by 30%, which is expected with the current economic outlook. In our view, this shows restraint on the part of management, rather than going further into debt to fuel growth, as the company has done in the past.

The company has bought a number of Master Limited Partnerships (MLPs), and continues to be able to absorb smaller companies in its sector. If organic expansion becomes less of a possibility, then growth by acquisition is likely to become more of a factor. Kinder Morgan will be a lot more boring than it was five years ago, but that's a good thing for income investors who want a company that produces reliable cash flow and is now more focused on paying and growing its dividend.

People's United Financial Inc. (NASDAQ:PBCT)

◇ Market Cap - $4.71 billion

◇ 52 week high/low - 17.22/9.37

◇ Current yield - 6.6%

◇ Beta - 1.18

◇ Number of years of dividend increases - 49

This is a company that Warren Buffett would love: a well-run business that exercises great capital management while expanding within its circle of competence. People's United is much smaller than the other companies on this list. It isn't even a large cap. However, given its stellar performance, we're optimistic that there are great things in store for this company.

As a bit of a background, at the time of writing, we've just come out of the strongest 100-day rally in market history, with the S&P 500 up 50.8% in that time. The index now trades at a forward PE of 22.8x, over two standard deviations from the mean. This forward PE level has only been experienced around five other times in the market's history. The last time prices were this high was in 1999 before the DOTCOM crash.

One sector which didn't experience much of a rally was the banking sector. The sector has come under a lot of stress over the past six months, with large national banks bearing most of this. However, there are still many opportunities in the regional banking sector.

PBCT is based in the Northeast and controls over 400 bank branches in the region. Most importantly, the bank is diversified. No loan category makes up more than 35% of the commercial real estate portfolio and no category counts for more than 26% in the bank's equipment financing, commercial and industrial loan portfolios. This is key because it means there is no liability for a single point of failure like there would be, for example, if 90% of its loans were to the restaurant or retail industry.

The bank has no material exposure to loans in airlines, cruise lines, casinos, student loans, auto lending, or consumer credit cards - industries that are deemed to be higher risk in the currently uncertain market environment. Both Q1 and Q2 earnings were up year on year, despite uncertainty due to COVID-19. Its balance sheet is strong, with a debt-to-equity ratio of 0.31.

An important metric in the banking sector is credit rating, because this correlates with risk of bankruptcy in the long term. PBCT currently has a rating of BBB+, which roughly equates to a 0.6% chance of bankruptcy over the next 30 years. In terms of dividends, the bank returns 34% of its capital as dividends, roughly triple the S&P 500 average.

The company is still growing. It made 16 acquisitions over the past decade, which have roughly doubled its total assets to around $45 billion. Its last three acquisitions added $16 billion worth of assets to its balance sheet. PBCT continues to expand its wealth management business to keep up with increased demand from people looking for portfolio guidance in this uncertain market environment and is expanding its digital offerings to clients.

Currently the company trades at a PE of just 9.7x compared to the market average of 27x. It is also a potential acquisition target if one of the national players wants more exposure to the Northeast market. Dividends of $0.71/share will net you an annual income of $643 on a $10,000 initial investment, paid quarterly.

In short, PBCT is a great dividend player as well as a value stock to hold for the next decade (unless it gets bought out, but then you'll get a great payday to make up for it).

Now that we've covered our seven favorite dividend growth stocks, it's time to look at another sector that income investors favor, real estate.

Chapter 10

OUR 2 FAVORITE REITS

"The best investment on earth is earth"

-Louis Glickman

Real estate is widely considered one of the best investments on the planet because land is limited and growing populations always need a place to live and work. The typical method of investing in real estate is to buy property via financing.

However, owning physical property poses a few challenges. First, it requires you to have enough money for a down payment, which can be substantial. Second, it's not a passive investment. If a pipe in your property bursts at three in the morning, you'll need to attend to it.

Real Estate Investment Trusts (REITs) provide a more comfortable alternative. For example, what if, in addition to investing in Amazon, you could also invest in Amazon's Landlord?

There are many different kinds of REITs you can invest in. Some are diversified across all forms of real estate, while others specialize in certain property types (residential, commercial, shopping centers, hospitals, raw land, etc.)

For income investors, the big benefit of REITs is that they are legally mandated to pay out 90% of their profits to shareholders, making them income-generation machines. Stag Industrial is one such REIT. They own many of the warehouses which are then leased to Amazon as they store and ship goods; because of this, the company is often referred to as "Amazon's Landlord".

Most significantly, over the past 30 years, the U.S REIT index has outperformed the S&P 500 and has posted returns of 10.6% per year on average. All of this means a well-diversified portfolio of REITs can help you achieve your income and capital gains goals.

Important REIT Metrics

Analyzing individual REITs isn't as complicated as it seems. Here are the key metrics you need to look for when examining REITs.

Funds From Operations

Think of FFO as equivalent to the net income per share for a REIT. You can calculate FFO by adding non-cash expenses back to net income. Depreciation is a substantial non-cash expense that REITs experience. However, depreciation as an expense makes no sense when evaluating a REIT.

Accounting rules state that all assets must be depreciated. This makes sense if the asset is a physical good or a factory with a definite term of use. However, well-maintained real estate doesn't decrease in value. Instead, it appreciates. This means REITs write down perfectly good assets on their books through large depreciation expenses when, in reality, these assets are appreciating in value.

Large depreciation expenses mean that many REITS pay dividends above their net income. Don't mistake this for irresponsibility when you notice it. It's merely a quirk of how accounting works. REITs will clearly indicate their FFO numbers in their financial reports since this is a more relevant metric.

FREEMAN INCOME INVESTING RULE #5

GOOD REITS INCREASE THEIR FFO ON AN ANNUAL BASIS.

Credit Ratings

REITs make money by managing large properties and collecting rents from their tenants. Like every other real estate purchase, they finance their properties through mortgages and lines of credit. This means their credit ratings are important because it reflects the degree of confidence creditors have in the company. A high credit rating means lenders think that the REIT will repay its debts and is managing its properties well. A low credit rating implies the opposite.

Rent Collected

Ideally, REITs will be able to collect 100% of the rents they're owed from their tenants. However, we don't live in an ideal world. The pandemic shined a light on which REITs were efficient at collecting rents and which ones weren't. REITs manage hundreds of properties, and it's impossible to collect 100% of the rent all the time.

However, good REITs attract high quality tenants who are less affected by sudden disruptions. During the lockdown period, we paid particular attention to the rent collected by REITs. Some low quality companies weren't able to collect even half of the rents they were owed. Others, high quality ones, were relatively unaffected.

Here are the two best REITs that we have identified.

Realty Income (NYSE:O) has reliably paid monthly dividends for more than 25 years now, making it the perfect stock for retirement investors. It's also one of the few monthly dividend payers that are worthy investments. The company leases single-tenant properties to retailers that are largely immune to e-commerce headwinds and that are recession-resistant. These are businesses such as convenience stores, drugstores, dollar stores, and others that do well in all economic conditions.

The company currently has a $28 billion market capitalization. Typically, tenants sign long-term net leases, which require them to pay for property taxes, insurance, and maintenance. This shifts the variable costs of the property to the tenant (Frankel, 2020).

Realty Income has declared over 600 consecutive monthly dividend payments without interruption and has increased its dividend 107 times since its initial public offering in 1994. It has a 20-year annualized return of 15.3%.

To put this kind of performance in perspective, if you invest $5,000 per year and your money grows at this rate (15.3%), you'll end up with $530,000 after 20 years. After 30 years that's $2.3 million. You could become a real estate millionaire without owning any real estate!

At the same time, the company's beta is just 0.4. This means not only did Realty Income thus easily outperform the broad market, but it also did so while being a less risky/less volatile investment at the same time. In the 2020 second quarter, adjusted funds from operations per share increased 4.9% to $0.86 year-over-year (*Realty Income Announces Operating Results For Secon• Quarter An• First Six Months Of 2020*, 2020). Realty Income collected 86.5% of contractual rent across the total portfolio. AFFO (FFO minus revenue accruals & capital expenses) growth was due to a combination of rental increases at existing properties, as well as contributions from new properties.

Average lease term remaining is a healthy nine years, which means there aren't likely to be many cash flow shocks in the near future if tenants do not renew their leases. It's one of the two REITs which is both A rated by Moody's and has had increasing dividend payouts for the past 25 years. A strong management team is committed to the cause, and insider buying numbers continue to increase year on year.

While other REITs have been struggling to collect rent and maintain their dividends, **W.P. Carey (NYSE:WPC)** has sailed through the COVID-19 downturn without breaking a sweat.

And while other REITs cut dividends during the pandemic, W.P. Carey was one of the few to raise dividends (as did Realty Income). The company collected 97% of rents in April, the highest of any major REIT. Meanwhile, W.P. Carey's closest competitor, National Retail Properties, collected just 52%.

The reason for this outperformance was W.P. Carey's diversified portfolio. It currently owns a portfolio composed of 24% industrials, 23% office space, 22% warehouse, and 17% retail. Like Realty Income, it's a net-lease provider. It buys properties from companies and then instantly rents them back to the seller with a long-term lease. The seller, meanwhile, is responsible for most of the operating costs of the property they occupy. It's really more of a financial transaction, with the seller raising cash it can put to better use elsewhere. And since the lessee is responsible for most of the operating costs, W.P.Carey just gets to sit back and collect the rent.

The company is more active than other REITs and is continuously looking for opportunities to expand its portfolio across the world. In the previous decade, management believed US retail space was overvalued, so they focused more on Europe which now generates around a third of the company's rents. This gives them good protection from potential US civil unrest. They're also targeting industrial, and warehouse sectors, which they foresee will not be as affected by a post-COVID landscape.

The REIT boasts a solid 5.9% dividend yield with an annual payout of $4.17 per share, paid quarterly. It's an ideal stock to own as a hedge against another recession. If the company can still collect 97% of its rents during the biggest mass layoff in US history, that bodes well for future uncertainty. We're positive that it's strong enough to weather another storm in the long run though.

Note that we also included two other single industry-focused REITs with fantastic long-term outlook in our first book *The 8 Step Beginner's Guiⅰe to Value Investing.*

Private REITs

These days you also have the opportunity to invest in private REITs. These REITs aren't traded on the stock exchange, as their names imply. In the past, only accredited investors (those who are worth at least $1 million) could invest in them, and these instruments had high investment minimums.

However in the past decade, private REITs have become extremely popular, and you'll hear of them being also pushed as "crowdfunded REITs", with one of the more prominent examples being Cardone Capital, run by entrepreneur and YouTube influencer Grant Cardone.

When you buy a private REIT, you're buying units in the fund directly from the company. There are no shares since these companies are not publicly traded. If you wish to sell your units, you'll have to sell them to other investors or back to the REIT itself. This makes it tough to exit your investment. However, private REITs tend to have a few advantages over the average public REIT.

They pay a much higher yield for starters while only requiring a $1,000 minimum investment (on average.) Streitwise, for example, pays 9.75% per year, and you can invest in them through your IRA account. However, there are some catches you must keep in mind before investing in a private REIT.

Your money is being placed in a private fund, which means you'll have to do as the fund manager says. Typically, REIT fund managers impose lockup periods. A lockup is a phenomenon borrowed from the hedge fund world where investors have to keep their money in the fund for a certain period of time before they're allowed to withdraw it. The typical lockup lasts for around six months, but some private REITs have lockups that are as long as a year.

Many funds also impose redemption fees. For example, private REIT Upside Avenue charges two percent early withdrawal fees in the second year and a one percent fee in the third. This fee is referred to as "early withdrawal" since the fund manager expects investors to remain in the fund for the fund's entire lifespan. Each fund is typically tied to a single property, and investors earn returns directly from the rents and capital gains that the property experiences.

Most REITs can last for as long as a decade and might impose a minimum investment period of five years. Understand that the lockup is different from the minimum investment. During the lockup period, you won't have access to your funds, no matter what.

The bad news doesn't end there, though. According to an article by Michael Finke, a 2014 report by an independent REIT rating publication called Green Street Advisors concluded that privately held REITs underperformed publicly traded REITs by about 3.6 percentage points per year (Finke, 2020).

For this reason, as well as the ones listed above, we recommend you stay away from private REITs. The regular income investor can get just as good results with larger public REITs like Realty Income and W.P. Carey.

Chapter 11

PARTNERSHIPS - THE UNDERGROUND SECRET TO MASSIVE DIVIDENDS

Master limited partnerships or MLPs have long been a source of great dividends for wealthy investors. These legal structures used to be employed by companies to help pay their owners' massive dividends and avoid the resulting tax burden.

But now with many MLPs trading on public stock exchanges, it's now easy for regular income investors to realize the benefits of these vehicles.

First, what is an MLP? An MLP is a partnership that derives its income from a resource. To qualify as an MLP, the partnership must derive at least 90% of its income from either commodity operations, natural resources, or real estate (McClay, 2020). MLPs are usually founded by parent firms and their largest shareholders often own stock in the parent company as well. Thus the biggest shareholders of the MLP are traditionally the management team of the parent company.

Partnerships are taxed differently from other legal structures. In the past, many MLPs were used to reduce taxes on the primary companies they were tied to. The partners in an MLP would charge these firms massive fees, on paper. Thus, the firms would get to declare a loss while the partners of the MLP would withdraw their profits as dividends.

Another way to reduce taxes on the MLP's payouts would be to declare these dividends as ROC or return of capital. This is why the IRS treats ROC as a reduction of the cost basis of your investment. We'll discuss what this means shortly. For now, let's dive deeper into MLPs and look at how you can put them to use.

How MLPs Work

MLPs are income-generation machines, and best of all, you can buy shares in them on a public stock exchange. As we just outlined, there are many companies that use MLPs to create losses on their books. Large public companies don't do this anymore due to the reputational damage they'd sustain. However, many smaller MLPs and firms continue to rely on this tactic and you ought to watch out for them.

These partnerships have gained a poor reputation amongst the online investment community, but as we've repeatedly highlighted so far, this doesn't mean MLPs are a bad investment. You need to conduct your research into them before investing. Not every MLP is the same.

For example, MLPs are used by oil and gas companies to hold assets such as tankers and pipelines. These assets usually depreciate and decrease the parent company's earnings. To remove this burden from their books, companies offload them onto an MLP, pay fees to the MLP, and use that to offset the depreciation expense. The result is two profitable companies, with the MLP paying massive dividends to its partners (shareholders).

Given the fact that MLPs operate in the energy and natural resources field, you'd be right to worry about exposure to commodity price fluctuations. However, most MLPs are structured to merely hold assets and earn fees based on the volume of the resource that flows through them.

There is some jargon you need to learn before investing in MLPs. Natural resources companies typically divide their operations into three segments: upstream, midstream, and downstream.

Upstream refers to operations and earnings that are generated early in the resource extraction process. For example, exploration and drilling are considered upstream activities.

Midstream typically includes processing, storage, and marketing of the resource. Most MLPs are midstream operations. For example, Energy Transfer Partners is a midstream natural gas MLP that earns fees and pays dividends based on the volume of natural gas that flows through the pipelines it owns.

Downstream deals with all post-production activities. For example, refining crude to produce gasoline and other products is downstream activity. Upstream and downstream operations are exposed to commodity prices, but midstream operations typically aren't. The fees that a midstream MLP generates are tied to the volume of products in its storage facilities.

Upstream and downstream MLPs exist, and they do contain exposure to resource prices. Therefore for the safety of your income stream, we recommend you stick to midstream MLPs.

Taxes

No discussion of MLPs is complete without diving into how they're taxed. There's a lot of misrepresentation when it comes to the topic. MLPs are often marketed as tax-deferred entities, and this isn't strictly true. The tax implications of owning an MLP depend on the MLP itself. The matter of taxation hinges on the type of payouts that the MLP makes to its shareholders.

Dividends are usually taxed as ordinary income and treated the same as the salary you receive from your employer. This means you pay taxes at your marginal income tax rate. However, MLP dividends can be classified as ROC as we mentioned previously. ROC payments aren't taxed since they reduce your cost basis in the investment.

For example, if you bought an MLP for $100 and received $10 back as ROC, the IRS will treat your investment as if you bought it for $90 (100-10). Therefore, you won't pay taxes on the dividend payment you received.

However, you will pay taxes when you sell your investment. Let's say you sell your MLP shares after you receive the $10 dividend payment. Let's also assume that the market price of the shares of the MLP is $110. Since you bought it for $100 and are selling it for $110, your capital gains on the investment are $10 right? Wrong. Remember that the dividend reduces your cost basis. This means your effective purchase price is $90. Your capital gains are therefore $20 from the investment.

The IRS treats Capital gains taxes as two separate categories, short or long-term. We'll discuss this in more detail in the chapter on taxes. For now, understand that long-term capital gains taxes are a lot lower than short-term ones.

Over time, it is possible for your cost basis in the MLP to reduce to zero. Once this happens, you'll pay long-term capital gains taxes on your dividend payment. Remember that the ROC classification of MLP dividends depends on the MLP itself. There are MLPs that classify their payments as ordinary dividend income. These payments won't be treated as ROC. You'll need to read the annual filings of the MLP and do your research to figure out how the dividend payments are classified.

One of the biggest perceived drawbacks of investing in MLPs is the unwieldy tax form that accompanies them. Typically, you'll receive a 1099 form when investing in dividend-paying instruments. However, an investment in an MLP is treated as though you are investing in a partnership, and this means you'll receive the K-1 form. This form has acquired a notorious reputation, and many income investors shy away from MLPs because they consider it too painful to deal with.

While the K-1 isn't as straightforward as a 1099, handling it is as simple as passing it on to an accountant who'll figure it out for you. The K-1 will mention the portion of dividend payments that are ROC, ordinary income, and capital gains. Your accountant will need to keep track of your adjusted cost basis over time. When you sell your investment, they'll probably ask you to furnish them with your prior K-1s to verify your cost basis for tax purposes.

The great thing about ROC is that it works very well if you hold onto your investment indefinitely. Let's say you buy an MLP for $100 and receive $10 as dividends every year. Within ten years, your cost basis is zero, and you'll pay long-term capital gains taxes on dividends you'll receive from that point on. However, if you never sell your MLP investment, you'll never pay taxes on the $100 you received as dividends.

What's more, when you pass away, you can transfer your MLP shares to your heirs. Their cost basis is adjusted to the stock price on the day of your passing. This resets the ROC clock and once again, they'll enjoy the advantages of deferred taxes until their cost basis resets to zero.

Disadvantages of MLPs

Like with everything else, MLPs have certain disadvantages. For starters, the K-1 form poses a few challenges. This isn't to do with the way the form is treated. Rather, it usually arrives late and close to the filing deadline. In some cases, you might receive it after the deadline, and you'll need to file for an extension.

The way the MLP operates can also pose challenges to your accountant. If an MLP operates in multiple states, you might need to file separate returns with each state and will pay taxes according to the K-1. This is a headache for your accountant to deal with. Additionally, some accountants will charge you extra fees for filing a form in each state. This is something to address with your accountant *before* you begin investing in MLPs. You also can't deal with MLP taxation by yourself unless you happen to be an accountant. For some investors, the hassle of dealing with all of this for a few additional points of yield isn't worth it.

Speaking of yield, many MLPs pay high yields, greater than eight percent per year. Because of this attractive headline figure, there is much unscrupulous marketing surrounding a few of them, so you need to be careful about evaluating the company. Like regular stocks, don't invest in an MLP solely for the yield since this will only lead you to yield traps. You'll need to evaluate them as you would any individual stock or fund.

An option you can choose to avoid the K-1 is to invest in mutual funds or ETFs that invest in MLPs. This way, you'll receive the 1099 form at the end of the year while the fund deals with the K-1. However, keep in mind that there aren't many low-cost ETFs that invest in MLPs. They're a more complicated investment than just buying stocks, and as a result, active management is required. The fees associated will, therefore, be higher. You'll need to evaluate how much you think the reduced tax filing burden is worth before investing in a managed fund.

Given their relatively high yields, MLPs don't provide the best capital appreciation. To understand this, we need to look at how companies use them. Most of them are structured as special vehicles used to offset losses resulting from regular operations. For example, an upstream MLP is used to capture the losses associated with the surveying and exploration process. The MLP draws depreciation and capital losses away from the parent company and boosts the latter's profits. While such an MLP might pay high dividends, its stock price might decline over time.

Midstream MLPs are far more stable, but again, they're asset vehicles. Once the assets have been written down, the parent company might decide to create another MLP and might wind the existing one down. This means you'll have to find another vehicle to fill that dividend income hole. This isn't a disadvantage per se. It's just that you need to be aware of how MLPs work and how parent companies treat them.

This is why it's important to invest in the right structures, backed by reputable companies. Any high-yielding MLP won't work since the structure might not be beneficial to you. You'll see some MLPs yielding 25% annually. These are yield traps and have such high payouts due to declining share prices, not just because of increased dividends.

The annual filings are the best way of figuring out what an MLP is all about. Some of the standard shenanigans that occur with low quality MLPs are asset maneuvering and yield inflation. Asset maneuvering refers to when a parent company will suddenly decide to transfer all of an MLPs assets to another vehicle without notice. Technically speaking, every MLP investment runs this risk. However, you want to watch for the reputation of the parent company.

Yield inflation occurs when a company aggressively pushes its high yield nature on investors. Such companies are usually looking to dump their stock onto new shareholders while the older ones exit. Look for a breakdown of their dividends. Typically, most of their payments will be ordinary income, which means you won't realize any tax advantages. Combine this with a falling stock price, and you'll end up having your money dwindle quickly. As a rule of thumb, the easier it is for you to understand how the MLP works and generates money, the better your investment will be.

Two MLPs Worth Investing In

Here are two high quality MLPs that we believe are worth an investment.

Enterprise Products Partners (NYSE:EPD)

◇ Stock Price: $20.21

◇ 52 week high/low: $29.22/$10.27

◇ Market Cap: $44.8 Billion

◇ Dividend yield: 10%

◇ Number of consecutive years with dividend increases: 23

Enterprise Products Partners is a high income instrument that boasts a stable 10% yield. Stable and 10% yield might sound like an oxymoron, but thanks to the MLP structure, it's not just a possibility; it's a reality.

This midstream MLP is a play on the energy sector. While the sector has been hammered in 2020, there are still a number of great opportunities for investors looking for reliable income streams. There is a misconception in this sector that all "oil companies" make their money from drilling expeditions, which leaves them highly exposed to falling oil prices. This isn't true. As we explained previously, upstream, downstream, and midstream operations are very different.

Enterprise operates in the midstream segment. Upstream companies that drill for oil and gas (like ConocoPhillips or Schlumberger) suffer from volatile commodity prices that don't dictate Enterprise's top or bottom-line results. Downstream companies (like Marathon Oil) refine oil and gas or make chemicals. For these companies, earnings are driven by the difference between input costs and the final sale price of its products.

By operating pipelines and transportation services, Enterprise is what you might think of as a "toll booth" stock in that it collects fees regardless of oil prices. This makes it a fundamentally safer business model than that of upstream or downstream companies. To illustrate this, Enterprise's earnings rose during Q1 2020, when drilling companies were suffering. Best of all, it has covered its distributions by 1.6x in Q1, meaning that it isn't paying out shareholders with debt.

EPD does have its share of competitors. Enbridge is often referred to as EPD's biggest competitor. However, the biggest drawback with Enbridge is that it is a Canadian company, therefore the dividend is paid in Canadian dollars, which leaves you exposed to foreign exchange risk, and you may not be able to exercise DRIPs on your broker platform. Besides, EPD has a more conservative balance sheet with Debt to EBITDA of 3.7 vs. 7 for Enbridge. With dividends at $1.78 per share this represents around a 10% yield based on current market prices. Dividends are paid quarterly.

Slow growth is expected in the next 5-10 years, but this should be considered a pure income play with a 8-10% distribution from a solid company - near impossible to find anywhere on the market.

Brookfield Renewable Energy (NYSE:BEP)

◇ Stock Price: $62.53

◇ 52 week high/low: $64.94/$30.09

◇ Market cap: $11.5 Billion

◇ Dividend yield - 3.1%

◇ Number of consecutive years with dividend increases: 7

Brookfield is the new renewable energy kid on the block and competes against the legacy oil industry. A huge run from March lows has now pushed the stock above February highs again, meaning over the past three years, it has nearly tripled the returns of the S&P 500. Despite this growth, it still has a healthy distribution coverage of 1.4x. Management targets between 1.4 and 1.67x distribution coverage as a long-term sustainable level.

The great thing about Brookfield is that it isn't just a pure income play. You can expect significant capital gains growth in addition to earning a steady dividend income. When it comes to the stock market valuing a company, there are a couple of ways in which it might happen.

First, the market might get caught up with the hype surrounding a company and send its stock to dizzying heights. Nio, dubbed "The Tesla of China" is a good example of this. The company manufactures just 16,000 vehicles per quarter, each one at a loss, and yet it currently has a higher market cap than Honda and Ford. Nio is an example of how emotions often drive lofty valuations in stocks.

Brookfield is an example of the second way in which the markets value companies. Its valuation is backed by solid financials instead of hype. The company owns and operates a portfolio of renewable power generating facilities including 193 hydroelectric generating stations, 11 wind facilities and two natural gas-fired plants in the USA, Canada, and Brazil.

The demand for electricity is consistent compared to oil or gas, which gives the company predictable, reliable cash flow. It sells the bulk of its power through long-term fixed contracts, so its income is not directly dependent on plant output. Brookfield acquired TerraForm Power in July, and when combined they will be one of the largest renewable energy companies on earth with a capacity of 19,000 MW.

Management predicts that cash flow will grow by 6-11% over the next two years, despite the current worldwide economic situation. Including growth, Brookfield shareholders are looking at a 10-14% annual growth rate, which is fantastic for a company with high distributions as well. What's more, distribution payouts have increased by over 300% in the past decade. Management aims to increase payouts by eight percent a year going forward.

We'd like to mention that in your brokerage account, you may see two companies trading under similar names: Brookfield Renewable Inc. and Brookfield Renewable Partners L.P. The MLP is Brookfield Renewable Partners L.P. and trades under the symbol (NYSE:BEP).

FREEMAN INCOME INVESTING RULE #6

STICK TO MIDSTREAM MLPs IF YOU DON'T WANT TO BE EXPOSED TO FLUCTUATIONS IN COMMODITY PRICES

Now we've covered stocks, REITs and MLPs. It's time to look at the "cherry on the cake" of income investing.

Chapter 12

CLOSED-END BOND FUNDS – AN INCOME INVESTOR'S DREAM

You've already read that we aren't the biggest fans of mutual funds or managed funds, because while they target outperformance, they rarely ever achieve it. If you want to stick to funds rather than individual stocks, targeting the market average and minimizing expenses is the way to go. However, there is one significant exception to this, namely the Closed End Bond Fund or CEF.

Most mutual funds suffer from underperformance due to their structure. The average mutual fund manager needs to be a marketing machine while figuring out how to invest the money they're charged with. The stock market allows people to buy new units in the fund, and this means they need to constantly find ways to make more money with an increasing capital base. This leads to less than optimal asset allocation and underperformance is the result.

Not every mutual fund is set up to fail like this. The fact that you can always buy new units of a mutual fund means that it is open-ended. However, there are also closed-ended mutual funds. These funds raise a fixed amount of capital from investors and then close the fund to new subscriptions. Their shares trade on the market, but since you'll be buying shares from existing investors, their capital base doesn't increase. This means the fund manager can concentrate on allocating capital to the best of their abilities, and not worrying about finding new places to park money.

You'll notice that we've mentioned bonds in the title of this chapter. As you grow older, your investment focus will naturally shift towards income generation instead of capital gains. We've already mentioned the 60/40 and "subtract your age from 100" rule of thumb asset allocation calculations that most financial advisors resort to. Despite the fallacy of that method, there's no denying that as you get older, you need to focus more of your investments toward bonds or fixed income assets.

Closed-ended bond funds are a great choice since they're both actively managed, and their pricing structure often results in bargains. Why are these two such huge advantages?

Fund Structures

Why is active management a good thing in this case? We've highlighted previously that passively managed funds do better in the long run. However, bonds are an exception to the rule. The reason being that bonds are more complex than stocks and require active management.

Bonds are primarily traded by institutions. Despite the bond market's size being much bigger than the stock market, almost $40 trillion compared to $15 trillion for stocks, the number of traders and participants in the market is less than the stock market. However, thanks to every participant being an institution of some kind, the average trade size runs well into the hundreds of millions of dollars.

The other thing to note about bond markets is that there are no insider trading laws or other investor protections like those in the stock market. The financial authorities figure that everyone can take care of themselves and know what they're doing when trading bonds. This makes it crucial for a money manager to be on top of things and react quickly when they need to. This is also why active management is much more preferable in the bond market.

The second reason for investing in closed-ended bond funds is the price structure. This is unique to closed-ended funds in the investment world. Every fund (whether passive or active) has a net asset value or NAV that indicates the total monetary value of the units the fund holds.

For example, if a fund raises $100 million from investors and invests it in securities that rise to $200 million, the fund's NAV is $200 million. You would expect that the NAV divided by the number of units would be equal to the price at which the fund trades in the market.

This is how mutual funds work. Their NAV is calculated at the end of a market day and that is the price at which investors can buy or sell the fund's units. With closed-ended funds this doesn't happen. Their prices fluctuate during the day as stocks and ETFs do. This means their unit prices won't always match their NAV. Some funds trade at a premium to NAV and some at a discount.

You might think that the ones trading at a premium are high quality and the discounted ones are of a low quality. However, this isn't the case. There are many reasons why a fund can trade at a discount, such as market perception, bad analyst ratings, and current events. Like any company whose stock price can get depressed for various reasons, closed-ended funds' unit prices are subject to emotions of short-term market participants.

This is an opportunity for you to jump in and earn a high yield on your investment. A fund that would normally yield five percent to NAV might be yielding 10% or more thanks to the discount at which it trades. Remember that the fund does not issue new units to the market. You'll be buying from existing investors. This is often a reason for steep discounts in prices.

The reason is that smaller closed-ended funds suffer from a lack of liquidity. If existing investors in a fund don't wish to sell, and if the fund isn't issuing new units to bring new investors on board, the market for selling existing units is pretty small. This leads to a price discount. Liquidity is an important factor when investing, but if your outlook is longer than a decade, you won't have to worry about it. This is because you'll capture the capital appreciation over time, and even if you sell at a discount to NAV in the future, you'll still be selling at a higher price than what you bought the fund for.

Many income investors buy closed-ended funds with the hope of trying to capture the price rise from a discount to NAV. This is the wrong way to do things. It's a lot like buying a stock before it goes ex-dividend since you know the dividend is on the way. It's a short-term method of trying to make money, and it doesn't work. You can't control the discount at which the fund's units sell. Instead, understand what the fund does and seek to remain invested over the long term. The discount merely gets you a good entry into a great asset.

Since they seek outperformance, closed-ended funds charge high performance and management fees. You won't be charged loading fees though. You're buying their shares in the market and this means the manager doesn't have to deal with new funds to allocate. However, the fact that the investor base is small results in funds charging higher than normal fees. Some of the best closed-ended funds charge as much as 1.7% in annual fees, which is a high hurdle (*What to know about buying close*r*-en*r *fun*r*s at a* r*iscount*, 2020).

Bond funds charge lower fees since their capital returns are lower. However, these fees are still greater than what you can expect with a passively managed ETF. The idea is to offset the higher fees against the promise of outperformance. Some bond funds have returned as much as stock funds, though. A shining example is the AllianceBernstein High Income Fund that has returned 10.9% annually over the past 25 years. The fund currently holds over 1,163 corporate bonds.

Other Advantages

Closed-ended funds are treated differently by the SEC than mutual funds. Mutual funds operate in a strict regulatory environment and cannot deviate from their guidelines no matter what. The same isn't true of closed-ended funds. This is not to say that they have a hedge fund-like independence. It's just that they have a more comprehensive array of choices for assets they can invest in.

For example, closed-ended funds can invest in below investment grade bonds. Each bond is given a grade or credit rating by Standard & Poor's and Moody's, the two ratings agencies. The rating scale that each agency uses is slightly different, but generally speaking, anything below an A grade is considered less than investment worthy.

The thing about these riskier bonds is that this is where true bargains are found. The moment a bond is downgraded to less than investment worthy, its price plummets, and its yield rises.

As we mentioned earlier, bond prices are quoted in percentages, so let's look at an example of this. Let's say a bond was trading at 100 (100% of its face value) and was yielding two percent. Once the downgrade hits, its price could plummet to 60 or 50. If it falls to 50, the yield on the bond is now four percent.

There is the risk of default, but this is why you need an active manager to step in and assess opportunities. We should also note a big difference between a bond rated below investment grade and junk bonds. For example, a bond rated BBB would be considered below investment grade, but above junk bond grade. Anything below a B rating is considered junk.

When investing in closed-ended funds, pay attention to the issuer. Here are some of the fund issuers in the market who have the best track record:

◇ AllianceBernstein

◇ PIMCO

◇ Nuveen

◇ DoubleLine

What To Look For in a Bond CEF

So what should you look for when choosing a closed-ended fund to invest in? For starters you should stick to funds that are trading at a discount to NAV. There's no specific number that you should look for. Obviously the deeper the discount, the greater your yield will be. You'll also be potentially locking in capital gains equal to the discount in case the fund rises to par value. However, as we previously mentioned, this shouldn't be your primary goal.

You can check fund discounts at https://www.cefchannel.com/screens/discount-to-nav/. You'll find quite a few high quality funds trading at a discount. For example, Calamos Dynamic Convertible and Income Fund (CCD) CEF has returned 19.39% YTD, has an annual distribution of 8.87%, and still trades for an 11.37% discount to NAV. Don't be swayed into buying funds that trade for a premium. There's less upside to these investments than there is in stocks. Income is what you should be after. This is why choosing a high quality fund with the biggest discount works best.

A larger discount also means you'll have the fund's management fee paid for. For example, if you buy a fund that charges one percent management fees at a five percent discount, you're still ahead after fees. Since income is your primary goal, you want to look for funds that consist of BB or BBB grade bonds. These bonds are below investment grade, but they are above the junk category. Some of them might default, but the majority of them will recover their value. Generally, these bonds trade between 70 and 90 (remember bonds prices are quoted as a percentage of their face value). Their yields aren't as high as lower-rated bonds, but they're in a sweet spot in terms of safety and yield.

You can find a fund's portfolio composition on its web page or in its prospectus. You also want to invest in funds that own bonds in stable markets. While emerging markets (countries with faster economic growth than developed countries like the US or Japan) are sexy investments, they aren't the most stable. Putting money in emerging market bonds isn't all that different from speculating in those stock markets. Stay away from taking on such risk.

Pay attention to the fund manager. The longer their track record is, the better. The issuers we highlighted previously hire excellent managers with great pedigrees. At the very least, you want a manager who has a track record that spans ten years. Check to see if the fund has outperformed its benchmark. The longer the outperformance, the better. The best sign of a good manager is someone who invests their own money into the fund.

A good example of a fund that ticks all of these boxes is the AllianceBernstein Global High Income Fund. The fund has a 10.79% annualized return over 22 years ($10,000 invested in 1998 would be worth $74,222 today). The same investment in the S&P 500 over the same time period would be worth $26,283. It has significant insider ownership as well, which makes it extremely attractive.

This fund is also a good example of how a discount can compensate for high fees. Currently, there's a 1.05% fee, but it trades at a 13% discount, so you're paying 87 cents on the dollar. That fully covers your fee, making the management essentially free. The fund currently holds 65% of its bonds in the US, with no other country making up more than five percent. 98% of its exposure in USD, so there's no foreign exchange risk. Best of all, its yield is 6.38% and is distributed monthly.

FREEMAN INCOME INVESTING RULE #7

IF YOU BUY A CEF FOR A DISCOUNT TO NAV,
THEN YOU ARE ESSENTIALLY GETTING
ACTIVE MANAGEMENT FOR FREE.

Chapter 13

THE 3 BEST DIVIDEND ETFS FOR HANDS-OFF INVESTORS

While closed-ended bond funds are a good investment choice, they do come with risks. Outperformance isn't guaranteed, after all. If you're someone who wants income but is conservative when it comes to investing, dividend ETFs are a good option. While your yields will be lower, they'll be pretty stable. Like with everything else, there's a tradeoff between safety and yield.

The Best Low-Fee ETF Issuer

The best low-fee dividend ETFs are issued by the Vanguard Group. With this in mind, here are three dividend ETFs that have conservative strategies and yield a good amount of cash.

Vanguard Dividend Appreciation ETF (NASDAQ:VIG)

This is a popular ETF that tracks the Dividend Achievers index. Because the fund incurs costs when buying and selling securities in the index, it trails the index by a negligible amount. It consists of 182 companies that have increased dividend payouts for at least the past ten years.

The Dividend Achievers index is different from the Aristocrats and the Kings index in that it prioritizes capital gains along with income generation. Since companies need to have paid dividends for just ten years in a row, most companies in the index have a history of capital appreciation.

For example, VIG's biggest holdings are currently Microsoft, Visa, and Procter & Gamble. Microsoft has been one of the stock market's best performers over the past decade and has led the way with its massive capital gains. Visa has been a huge beneficiary of the pandemic, even if it has stayed away from the headlines that other tech companies have garnered. Procter & Gamble is an example of a stable dividend-paying stock that won't witness much capital appreciation but will provide steady income flow.

Some of the fund's other major holdings include Walmart, McDonald's, and Johnson & Johnson. With these three holdings, Walmart is an example of a company that has been stable in terms of both growth and dividend payouts.

It's no surprise that VIG as a fund has achieved stellar performance. It has returned 350% over a 10-year period. $10,000 invested in the fund a decade ago would have turned into $35,000 by now.

Best of all, VIG charges a low fee of just 0.06% per year. This is fantastic compared to mutual funds that charge upwards of one percent per year or some closed-ended bond funds that charge three percent or higher. The dividend yield is around 1.8%, which might sound low compared to some of the other options we've highlighted so far in this book. However, you are making up for it with higher growth rates from companies like Microsoft.

VIG is best suited if you're not looking for the highest dividend yields but want capital appreciation to balance it out. Your investment principal will be safe with VIG for the long term and you'll manage to earn steady dividend payouts as well. DRIP these payouts back into the fund and you'll grow your capital significantly.

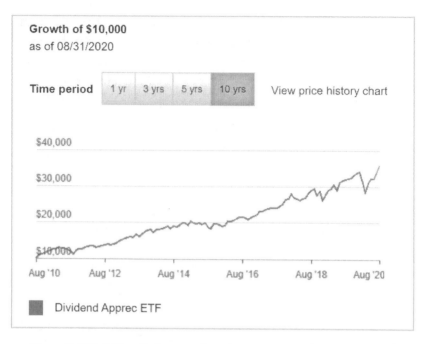

Figure 11: VIG 10 Year Performance from August 2010-2020 (Source: Vanguard)

Vanguard High Dividend Yield ETF (VYM)

Vanguard describes VYM as a high yield ETF. To this effect, the ETF tracks the FTSE High Dividend Yield Index. This index isn't as widely followed as the Dividend Achievers index, but it is a valid and thoroughly researched index nonetheless. VYM holds 426 dividend-paying companies across all industries. Currently, financials and healthcare account for the largest holdings.

Its biggest holdings are Johnson & Johnson, Procter & Gamble, and JPMorgan Chase. These companies offer a lot of stability coupled with reliable dividend payments. Other portfolio holdings include AT&T and Intel for some higher yields. Despite the high yield moniker attached to the fund, its holdings aren't exactly risky. It invests mostly in large cap companies, which means its payouts are stable.

Not only are payouts stable, the yield is a lot higher as well. VIG yields less than two percent, but VYM currently yields 3.59%. Its expense ratio is the same as VIG, coming in at 0.06%. While it is slightly more volatile than VIG, it is still less volatile than the S&P 500. This makes it an excellent choice for conservative investors.

Keep in mind that despite the low volatility, it's still a riskier investment compared to VIG. Again, the higher yield implies more risk and reward.

Figure 12: VYM 10 Year Performance from August 2010-2020 (Source: Vanguard)

Vanguard Long-Term Treasury ETF (VGLT)

VGLT is primarily a bond ETF, specifically a US Treasury Bond ETF. The fund aims to provide stable dividend income at sustainable yields. It's extremely useful for long-term treasury exposure. 99.9% of the holdings are in US government treasuries with a weighted average of 10-25 year maturity. This is a great choice for older investors looking for additional stability in their portfolio.

VGLT currently yields 1.39%, but this is offset because it performs well in volatile market environments when stocks are falling. This is because bonds naturally become a safe haven when stocks are in turbulent waters.

Between March and September 2020, VGLT returned 25.38% compared to 6% for the S&P 500 on a YTD basis. However, the ETF underperforms during growth markets as we experienced from 2011-2020.

VGLT has monthly distributions of $0.14 per share (roughly a two percent annual yield), which is great if you want more frequent payouts. Its expense ratio is just 0.05% as compared to similar funds that charge anywhere from 0.07% up to 1%.

Vanguard places this fund squarely in the middle in terms of risk versus reward, with the previous two funds a rung above in terms of risk. This is primarily because of the bond concentration in the fund's portfolio.

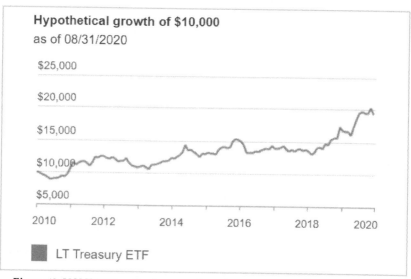

Figure 13: VGLT 10 Year Performance from August 2010-2020 (Source: Vanguard)

FREEMAN INCOME INVESTING RULE #8

IF YOU CAN'T (OR DON'T WANT TO) DEDICATE 30 MINUTES A DAY TO YOUR INVESTMENTS, THEN PASSIVE INVESTING WITH ETFS IS A SUPERIOR APPROACH

Chapter 14

TAX IMPLICATIONS OF DIVIDENDS

E arning steady income through dividends is great, but you have to take taxes into account. Many income-seeking investors get confused by how the IRS handles taxes, and in this chapter we'll be diving deep into this topic. Don't worry though. You don't need an accounting degree to understand all of this.

We'd also like to mention that given our audience's demographics, we'll be dealing primarily with the way the US government handles dividend taxation. For our readers outside the US, be sure to check your country's laws with a qualified tax professional.

To address the biggest question you might have, the majority of dividend taxation is fairly simple to understand. The most complex taxation requirements concern MLPs as we've discussed already. The average income investor will receive the Form 1099-DIV from their broker and will simply have to input the numbers on this form into their tax return software. Popular DIY tax software like QuickBooks, H&R Block and TurboTax have instructions on their website for how to enter information from your 1099-DIV form into your standard 1040 Tax Return form.

If there's no complexity in terms of filing, why should you pay attention to taxation? Simply put, it has implications for the way you choose to invest your money. Some high yield investments might not be suited for you thanks to the way they're taxed, while lower yield instruments might work better.

Before we dive into dividend taxation, we'd like to mention that you should take full advantage of all the tax perks you're provided. If you have a retirement account or multiple accounts with employer matching, you must take advantage of this. The dividends you earn in these accounts will not be taxed until you withdraw your capital at the age of 59 and a half.

While the topic of retirement accounts is beyond the scope of this book, we'd like to merely mention that the tax deferment qualities of these accounts allow you to compound your dividend income tax-free. If you elect to DRIP your dividends, then your compounding is both automatic and tax-free.

The flip side is that you can't withdraw this money without incurring penalties before the age of 59½. However, as long as you maximize your contributions into all of your retirement accounts and manage your expenses properly, you'll find that you won't need to touch your retirement nest egg. Having covered all of that, let's look at how dividends are taxed.

Dividend Taxation

All dividends are classified into two categories: ordinary and qualified. A company earns profits in two ways. One way is through their regular operating activities, and the other is by selling their assets. The money earned from selling long-term assets is classified as capital gains. If any portion of this money is paid out to you, it's a qualified dividend. The rest of it is ordinary income.

A single dividend payment will contain portions of ordinary income as well as qualified dividends. Ordinary dividends are taxed at prevailing income tax rates. This means they're treated as an extension of the income that you earn every year. You'll pay income tax on it according to the marginal tax rate at which you usually pay income tax.

The Form 1099-DIV will list the total amount of ordinary dividends you've earned over the year. Ordinary dividends are the default mode of payment. If a company doesn't specify a category, you should assume that the money being paid is an ordinary dividend.

Qualified dividends are treated as long-term capital gains. Capital gains come in two flavors: long-term and short-term. If you were to buy a stock and sell it within a year, this is a short-term sale. Any stock that you've held for more than a year is a long-term investment. Long-term capital gains tax rates range from zero to 20%. They're lower than ordinary income tax rates, which can be as high as 37%.

The amount of capital gains tax you pay depends on your filing status and your income tax bracket. For 2020, here's what the tax rates look like (O'Shea, 2020):

◇ Single filers

   a. 0 - $40,000 - Zero

   b. $40,001 - $441,450 - 15%

   c. $441,451 and above - 20%

◇ Married filing jointly

   d. 0 - $80,000 - Zero

   e. $80,001 - $496,600 - 15%

   f. $496,601 and above - 20%

◇ Head of household

   g. 0 - $53,600 - Zero

   h. $53,601 - $469,050 - 15%

   i. $469,051 and above - 20%

◇ Married, filing separately

   j. 0 - $40,000 - Zero

   k. $40,001 - $248,300 - 15%

   l. $248,301 and above - 20%

That's all there is to dividend taxation. Depending on the category your dividend is classified under, you'll pay different tax rates. Something to note is that if you DRIP your dividends into your investment in a regular brokerage account, you'll still be liable to pay taxes. Your broker will invest the entire dividend amount into the stock or fund. At the end of the year, you'll be liable to pay taxes on those dividends. This means you'll have a cash outflow at the end of the year if you elect to DRIP. Some investors forget about DRIP taxes since they don't receive cash payments. However, you're still liable for those taxes.

The two categories mostly apply to dividends earned from stock investments. In the case of bond or bond fund investment, dividends are technically interest income, which is the same as ordinary income.

REITs

REITs are slightly more complex than stock dividends, but these complexities work in your favor. The entire issue with REIT taxation hinges on how accounting principles work. These principles are referred to as Generally Accepted Accounting Principles or GAAP. GAAP is intended to cover every single industry and company in the United States and accounts for the quirks of every one of these industries. Understandably, sometimes the rules don't make much sense.

Nowhere is this more evident than with REITs. REITs are companies that own real estate and collect rent from those properties. Consider how the average landlord handles the issue of property valuation. Over time, the value of a real estate asset rises if it's well maintained. REIT companies, therefore, own properties whose values increase as time goes by, assuming they maintain them well.

However, GAAP has a different take on how assets ought to be handled. As far as GAAP is concerned, there's no difference between an asset such as furniture and real estate. Furniture and other typical company assets depreciate over time. On a company's balance sheet, this asset's value is reduced by a fixed percentage every year, over a fixed number of years. The length of the depreciation period is referred to as the useful life period. Real estate typically has a useful life of 20 years.

This means a REIT reduces the value of its assets by a certain percentage every year. Older properties decrease in value on paper as the years go by, irrespective of their true market value. There's another issue with depreciation. It's considered an expense under GAAP and has to be subtracted from a company's revenues. This means a REIT collects rent, pays salaries and administration expenses, and further reduces their revenues by depreciating expenses. This is a non-cash expense and makes no sense for a REIT (due to the nature of their assets), but they still record it to comply with GAAP.

So what does all this have to do with dividends? Dividends are paid from the income a company produces. If REITs are decreasing their revenues through unjustified depreciation, this means REIT dividends will be greater than their recorded net income on paper. After all, depreciation isn't a cash expense. It isn't even real for the most part when it comes to a REIT (since assets are *increasing* in value). The company would rather distribute that cash than hang on to it.

This is why you'll often see payout ratios exceed 100% when it comes to REITs. Remember that the payout ratio is calculated by dividing the dividend payment by the net income. It might seem as if the REIT is paying an unsustainable dividend on the surface of it, but this isn't the case. GAAP-enforced depreciation distorts the picture. While this rule makes no sense in business terms, it makes REITs quite attractive in terms of taxation.

Here's how the IRS categorizes REIT dividends. There are two categories: ordinary dividends and Return of Capital or ROC. Ordinary dividends are treated the same way as stock dividends of the same category are; you'll pay taxes equal to your marginal income tax rate on them. However, the rub is that the IRS considers just the net income per share amount equal to ordinary dividends. The rest is ROC.

For example, let's say a REIT declared a net income on paper of $1.50 per share and paid a dividend of $2.50 per share. Here's how the dividend payment will be categorized. $1.50 (which is equal to net income) is ordinary income and $1.00 (the remainder) is ROC. From an earlier chapter on MLPs, can you recall how ROC is treated?

ROC isn't taxed immediately. Instead, it reduces the cost basis of your investment. If you bought the REIT in the preceding example for $50, your adjusted cost basis is now $49 ($50 minus $1 of ROC). The longer you hold your REIT, the less your cost basis becomes until it eventually reduces to zero. Once that happens, you'll pay long-term capital gains taxes on the ROC distribution, depending on which bracket you fall into. We've highlighted these brackets in the previous section.

If you hold onto your REIT beyond the date of your death, you'll never pay taxes on the amount by which your cost basis was reduced. In the previous example, if you keep receiving $1.00 ROC payments for 50 years, your cost basis will drop to zero. Subsequent ROC payments will attract long-term capital gains. However, the $50 worth of ROC payments that decreased your cost basis will not be taxed until you sell your investment.

Let's say you sell your REIT for $100. Your purchase price in cash was $50, but your adjusted cost basis is $0. This means the IRS will treat this as you having earned $100 in long-term capital gains from this investment. If you never sell it, you won't pay taxes. You can transfer your REIT holdings to your heirs. In this case, the IRS will record the price of the REIT on the day of your passing, and this price is now the cost basis for your heirs.

Let's say the REIT is selling for $200. The ROC clock is now officially reset to this level. Your heirs will continue to receive tax free ROC payments that will reduce their cost basis from $200, until the day they decide to sell the REIT (if at all). ROC is what makes MLPs such an attractive investment as well. If you were to invest in a REIT ETF, you can technically hold on to it forever throughout generations and earn tax-free dividend income.

Do note that this ROC method doesn't apply if you're holding REITs in a retirement account. Retirement account withdrawals are treated as ordinary income, no matter their source. The exception is in a Roth IRA where distributions are tax-free. In a traditional IRA or 401(k) you'll pay taxes on the entire principal since you contributed pre-tax dollars to those accounts.

Therefore, if you plan to hold on to a REIT indefinitely, it's best to hold it in a regular brokerage account. You will pay taxes on the ordinary dividends you receive, but as long as you don't plan on selling, the tax savings from ROC will boost your returns. If you DRIP this into your REIT, that boosts returns even further.

Like stock dividends, you don't need to do any heavy lifting when declaring taxes on the cash you receive. The REIT will indicate the amounts within the respective categories on Forms 1099-DIV and 8937. You'll simply input these numbers into your tax preparation software and pay whatever is due. If you choose to DRIP dividends, you won't see a cash distribution hit your account, so you'll need to set aside cash to pay the taxes you owe.

The 2017 Tax Cuts and Jobs Act brings two important benefits for REITs and their shareholders. Most notably, thanks to the new 20% deduction on pass-through income through the end of 2025, individual REIT shareholders can now deduct 20% of taxable REIT dividend income they receive (but not for dividends that qualify for the capital gain rates).

MLPs work in the same way, except the forms involved are different, as we previously highlighted. Generally, it's not a good idea to hold an MLP in a retirement account. This is because you'll lose the capital gains deferral advantage, as we just explained.

However, there's also another reason. MLP dividends sometimes consist of Unrelated Business Taxable Income or UBTI. If you receive UBTI greater than $1,000 in a year in a retirement account, you're in for a world of tax headaches. You'll need to report it via a 990-T form to the IRS and pay taxes on it at your top marginal tax rate. Like the K-1, this form also arrives late and it complicates matters. The bottom line is, invest in MLPs using a regular brokerage account and not a retirement account.

We've reached the end of the taxation chapter, and you can take a deep breath now. We appreciate this might not have been the most thrilling part of the book, but it is one of the most important. If you have any concerns, contact a tax professional, preferably one who has experience working with investors.

Chapter 15

OPTIMAL PORTFOLIO CONSTRUCTION FOR DIVIDEND GROWTH INVESTING

So far, in this book, we've covered a wide variety of financial instruments you can invest in. We've also hinted at how you can construct a portfolio that will give you a good level of income. It's time to put everything together and construct a portfolio that will bring you the best results for your goals.

Anytime the subject of portfolio construction is broached, the word diversification rears its head. We are fans of diversification, but the trick is to diversify to the right degree. Diversify too much, and none of your positions will have an impact on your overall portfolio. Diversify too little, and you'll live and die by the performance of a few stocks.

There's also the matter of individual stock investing to be considered. How many positions should you own, and how should you allocate money to them? These are just some of the questions we'll be answering in this chapter. Many investors focus on picking the best instruments but neglect portfolio construction. A well-constructed portfolio minimizes risk without harming the rewards it can earn. This should be the basis on which you invest.

Diversification

So how should you diversify your portfolio, and is it even worth diversifying? The primary reason for diversifying is to avoid the risk of ruin. If you concentrate your money on a single investment without taking portfolio volatility into account, then you have a single point of failure. It's the same reasoning as to why we don't like investing in companies whose revenues are tied to a single product or customer. You might earn a steady 7% per year investing in AT&T, for example, but you don't want your portfolio tied to a single stock.

Before jumping into individual stocks, let's understand the reasoning behind our diversification strategies. If you're not someone who has the time to dissect a company and understand its business inside and out, then you're better off constructing a passive portfolio. This means you'll concentrate on investing in ETFs and funds. Doing this reduces your risk of losing money. The flip side is that you'll be paying management fees, and this reduces your return. This is why minimizing fees is essential and why we believe ETFs are superior to mutual funds.

A passive fund that tracks an index shouldn't charge more than 0.06% because there isn't much work that the manager needs to put into allocating capital. They simply buy and sell whatever's on the index they're tracking. This is why we often prefer Vanguard ETFs because they tend to have the lowest fees.

This isn't the case with an actively managed fund that seeks outperformance. In these cases, you'll need to evaluate the effects of fees and inflation on the returns. For example, if the fund charges you two percent in fees and earns an average return of 10% per year, your real return after considering two percent inflation is six percent.

If a passive ETF returns eight percent and charges just 0.06% in fees, you're better off investing in the ETF, despite its lower annual returns. The passive ETF will be less volatile and will increase over time since all it does is track an index. An actively managed fund will experience volatility, and you'll have to spend more time tracking its performance.

Given that both investments return around the same amount after inflation, it's better to opt for the passive investment. If the active fund returns far more than the passive one, then you'd be justified in spending time monitoring it.

Fees are especially significant when you consider investing in closed-ended bond funds. Bonds as an asset class return less on an annual basis than stocks. There are exceptions like some of the funds we highlighted, but take fees into account before investing in any fund.

We recommend investing in closed-ended bond funds to boost your income. However, don't make the mistake of comparing bond fund returns to stock fund returns. For example, don't compare a bond fund that returns five percent to a stock fund that returns 10%. You need to compare apples to apples.

So how should you diversify your portfolio? To begin with, we recommend asking yourself whether you wish to invest in individual stocks. If the answer is yes, we suggest dividing your capital in proportions of 60/30/10 and allocate the majority towards managed funds, 30% towards stocks, and 10% towards alternative assets. All portions of your portfolio will have different asset allocation principles. You will need to diversify your investments in the fund portion of your portfolio.

Here is a sample asset allocation for the fund portion of your portfolio:

◇ Dividend ETF (35% Allocation) - Vanguard High Dividend Index (VYM) (3.15% yield)

◇ Treasury Bond ETF (30% Allocation) - Vanguard Treasury ETF (VGLT) (2.68% yield)

◇ Public REIT (15% Allocation) - Vanguard REIT Fund (VNQ) (4.53% yield)

◇ Closed-End Fund (10% Allocation) - Reaves Utility Income Fund (UTG) (7.43% yield)

◇ Master Limited Partnership (10% Allocation) - Brookfield

Infrastructure (BIP) (4.64% yield)

Let's dig a little deeper into our reasoning behind this division of capital. Remember we're talking about 60% of your capital if you plan on investing in common stocks. If you don't have the time to analyze the business behind a stock, you should allocate 90% of your portfolio towards managed funds and 10% towards alternatives.

The stock ETF gives you a balance between capital gains as well a decent yield. You don't have to choose VYM, you can choose VIG instead. VIG prioritizes capital gains more than VYM does. If you're older and need to prioritize income a lot more than capital gains, we recommend choosing VYM. If you can wait for another decade or so before you need to withdraw your dividends, VIG is a better choice for you.

The treasury bond fund VGLT might seem to be a laggard in the portfolio. In fact, when times are great it will pull overall portfolio performance down. However, given that our aim is to minimize risk, VGLT should be one of the pillars of your portfolio. The point behind this position is to minimize your downside risk when markets turn bearish. Government debt is a safe haven during such times, and while VGLT will limit your gains in good times, it'll make up for it by not falling anywhere near as much or even rising during bad times.

Allocating money towards REITs is an excellent idea because you get to keep more of the dividend income you earn thanks to Return on Capital. VNQ has a lower yield than most REITs on the market, but it makes up for this with a low expense ratio and stable strategy. The fund doesn't invest in any properties but instead tracks the MSCI US Investable Market index. The objective is to capture broad-based real estate moves, instead of concentrating funds on a particular type of property that could increase your risk.

VNQ's expense ratio of 0.12% is higher than most Vanguard funds, but its portfolio is well-diversified. Industrials are the biggest proportion of its portfolio, and for this reason it has suffered recently. However, VNQ is well-poised to rebound when the economy picks back up. From a risk perspective, it doesn't hold any foreign real estate, which is a good thing since there's no telling which factors will influence property values abroad.

UTG is the income-generating star in this portfolio. With a 7.4% yield, it'll generate enough income to keep you satisfied. As its name suggests, UTG is a utility fund and invests in both domestic and international utility providers. Its high dividend yield is quite safe since utility stocks tend to be stable thanks to high barrier to entry, and distribute the majority of their earnings to shareholders. They don't appreciate much in share price, which is why the high yield is necessary to compensate investors. If generating high levels of income isn't as much of a priority for you and you'd like to capture capital gains as well, consider other closed-ended funds or even allocate this portion of your portfolio to common stock.

Lastly, we have BIP, which is an MLP. BIP is an MLP of its parent firm Brookfield Asset Management (BAM), which is a prominent infrastructure investment firm. Both BAM and BIP have had a great decade, and you might be wondering which is the better stock to own. We've recommended BIP thanks to its high dividend yield.

Given the infrastructure focus of both of these companies, it's a good bet that they'll be able to withstand any recessionary pressure. BIP's high yield will also ensure that its stock price remains relatively stable. A decline in stock price will boost yield to greater levels. This will lead to more investors buying the stock and bring its yield back to its current level.

When combined with VGLT, your portfolio will withstand bearish markets quite well. Thanks to the exposure to real estate, a portion of your portfolio will move in a different cycle, which also helps mitigate risk. We had previously mentioned that 10% of your portfolio should be allocated towards alternative assets. We'll explain what alternative assets are shortly.

For now, understand that this level of diversification in your passive portfolio is ideal. You have investments in every asset class and aren't overly exposed to risk. Your portfolio is U.S.-concentrated, which is a very good thing. Despite its current troubles, the American economic system will stay strong in the near term. You might be tempted to buy Chinese tech stock ETFs, but consider the risk before doing so. It's hard enough to figure out what's happening in the American market, let alone trying to figure out how a government-manipulated stock market like the Chinese one will work.

Let's move on and take a look at the common stock portion of your portfolio. Remember that if you don't wish to invest in common stocks, you'll split your money in a 90/10 split between funds and alternatives.

If you have the time to evaluate individual businesses, you should split your money in a 60/30/10 split between funds, common stock, and alternatives.

Portfolio Concentration

When investing in common stock, your objective is outperformance. If you review the investment principles we outlined earlier in this book, you'll realize that every principle is intended to keep you invested in a great business that keeps delivering capital gains as well as dividends. The lower the dividends you get paid, the higher your capital gains will be.

If you're going to invest directly into a stock, it doesn't make sense to over diversify. This is a controversial statement and flies against most financial advice. However, it's what investors such as Warren Buffett, Charlie Munger, and Mark Cuban prescribe.

To understand why, you need to look at your investment in a company from a business perspective. Let's say you're really good at something and start a company. Once the company starts doing well, would it make sense to divide your time between your company and a full-time job? Would such diversification make sense?

We don't think so. If your skill is good enough to get you paid lots of money, you're better off investing time into developing that skill instead of taking time away from it and working a "stable" job just for the sake of diversification. Allocating money in your portfolio towards common stocks works the same way. If you're convinced that a business is excellent and that it has great prospects, you should buy as much of it as possible.

As long as you can buy it at a reasonable price, you should be buying all the time. If you have $1,000 and have spotted two companies that are selling for prices that are bargains, how should you proceed? There's no template in such a scenario. You can buy more of the company that is giving you the best bargain. Or you could split your cash between both companies. The prices you can buy those company shares at are what matter the most. As long as the business conditions remain the same and as long as the price you receive is fair, you should be buying.

Doing this will result in a concentrated portfolio. You'll be buying many great businesses without worrying about holding 50+ different stocks. For example, Charlie Munger holds just three positions in his personal portfolio. He understands all three businesses in there and doesn't bother adding more in the name of diversification. By investing in what he knows and by following his principles, he reduces his risk considerably. If you are new to investing, we generally recommend you stick to less than 20 individual stocks in your first 2-3 years.

Portfolio concentration will bring you massive gains when your businesses do well. However, it'll also sink or swim based on the fortunes of the companies you invest in. Many investors get scared away by this volatility and consider concentration a bad thing. We'd like to point out that there are many caveats you need to satisfy before you decide to concentrate your money into a few holdings.

First, you need to have enough time to be able to evaluate a business thoroughly. This doesn't need to be a full-time job, but you need to dedicate at least 30 minutes a day. Second, you need to follow the investment principles we've outlined in this book. Not only do you need to follow them, but you also have to understand why they're effective. Many investors think they understand successful investing principles. Still, when it comes to buying companies, they let their emotions get in the way and end up doing the exact opposite.

Lastly, it would be best if you got your stable passive portfolio in place before investing actively. This will ensure you'll have some degree of stability at all times. As Warren Buffett famously said

> *"There are two rules in investing.*
> *Rule No. 1: Never lose money.*
> *Rule No. 2: Never forget rule No. 1."*

Alternative Assets

Alternative assets refer to investments that don't always have a business tied to them. For example, a common stock or bond is attached to a business. Whereas alternative assets such as gold or silver are not businesses. Instead, their prices are driven by their individual economic cycles and the state of the global economy.

Many investors consider them speculative since most alternatives don't have any value beyond what someone else thinks they're worth. However, we contend that alternative assets have a place in everyone's portfolio, albeit in the right proportions.

Let's take a look at some alternative assets and how you should invest in them.

Precious Metals

Gold, silver, platinum, palladium, etc. fall under the precious metals category. The most famous precious metals are gold and silver, of course. Gold is an excellent example of an alternative asset that is speculative but still contains a lot of value. Gold doesn't have any value beyond what someone else thinks it's worth. However, human beings have attributed monetary value to gold for more than 5,000 years, which is why it's considered precious.

If everyone were to decide tomorrow that gold isn't all that attractive, then it wouldn't be worth anything. This hasn't happened, and as a result, gold has always played an important part in the global economy. Traditionally, it's viewed as a safe haven asset. People have always valued gold, and there's no doubt that if paper money were to get devalued, gold would still be a viable currency. This is why gold rises in value whenever the values of the dollar and other major currencies decline.

Gold is a particularly viable investment these days because of the money printing policies that are in place in the developed world. As the amount of cash in a system increases, inflation rises, and with it, the value of money drops. Therefore gold is currently viewed as a great hedge against a falling dollar. Which is why its value has risen steadily since 2011, when Quantitative Easing really started ramping up.

Silver closely tracks gold, but it isn't quite the same. Silver has industrial uses, and there is more of a supply and demand component to its prices. Over the long run, silver tracks gold's movements despite being much cheaper than gold. It's also viewed as a desirable currency, and this adds a speculative element to its price.

The main difference is that silver doesn't function fully as a hedge against a declining dollar. Investing in it isn't as straightforward as gold, thanks to the industrial element present.

The other precious metals don't receive too much attention from retail investors, and even institutional investors who operate in them are highly specialized. As a result, we don't recommend investing into them. Gold and silver are great choices and even if you restrict yourself to gold, that's more than enough.

You can add Gold to your portfolio in many ways. You can buy the metal in physical form, or you can invest in an ETF that tracks its price. You can also invest in an ETF that tracks the fortunes of companies whose businesses are closely tied to gold.

Our favorite way to get gold exposure is slightly different, though. You can purchase companies like Royal Gold Inc. (RGLD) (1.19% yield) or Franco-Nevada Corp (FNV) (1.41% yield). Both of these companies are gold streamers. Streaming is a great business that gives you exposure to the profits of individual companies without exposing yourself to price movements in gold.

Here's how it works. Mining companies are cash-dependent and have huge capital expenses. They routinely seek out loans and financing to fund their operations. Mining is also a risky business. If the mine doesn't produce the projected output of metal, companies face huge losses. Bank interest rates tend to be high for gold miners, and this is where miners turn to streaming companies. A streaming company provides miners with financing, but instead of charging interest, they buy metal yielded from the mine at a steep discount. The streamer then sells the metal back to the market at regular prices and earns a profit.

The risk in streaming is that the company is exposed to mine risk. This is why it's important to invest in streaming companies that know what they're doing and evaluate mines thoroughly. The companies we've highlighted produce not only capital gains but also pay steady dividends. This makes them good bets for an income-driven investor.

The most important thing to remember is that not all exposures to gold are created equal. To highlight this further, here are the returns for four different gold entities over the past ten years.

◇ Franco Nevada (streamer): 197.18%

◇ Physical Gold price: 37.97%

◇ Gold ETF (GLD): 32.62%

◇ Barrick Gold (miner): -47.27%

Even though physical gold rose in price, mining companies like Barrick Gold suffered, while streamers such as Franco Nevada outperformed the metal itself.

Oil

After gold, oil is the most talked about commodity. Oil prices influence entire economies, and wars are fought over it. However, it's a bad idea to invest money with an aim of profiting from its price moves through ETFs or futures.

This isn't because of the rise of alternative energy sources. Oil is a poor investment because it has its own supply and demand element, along with a liberal dose of speculation. The price of oil often fluctuates based on what some kingdom in the Middle East decides to do and how American demand fluctuates.

Retail investors are best served staying away from oil. Even ETFs and companies tied to oil aren't a good bet because their incomes aren't stable. It takes companies the size of Chevron and Exxon, with deep resources and multiple income streams derived from oil, to generate steady income.

Agricultural Commodities

Agricultural commodities are an obscure class of alternatives as far as retail investors go. They aren't easily traded, and despite there being a few ETFs around, they don't garner much attention. Corn and soybeans are the two most heavily traded commodities in this asset class. Their prices usually track one another.

Given that they're crops, their output heavily depends on weather patterns and conditions. To invest in them successfully, you'll need to understand how supply and demand work in this sector. Institutions that support them are highly specialized and typically don't invest in anything else. Therefore, individual investors should stay away from commodities.

Other Alternatives

There are an increasing number of alternative assets that pay dividends. Cryptocurrencies are a popular alternative asset, but they don't pay dividends. However, we believe dedicating a small portion of your portfolio (5-10%) to Bitcoin is worth it as a hedge against the broad stock market. We will be covering Bitcoin in greater depth in our next book *The Only Bitcoin Investing Book You'll Ever Need*, which is scheduled for release in late February 2021.

Artwork, wine, jewelry, and classic cars are good places to park your money. However, these are mostly one-off purchases, and as such, we won't spend time discussing them since it's hard to develop a repeatable and consistent system. If you have a significant advantage in this area, then, by all means, go ahead.

Shipping containers have become more popular of late, with some companies advertising 25% returns per year. In our experience, most of these companies are flat-out frauds so it's best to stay away from this field entirely.

When it comes to alternative assets, stick with gold. Then add some Bitcoin in as a hedge. Most importantly, don't overcomplicate things.

Remember that your primary aim with alternative assets is to create your own personal financial fortress, not spend time learning the ins and outs of various obscure asset classes.

FREEMAN INCOME INVESTING RULE #9

HAVING 5% OF YOUR PORTFOLIO IN BITCOIN IS A GREAT HEDGE AGAINST A BROAD MARKET COLLAPSE

CONCLUSION

If you're looking for income from your investments, then the dividend growth strategy is your best bet. We hope this book has opened your eyes to the benefits of this approach.

It's important for you to remain realistic when seeking income from your investments. First things first, look at minimizing costs wherever possible. If your financial advisor is charging 1-2% to tell you to invest in a mutual fund that also charges 1% per year, you already need to make an extra 2% per year just to cover your fees.

Remember that with the rise in passive ETFs, you no longer have to pay 1-2% for a broad market fund, and can pay as little as 0.03% per year. By simply switching from a mutual fund to a passive ETF, your savings compound to a significant amount over the course of 10-20 years.

By concentrating on stability and avoiding yield chasing, you'll avoid most of the income investing traps out there. Stay focused on minimizing risk as much as possible, and this won't be an issue for you.

Remember that capital gains are just as crucial as dividends are. Without steady capital gains, you'll end up losing your investment principal, and your dividend income will inevitably decline because of it, if the company slashes its payouts. These days, low interest rates have created a ton of dividend and yield traps, so watch out for these stocks. Don't automatically assume a high yield is a good thing.

What truly matters is a stock's payout ratio and a history of growing dividend payments. A sustainable payout ratio varies from one industry to another. But as long as the dividend payment is growing and the payout ratio remains stable, you'll end up earning more income as time goes by. This is the essence of income investing, and it's what you should aim for. Don't chase monthly dividend payments for their own sake. A monthly payment that yields five percent is no different from a semi-yearly payment that yields the same amount.

We've provided you with a set of investment options within the managed fund sphere, but if you wish to invest in individual companies, you need to follow a repeatable investment process. We've outlined the 11 principles in our approach. These principles will help you unearth great companies that pay steady dividends and will grow over time. The most important thing to look for is a quality business. Everything else comes second.

Constructing a portfolio can seem overwhelming at first, but we're positive that you've gained some insight into how you should approach it and will find a simplified 60/30/10 approach practical. You can build a diversified portfolio or one that has elements of diversification and concentration within it. A concentrated portfolio is best when investing in individual companies. Keep in mind that there are a few caveats you need to satisfy before you decide to concentrate your holdings into a few stocks. Above all else, you need to follow the sound investment principles we've elaborated on in this book.

Feel free to use our recommended stocks such as AT&T, ExxonMobil, and Realty Income as a starting point for more research or as parts of your portfolio. For further research, we recommend examining the latest 10-K reports from each company, as well as checking key financial metrics using our *Company Valuation 101* criteria, which you can access for free at https://freemanpublications.com/bonus

Investing for income is critical as you grow older, but it doesn't have to be complicated. Make it a point to refer to this book whenever you have any doubts.

Alternatively, you can email us at admin@freemanpublications.com if you would like something clarified. We answer every single reader's email.

2020 was a chaotic year, so as we move into 2021, we wish you the best of luck with your investing!

One final word from us. If this book has helped you in any way, we'd appreciate it if you left a review on Amazon.

Reviews are the lifeblood of our business. We read every single one and incorporate your feedback into our future book projects.

To leave an Amazon review, go to https://freemanpublications.com/leaveareview

OTHER BOOKS BY
FREEMAN PUBLICATIONS
(AVAILABLE ON AMAZON & AUDIBLE)

 The 8-Step Beginner's Guide to Value Investing: Featuring 20 for 20 - The 20 Best Stocks & ETFs to Buy and Hold for The Next 20 Years

 Bear Market Investing Strategies: 37 Recession-Proof Ideas to Grow Your Wealth - Including Inverse ETFs, Put Options, Gold & Cryptocurrency

 Iron Condor Options for Beginners: A Smart, Safe Method to Generate an Extra 25% Per Year with Just 2 Trades Per Month

 Covered Calls for Beginners: A Risk-Free Way to Collect "Rental Income" Every Single Month on Stocks You Already Own

 Credit Spread Options for Beginners: Turn Your Most Boring Stocks into Reliable Monthly Paychecks using Call, Put & Iron Butterfly Spreads - Even If The Market is Doing Nothing

REFERENCES

2Q20 Earnings Conference Call E•ite• Transcript. (2020). Chevron. https://chevroncorp.gcs-web.com/static-files/10f71f7d-4347-40af-a329-baef3615e2bf

2015 Letter - Klarman tell investors he is looking for bargains ami• "stealth bear market." (2020, November 4). 2015 Letter - Klarman Tell Investors He Is Looking for Bargains amid "Stealth Bear Market." https://valuewalkposts.tumblr.com/post/138102275370/2015-letter-klarman-tell-investors-he-is

Bengen, W. (2020). *DETERMINING WITHDRAWAL RATES USING HISTORICAL DATA.* https://www.retailinvestor.org/pdf/Bengen1.pdf

Chen, J. (2020, November 4). *K-Shape• Recovery Definition.* Investopedia. https://www.investopedia.com/k-shaped-recovery-5080086

de Haas, B. (2020, October 13). *Why Dan Loeb Wants Disney To Cease Its Divi•en•.* https://seekingalpha.com/article/4378797-why-dan-loeb-wants-disney-to-cease-dividend

Facebook's a•vertising revenue worl•wi•e from 2009 to 2019 (2020). Statista https://www.statista.com/statistics/271258/facebooks-advertising-revenue-worldwide/

Finke, M. (2020, November 4). *Are Nontra•e• REITs Right for Clients?* ThinkAdvisor. https://www.thinkadvisor.com/2014/11/24/are-nontraded-reits-right-for-clients/

Foelber, D. (2020, July 29). *Is Kin•er Morgan Stock a Buy?* The Motley Fool.https://www.fool.com/investing/2020/07/29/is-kinder-morgan-stock-a-buy.aspx

Frankel, M. (2020, November 4). *Pros an* Cons of Single-Tenant Net Leases for Investors*. Millionacres. https://www.fool.com/millionacres/real-estate-investing/articles/pros-and-cons-single-tenant-net-leases-investors

Graham, B., & Dodd, D. L. (2009). *Security analysis : principles an* technique*. Mcgraw-Hill.

*He*ge Fun*s: Higher Returns Or Just High Fees?* (2019). Investopedia. https://www.investopedia.com/articles/03/121003.asp

*Here's How Much Warren Buffett Has Ma*e on Coca-Cola*. (2019, November 19). Nasdaq.Com. https://www.nasdaq.com/articles/heres-how-much-warren-buffett-has-made-on-coca-cola-2019-11-19

Is Tesla Losing Money on Every Car Sale? (2019). Investopedia. https://www.investopedia.com/articles/markets/070116/tesla-losing-money-each-time-it-sells-car-tsla.asp

Japan's Expansionist Policies Have Brought Unexpecte Results*. (2019). Investopedia. https://www.investopedia.com/articles/markets/052516/japans-case-study-diminished-effects-qe.asp

Lynch, P., & Rothchild, J. (2000). *One up on Wall Street*. Simon & Schuster.

Maverick, J. B. (2019). *What is the average annual return for the S&P 500?* Investopedia. https://www.investopedia.com/ask/answers/042415/what-average-annual-return-sp-500.asp

McClay, R. (2020, November 4). *The Benefits of Master Limite* Partnerships*. Investopedia. https://www.investopedia.com/investing/benefits-master-limited-partnerships/

*Me*ical Cannabis Market – Global In*ustry Tren*s An* Forecast To 2027* (2020). | Data Bridge Market Research. https://www.databridgemarketresearch.com/reports/global-medical-cannabis-market

Nikola: How to Parlay An Ocean of Lies Into a Partnership With the Largest Auto OEM in America. (2020, September 10). Hindenburg Research. https://hindenburgresearch.com/nikola/

O'Shea, A. (2020, November 4). *2020 Capital Gains Tax Rates & How to Avoi♦ a Big Bill.* NerdWallet. https://www.nerdwallet.com/article/taxes/capital-gains-tax-rates

Pisani, B. (2019, March 15). *Active fun♦ managers trail the S&P 500 for the ninth year in a row in triumph for in♦exing.* CNBC; CNBC. https://www.cnbc.com/2019/03/15/active-fund-managers-trail-the-sp-500-for-the-ninth-year-in-a-row-in-triumph-for-indexing.html

Realty Income Announces Operating Results For Secon♦ Quarter An♦ First Six Months Of 2020. (2020, November 4). Www.Realtyincome.Com. https://www.realtyincome.com/investors/press-releases/press-release-details/2020/Realty-Income-Announces-Operating-Results-For-Second-Quarter-And-First-Six-Months-Of-2020/default.aspx

Shah, A. (2020, November 4). *Obscure Berkshire Hathaway Filing Reveals What Warren Buffett Thinks About Kraft Heinz.* Forbes. https://www.forbes.com/sites/alapshah/2019/08/12/obscure-berkshire-hathaway-filing-reveals-what-warren-buffett-thinks-about-kraft-heinz/#7947aaec3b82

Sparks, D. (2020, January 15). *Battle of Divi♦en♦s: Apple vs. Microsoft.* The Motley Fool. https://www.fool.com/investing/2020/01/15/battle-of-dividends-apple-vs-microsoft.aspx

Tra♦e Signals - FANG Stocks Up 400%, S&P 500 In♦ex ex-FANGs up 35%, S&P 500 In♦ex up 45% (2015-Present). (2020, November 4). CMG. https://www.cmgwealth.com/ri/trade-signals-fang-stocks-up-400-sp-500-index-ex-fangs-up-35-sp-500-index-up-45-2015-present/

US ♦ivi♦en♦s for the long term. (2013). JP Morgan.

What to know about buying close♦-en♦ fun♦s at a ♦iscount. (2020, November 4). Nuveen. https://www.nuveen.com/en-us/thinking/closed-end-funds/what-to-know-about-buying-closed-end-funds-at-a-discount

Why the Fe♦ save♦ AIG an♦ not Lehman. (2020, November 4). Fortune. https://fortune.com/2010/09/02/why-the-fed-saved-aig-and-not-lehman/

Williams, D. (2020, November 4). *Where Does The U.S. Housing Market Go From Here? Five Experts Share Pre♦ictions For The Rest Of 2020.* Forbes. https://www.forbes.com/sites/dimawilliams/2020/07/10/is-it-going-to-get-better-before-it-gets-worse-five-experts-share-predictions-for-the-us-housing-market-in-the-second-half-of-2020/#6730e1a07026

Williams, S. (2020, July 24). *The 4 Biggest Divi♦en♦ Payouts on Wall Street.* The Motley Fool. https://www.fool.com/investing/2020/07/24/the-4-biggest-dividend-payouts-on-wall-street.aspx

Winck, B. (2020, April 24). *Ninten♦o cuts 'Animal Crossing: New Horizons' interest rates to boost virtual spen♦ing.* Business Insider. https://markets.businessinsider.com/news/stocks/nintendo-cuts-interest-rate-animal-crossing-new-horizons-stimulate-spending-2020-4-1029127954#:~:

PART - 2

REIT
INVESTING
for
BEGINNERS

HOW TO GET RICH IN REAL ESTATE WITHOUT OWNING A SINGLE PHYSICAL PROPERTY

+BEAT INFLATION WITH CONSISTENT 9% DIVIDENDS

HOW TO GET THE MOST OUT OF
THIS BOOK

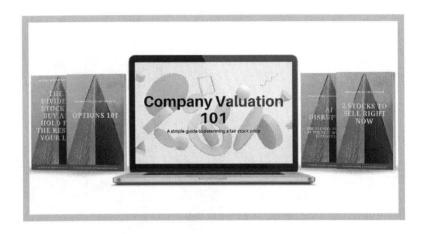

To help you along your investing journey, we've created a free bonus companion course that includes spreadsheets, bonus video content, and additional resources that will help you get the best possible results. We highly recommend you sign up now to get the most out of this book. You can do that by going to the link below or scanning the QR code with your cell phone

https://freemanpublications.com/bonus

Or text the word BONUS to 844-968-4152 (US only)

Free bonus #1: Company Valuation 101 video course ($97 value)

In this 8 part video course, you'll discover our process for accurately valuing a company. This will help you determine if a stock is overvalued, correctly valued, or a bargain. Giving you an indicator of whether to buy or not.

Free bonus #2: Guru Portfolios Analyzed ($37 value)

In these videos, we analyze the stock portfolios of Billionaire investors like Warren Buffett. As well as top entrepreneurs like Bill Gates.

Free bonus #3: Crypto 101 ($47 value)

When you have a paradigm-shifting technology like cryptocurrency and blockchain … there are multiple ways to profit from it.

But before you rush out and buy every altcoin under the sun… there is a smarter way of doing this.

The ways used by hedge funds and Billionaire investors to make massive profits from the price of Bitcoin and other cryptocurrencies.

And you don't need anything more than a regular brokerage account to do so.

We covered exactly how to do this in a private call for our premium members recently and you ll get access to this video for free.

Free bonus #4: 2 Stocks to Sell Right Now ($17 value)

These 2 stocks are in danger of plummeting in the next 12 months. They're both popular with retail investors, and one is even in the top 5 most held stocks on Robinhood. Believe us; you don't want to be holding these going into 2021 and beyond.

Free bonus #5: AI Disruptor - The $4 Stock Poised to be the Next Big Thing in Computing ($17 value)

This under the radar company, which less than 1% of investors have heard of, is at the forefront of a breakthrough technology that will change our lives as we know them. Soon this technology will be in every smartphone, tablet, and laptop on the planet.

Free bonus #6: Options 101 ($17 Value)

Options don't have to be risky. In fact, they were invented to *re uce* risk. It's no wonder that smart investors like Warren Buffett regularly use options to supplement their long-term portfolio. In this quick start guide, we show you how options work and why they are tools to be utilized rather than feared.

Free bonus #7: The 1 Dividend Stock to Buy and Hold for the Rest of Your Life ($17 Value)

Dividends are the lifeblood of any income investor, and this stock is a cornerstone of any dividend strategy. A true dividend aristocrat with consistent payouts for over 50 years which you'll want to add to your portfolio for sure.

Free bonus #8: All the images inside this book in color ($17 Value)

As much as we'd like to print these books in full color, the printing costs prohibit us from doing so. So on our website, you can get all the images from the book in full color.

Free Bonus #9: Our #1 High Yield Stock for 2023 ($17 Value)

A company with a virtual monopoly in its industry. The stock pays a 10% yield while offering capital appreciation. Best of all? It's only $9/ share

All of these bonuses are 100% free, with no strings attached. You don't need to enter any details except your email address.

To get your bonuses go to

https://freemanpublications.com/bonus

Or text the word BONUS to 844-968-4152 (US only)

INTRODUCTION

"They made all their money in real estate"

Oh how often we hear that phrase.

As I write this chapter, I'm currently on a flight between London (where I was born), and Austin, Texas (where I currently reside). On both sides of the pond, real estate investment is often looked at as the holy grail asset class. There's something about owning a physical item that sounds so captivating to the investment minded individual.

However real estate investment is not without its downsides. Flaky tenants, leaking pipes and hidden costs all make the act of being a landlord less appealing in reality. Which is why I've always gravitated towards Real Estate Investment Trusts.

REITs have exploded in popularity over the past decade, and for good reason. I believe they offer a best of both worlds approach where you can benefit from the upside of owning real estate, without the hassle of owning physical property.

This unique asset class also allows you to branch into areas of real estate which are unavailable to most of the population. It's one thing to own a duplex, but it's another to own 300 datacenters, 441 hospitals or 40,000 cellular towers. However with REITs, that is entirely possible, all using your regular brokerage account.

I suppose I should address the elephant in the room, that being the current economic climate. There are no 2 ways about it, 2022 has been a horrid year for investors. For the first time in recorded history, both stocks and bonds are down more than 10% in a calendar year. Crypto is down roughly 50% from its previous highs, and the physical real estate bubble in the US seems to be on the brink of bursting.

Now if you've never read The Intelligent Investor, then it's worth buying just to read Chapter 8. This chapter is one of the most crucial pieces of writing about investing that has ever existed. In the chapter, Benjamin Graham describes the Mr. Market phenomena, where short term stock prices divorce from business reality, purely on the current market sentiment. Using a property example, it'd be like if a stranger came to your house one day and told you it was worth $100,000. Naturally if this happened, you'd laugh them off. Then the next day another strange appears offering you $10 million for the same house. Once again, you'd laugh them off. This might sound crazy but the exact same phenomena happens every day in the stock market. Companies which were valued at a market cap of $50 Billion last year, are now viewed as only worth $10 Billion.

The key lesson being that stock prices can and do decline even if the underlying business is sound.

Right now is one of those times. While there is no doubt that many companies are facing a tough economic environment, one thing that you can benefit from in recent times, is bargain prices for quality companies.

In fact, there are many stocks which have declined in price by 30% or more, despite strengthening fundamentals. So it's times like these when truly great investors are made. Because if you can separate the signal from the noise, right now is when you can pick up quality companies for fifty cents on the dollar. This book will help you do just that.

If you've been following our work for a while, then you'll know that we're not about get-rich-quick schemes or financial gimmicks. Instead we focus on sound, long-term investing principles. The same principles adhered to by the likes of Warren Buffett, Howard Marks and Peter Lynch. The same principles that aim to create generational wealth. Wealth which can facilitate financial freedom for you and your family.

If you're new to our work though, first of all, welcome to the family. It's our mission to empower individual investors to reach their financial goals, while avoiding the pitfalls, scammers and shysters which are rife in this industry.

Our books are the first step in that process, this being our 11th title. We aim to first give you the necessary context for why REITs are so desirable. So in part 1, we'll explore how we reached the current inflationary environment along with the short to medium term consequences of high inflation and interest rates. Then we'll explore how REITs can not only generate a healthy source of income for you, but also provide downside protection for the rest of your portfolio.

After that, we'll dive deeper into how REITs work, plus some traps that inexperienced investors can fall into. Then we'll cover specific examples from REITs in different sectors and why we believe these companies are worthy additions to your portfolio.

One final thing, it doesn't matter what the size of your portfolio is now. You don't need a special investing account either, all you need is a standard brokerage account or a retirement account.

The companies and strategies we're going to highlight will eventually help you generate a full time passive income and supercharge your retirement. We'll also show you how you can grow a small account to a much larger one thanks to the power of compounding and dividend reinvestment.

All it takes for you to realize this potential is a little work and dedication. Put in the work today, and you and your family will benefit tomorrow.

Oliver El-Gorr

Founder & CEO, Freeman Publications

30,000 feet above the Atlantic Ocean, October 2022

Chapter 1

WHY AMERICANS ARE FACING THE HIGHEST COST OF LIVING IN FOUR DECADES

The consumer price index jumped to 8.2% in October 2022, continuing the highest 12-month rise in four decades. While this is the figure that makes the headlines, the inflation you and I actually feel on a day to day basis is even higher. According to the US Bureau of Labor Statistics, food prices are up 11.2%, gas is up 18%, and electricity is up 15%.

Runaway inflation has encouraged the Federal Reserve to keep hiking interest rates to attempt to drag inflation toward the targeted two percent level. This led to rates for a 1 year treasury bill hitting over 4.5%. The same bond which paid just 0.1% in October 2021. With more rate rises looming, let's dig deeper into what caused this recent inflation surge, along with the near term consequences of higher interest rates.

What caused this recent surge in inflation?

On its purest level, inflation occurs when demand outweighs supply. This is a fundamental law of economics. So the first question we should ask is, "Why is demand outpacing supply?"

The answer to this question takes us back to the times when COVID-19 halted most global economies. The U.S. was no exception.

COVID-19 halted economic activities weeks after the initial spread to the US in March 2020. Other aspects of typical American life stopped, including schooling, recreation, and sporting activities. The damage that the virus was inflicting had never been seen before; it was ferocious and infected the public at a fast pace. Most states were forced to shut down nonessential businesses to curb the spread of the virus. One of the consequences of this was disruption to supply chains.

Therefore it shouldn't be a surprise to learn that the U.S. GDP (a measure of a country's income from its services and goods) plummeted by 5.1% in the first quarter of 2020 (Cox, 2021).

When some businesses temporarily shut down, it became clear that COVID-19 was a national health and economic issue. The state of the economy confirmed this in the second quarter of 2020 when it shrunk by 31.4%, the highest drop since 1947 when GDP quarterly records were first recorded (Cox, 2021).

The Federal Reserve wasn't going to watch as the country was being buffeted by coronavirus. It moved swiftly to ensure that businesses and banks had ample money to conduct their respective activities. For example, they wanted banks to continue lending money as they were unsure how long the pandemic would negatively impact the economy. The Fed lowered its target fed fund rate by one basis point, resulting in the new range being 0%–0.25% (Alpert, 2020). This meant that it became cheaper for consumers to get bank credit. The Fed also reduced the reserve requirement for banks to zero, meaning that banks could lend all money on hand.

In late March 2020, Congress moved fast to pass the Coronavirus Aid, Relief, and Economic Security (CARES) Act. This act provided financial relief to businesses and families to the tune of $2 trillion (Alpert, 2020). Toward the end of 2020, the Consolidated Appropriations Act provided up to $600 to qualifying taxpayers, which amounted to a $900 billion aid package (Alpert, 2020).

That wasn't the last government effort to stimulate the economy; Congress further ratified the American Rescue Plan Act in March 2021. This put $1,400 in the hands of eligible Americans and provided funds for vaccinations and other initiatives. Sadly, the various package aids further raised the federal deficit.

One of the consequences of a combination of low interest rates and being stuck indoors was a shot of adrenaline into the housing market from June 2020. This was due to families opting to buy homes to access features such as bigger yards and homes suited for remote working and learning. In the past, home builders were reluctant to keep large inventories for fear of a possible repeat of the Great Recession. This came to bite them in 2020 when the supply of homes lasted but a little more than two months.

The government's injection of money into the economy, coupled with vaccinations, saw the resurgence in demand for goods and services. Sadly, many businesses couldn't meet the excess demand as they struggled to find employees and supplies to meet customer orders. Supply chains battled as factories, ports, and other freight logistics increasingly became overwhelmed. This was exacerbated by China's "Zero-Covid" policies which left many of the world's biggest ports completely shut for weeks at a time.

Three Major Drivers of Recent Inflation Rises

The May 2022 inflation rocked many who thought it had peaked. The reason for that hope stemmed from April's rise of 0.3%, which was lower than the 1.2% in March. The May 2022 inflation rise was the second highest over the previous 12 months. It's clear that demand for goods and services is continuing to outpace supply. With possible interest rate hikes, there's a possibility the country could go into a recession. With that said, what amenities and services are pushing inflation higher and higher?

The biggest contributors in May 2022 were used cars and trucks, gasoline, and food. Energy costs jumped by 3.9% driven by fuel oil, gasoline, and utility gas services. This means that energy costs have risen by 34.6% in the previous 12 months (U.S. Bureau of Labor Statistics, 2022). It shouldn't come as a surprise that car owners are forking out an average of nearly $5 a gallon for gas. If you're in California, the cost is even higher at an average of around $6 a gallon (AAA Gas Prices, 2022). If you drive a car with a 15-gallon fuel tank, that tank which used to cost $45 to fill, now costs $75 or more.

It's not only gas that's costing more, but diesel prices are also leaping higher. Truckers are having to pay more to transport goods, which pushes them to charge higher prices.

Soaring energy prices are largely due to excess demand for crude oil. Some energy producers were forced to cut back during the 2020 pandemic, and when you couple this with Russia's invasion of Ukraine, the energy situation becomes dire. U.S. refineries have amped up plant utilization to September 2019 levels, but petroleum levels remain low (Paraskova, 2022). It appears there's no respite yet for Americans due to rising energy costs.

The war between Russia and Ukraine isn't only impacting energy prices, but it is also influencing food costs. Combined, these two countries supply about a third of global wheat and barley. Moreover, two-thirds of the sunflower oil many use for cooking comes from

Russia and Ukraine (Reuters, 2022). Food cooked at home and outside of the home has risen by 13% and 8%, respectively, in the previous year. Both these sorts of food items have risen to their highest levels in the last four decades.

It wasn't just food and energy which is driving overall inflation. Over the past 12 months, prices for used cars and trucks are up 7.2%. A shortage of new cars due to the supply chain constraints of semiconductors is causing the surge in used car and truck demand.

Sal Guatieri, a senior economist at BMO Capital commented, "There's little respite from four-decade high inflation until energy and food costs simmer down and excess demand pressures abate in response to tighter monetary policy" (as cited in Mutikani, 2022). Judging by recent inflation numbers, it appears Guatieri isn't far off in his assertion.

For investors, high interest rates are as much of a concern as rising inflation is a concern. It's hard to predict how long they will remain high. However based on past history, we can hypothesize that inflation will eventually stabilize at a lower level than today.

One thing to consider is that although we've been anchored to extremely low interest rates for the past decade, these are the exception rather than the rule. Before 2008, rates had never been below 1% (except for a short time in 2003), and from the mid 1980s to 2006, rates generally stayed between 3 and 6%.

So for our medium term thesis, we're taking the view that rates won't return to 2008-2021 levels, but rather will likely settle somewhere between 3-5%.

One thing I can't stress enough though, is the actions of the Fed are beyond your control. A key factor which separates great investors from the rest, is understanding what is and isn't within your control. Meaning there's no use driving yourself crazy over the latest inflation and interest rate data. That's why we're focused on what we can control, which is companies we own within our portfolios, and the process we use to pick those companies. Note that I said companies, not stocks. This small, but powerful tweak can make a big difference in your investing strategy, and it's a guiding principle we'll be using throughout the rest of this book.

KEY TAKEAWAYS

◇ At the time of writing – CPI inflation is 8.2% with key inflationary measures like food and gas being even higher

◇ Inflation and the subsequent actions of the Fed are beyond your control

◇ While we can't make predictions for when inflation will decrease – it is likely that in the medium term (3-5 years) we will see lower inflation than we have today

---

Chapter 2

HOW TO KEEP UP WITH INFLATION WITH REIT INVESTING

There's a way to keep up with rising inflation: invest for income. One of the best long-term choices for generating income is through investing in publicly listed Real Estate Investment Trusts (REITs). Having such assets can help ensure that you have a second income while you're working, and can safely withdraw money during your retirement without needing to touch your investment principle.

Build a Resilient Investment Portfolio

Inflation eats up your investment returns, making it necessary to generate even higher yields. This can be tough to achieve. For example, with the current incessant predictions of a recession, stocks are getting hit hard. As of October 15, 2022, the S&P 500 has tumbled 25% from its January 2022 record high, and is now trading at the same level as November 2020. (Subin & Imbert, 2022).

That's why you need a sound investment strategy that's likely to deliver results over the long term. Your strategy should consider the following:

Grow Your Investment Portfolio for 10 Years or More

You have three approaches when investing in the market: to invest in bonds, stocks, or both. The rationale behind this is that bonds will provide income and safety, while stocks while provide capital appreciation. There's a reason that nearly every target date retirement fund is a simple mix of a broad stock index like the Vanguard Total Stock Market Index and a bond index like the Vanguard Total Bond Market Index. With weighting skewing more heavy towards bonds as your target retirement date gets closer.

However, in the past decade, bonds have become less and less appealing for investors due to chronically low yields.

Therefore if you want to grow your portfolio, fixed-income securities aren't the best financial assets to buy. Instead a better approach is to invest in stocks that offer **both** capital gains and dividends. Since booms outlast dips, you could potentially make a killing if you select the right kind of stocks and invest for the long term.

The difficulty with investing is resisting the urge to focus on minutia. This is especially so when you rely on daily financial news for making investment decisions. As Charlie Munger so wisely said, judge people by their incentives. In the case of news sources, their incentives are to increase the number of eyeballs watching them, either on TV or their websites.

Minimize Risk to Your Portfolio

It's a fact that you can't create a portfolio that's completely risk-free. The best you can do is minimize risk. To be sure, investing risk means the possibility of losing capital. Over the short term, risk can increase when assets are highly volatile.

There are two methods for measuring risk: beta and standard deviation. With beta, you use it to establish the sensitivity of your investment to market gyrations. A beta of 1.0 signifies that your investment moves with the market. When beta is less than 1, your investment is less volatile than the market and the opposite is also true. With this in mind, it's advisable to select income focused stocks that have a beta of less than 1

It helps a great deal if your investments also have a narrow standard deviation. Like beta, standard deviation measures volatility. When it's large, an investment's price swings wider from an average value, meaning that your investment is highly volatile. As such, you may generate inconsistent returns, and perhaps register losses. Preferably, you should aim for investments with lower standard deviations.

Diversify Into Different Sectors

Having a properly diversified portfolio has been one of the best methods to mitigate this ripple effect in the market. At Freeman Publications we often spend a lot of time talking about growth stocks, which are smaller companies with the potential to return 10 or even 20x our original investment over the long run.

The reason we can do this is because we have "workhorse" stocks like REITs providing consistent income every single quarter, and in some cases, every single month. This gives us the downside protection necessary to be able to take swings at some of these more volatile, higher reward stocks.

Ability to live off the income rather than withdrawals

Withdrawal strategies are one of the most misunderstood elements of investing. The majority of them simply tell you to withdraw a certain percentage of your total investment annually. However, considering the current market situation and realistic scenarios, they often tend to fall short at providing you with consistent income. Let's look at the most popular strategy, and its flaws.

William Bengen's 4% rule

William Bengen is a retired financial advisor who invented the 4% Rule. In his paper titled *Determining Historical Withdrawal Rates Using Historical Data*, Bengen (1994) recommended that retirees withdraw four percent of their initial portfolio consisting of 50% stock and 50% bonds. In the succeeding years, the withdrawal rates get adjusted up or down based on inflation.

For example, if you have a $1 million-portfolio at the start of your retirement, you'll withdraw $40,000 (4% of $1 million) at the end of your first year of retirement. I'm assuming you'll make the first withdrawal a year after retirement. Suppose inflation has increased by one percent by then. You'd have to adjust your first-year withdrawal income upward by one percent to $40,400 ($40,000 + (1% of $40,000)). This approach, according to Bengen, would ensure a retiree never runs out of money in their portfolio for the next 33 years or so.

However the 4% rule is inherently flawed as retiree spending doesn't stay flat. According to the U.S. Bureau of Labor Statistics, mean spending for households headed by retirees aged 65—74 was about $10,000 lower than for those aged 55–64 in 2017 (as cited in Finch, 2018). Most expenses like clothing and transportation declined while health costs rose. This spending is higher in the early years of retirement due to factors such as aging parents that may still be alive and children that are finding their feet.

The problem with Bengen's approach is that the market might take a big hit in the early stage of your retirement. This is exactly what happened to people who retired during the mid and late 2000s. The Global Financial Crisis decimated their portfolios, forcing many to sell a portion of their shares at significant losses, which means they missed on capitalizing on the 10-year bull run that soon followed. Since you may need additional income in your early retirement years, you need a better alternative than the 4% Rule, and that's where REITs come in.

U.S. law demands each REIT to pay out 90% of its taxable income to its stockholders (FTSE Russell, 2016). It's for this reason that many REITs offer attractive dividend yields, often above 5% per year. Some even reach double digits, for example, Annaly Capital Management and Penny Mac Mortgage Investment Trust are paying shareholders dividends yielding around 14.86% and 13.83%. For the record, I'm not a fan of either company, or any Mortgage REIT, and I'll explain why in chapter 4.

There are however a number of great REITs which pay you anywhere between 5 and 10% per year. In fact, in chapter 8 we cover 7 specific REITs which we believe have the potential to outperform over the long term. For now, let's take a look at how REITs work, and how they've become so popular over the past decade.

KEY TAKEAWAYS

◇ One way to mitigate inflation is to get income from your investments

◇ REITs are a fantastic income provider as they average higher payouts than regular dividend stocks

◇ The 4% Rule is a flawed way at gauging how much income you'll need in retirement

Chapter 3

REITS 101

N ow that you know you can beat inflation by investing in REITs over the long term, it's time to discover more about this financial asset.

Where REITs came from

Before 1960's the risks and rewards of real estate were only enjoyed by institutional investors and business tycoons with a large amount of financial weight to push around. REITs were created in the 1960s by the U.S. Congress to remove the hurdles a retail investor would face while trying to enter the real estate market.

A REIT is a company that buys or builds, owns, and operates large income-generating real estate such as warehouses, office buildings, shopping malls, resorts, hotels, and apartments. A REIT pools money from retail investors like you and me and invests that money in real estate properties, then collects rental income, and distributes it to us.

For retail investors, REITs provide exposure to a wide variety of real estate properties including industrial buildings, data centers, self-storage facilities, as well as conventional housing.

To eliminate some confusion, all conventional REITs own real estate properties, but not every company that own real estate properties is a REIT. For a company to qualify as a REIT, it must meet certain conditions and requirements. The biggest 3 being that these companies must pay the majority of their net income as dividends, they can't invest in any assets other than real estate, and they can't have any other significant income source other than rental income.

How do REITs Differ from Ordinary Stocks?

Both public REITs and regular stocks are similar in that you can buy and sell them at a stock exchange. Like all stocks you own—for example, Nvidia is into computer technology, and Starbucks in the coffee business—REITs are into real estate properties.

However, a REIT differs in that the company itself has a special legal structure which minimizes its' tax liability.

All REITs must meet all 4 of these criteria

◇ The company must have a minimum of 75% of its total assets as cash or in real estate or U.S. Treasuries.

◇ A minimum of 75% of the company's gross income must be sourced from mortgage interest, real estate sales, or rents.

◇ **The company must pay at least 90% of its taxable income to its shareholders as dividends.** Yes, you read it right. REITs are legally mandated to distribute profits as dividends. This benefits the REIT as it means the company minimizes its tax burden, and it also makes REITs an attractive addition to your portfolio.

◇ The company must have a minimum of 100 shareholders after its first year as a REIT and no more than 50% of its shares held by five or fewer individuals. The 5/50 rule and 100 shareholders ensure less concentrated ownership and thereby less biased decision making. Additionally, it helps a REIT to display high quality and transparent governance of operations, prevents issues such as governance fraud, misreporting, and financial fraud.

Because of this structure, there are some differences when analyzing REITs compared to analyzing regular stocks. REITs are more like dividend stocks. They provide consistent dividend income due to its special legal structure. Therefore we analyze and value them like dividend stocks as opposed to stocks which don't yet pay a dividend.

In addition to this, there are a few metrics and parameters that we use solely for REITs. For example, while we use metrics like net income or earnings per share to value regular stocks, we use different metrics like funds from operations (FFO)/FFO per share in case of REITs. In chapter 8, we'll go deeper into why this is.

REITs also have a special legal structure which provides tax advantages, more transparency in governance and operations. We'll discuss this in more depth in the next chapter.

KEY TAKEAWAYS

◇ REITs were created in the 1960s to help regular investors gain exposure to real estate

◇ REITs have a unique structure which provides advantages for both the company, and individual investors

◇ The key benefit of REITs for income investors is that they must pay at least 90% of net income to shareholders as dividends (also called distributions)

Chapter 4

WHY REITS CAN BE
A GOOD INVESTMENT

Since 1971, publicly traded REITs have seen an increase in total market cap from $1.4 Billion to over $1.2 Trillion dollars in 2020 (Nareit, 2022). That's a thousandfold increase in just 50 years. From a mere 34 REITs, this number has ballooned to over 225 publicly traded REITs in the US alone.

What's more impressive is the overall performance of REITs vs. the broad stock market during that period.

Between 1972 and 2019, REITs offered an annual return of 13.3% vs. 12.1% for the S&P 500.

While this may not seem like a big difference, it really does add up over the long term.

A $10,000 investment in 1972 in each of the 2 indexes would be worth the following amount at the end of 2019.

$10,000 in the S&P 500 @ 12.1% annual returns: $2,867,237

$10,000 in the REIT index @ 13.3% annual returns: **$5,010,034**

Not only does this demonstrate the power of compound interest, but it also highlights how beneficial it can be to add REITs to your portfolio. Here are some other benefits of owning REITs.

Six Benefits of Investing in REITs

1. Tax Advantages

A REIT that pays at least 90% of its taxable income to shareholders, pays zero corporate tax. As a result, these REITs have a lot more money to distribute to shareholders than a regular company with an equivalent taxable income. This means you will receive almost 5% extra return. We have covered the detailed explanation including an illustration in chapter 12.

2. No Need to Fix Leaking Toilets

When investing in physical commercial real estate, you have to hunt for the right property, raise capital if you don't have it, prepare complex documentation of the property, and close on the property. Once you own the property, you'll need to perform due maintenance to prepare it for rental. After all this, you'll need to perform all the necessary property management activities, including finding tenants, doing regular maintenance, and collecting rentals. Alternatively, you may hire a property manager to do all the above in exchange for a fee that could be as high as 25% of the rental income eating away your margin.

When you've invested in a REIT, you don't directly buy real estate. This means that you don't have to worry about property management or complex legal documentation.

In summary, a REIT delivers consistent rental income without an investor directly owning a piece of land or buildings. What a fantastic method to collect regular income from a real estate investment without the hassle.

3. Consistent Dividend Income

As mentioned earlier, REITs collect most of their income from rentals or interest.

Interest and rentals are period-based payments and is often unaffected by market adversities. Thus, REITs are bound to generate consistent income despite being an equity REIT or mortgage REIT.

As discussed above, REITs are legally required to pay 90% of their income to shareholders, which promises consistent income to the investor.

The average dividend yield for REITs is about 4.3%, which is nearly 63% higher than for ordinary stocks (Vandenboss, 2022).

4. Portfolio Diversification

The classic portfolio composition of 60% stocks and 40% bonds is no longer a viable investment strategy. Stocks and bonds are exposed to unforeseeable market conditions such as a pandemic, bear and bull market conditions, or geopolitical uncertainties.

Having an investment portfolio of only stocks or only bonds expose you to too much risk and potentially lower returns. For example, AAA-rated corporate bonds returned a nominal annualized return of 5.57% over the 15 years between 2001 and 2021 (Steiner, 2020).

The best way to diversify your portfolio is by including real estate in the mix. You can do that by buying REITs without burning a hole in your pocket. It diversifies your portfolio without the downsides of owning a property.

From January 2011 to the end of 2019, large-cap equity REITs were 0.68 correlated with large-cap equities as measured by the S&P 500, making them good candidates for portfolio diversification (Guggenheim Investments, n.d.). This minimizes the overall volatility of your portfolio.

5. Liquidity and Transparency

Physical real estate is an illiquid asset. This means it could be hard to dispose of when you want cash. On top of that you do not have the choice of selling portions of the property as it is mostly inseparable. This means that your hard-earned money is stuck in the form of a property till you find a buyer.

REITs are publicly listed just like any other stocks you own. It's quite easy to dispose of shares held. You also have the freedom to dispose a portion of your REIT investment which is impossible with a physical property.

Since REITs are listed shares – and are required by law to disclose their finances, you can have a simple understanding of the company at any given time. By going to the investor relations section of a REIT website, you can look up key statistics like occupancy level and debt coverage ratio. This makes it easier for analysis and valuation.

6. Anyone can enter into real estate market with as little as $10.

A major hurdle towards entering the real estate market is its capital extensive nature. One of the most attractive features of REITs are the low capital requirement needed to start investing. Anyone with as little as $10 can start investing in REITs and gain exposure to the real estate market. Yes, you read it right! Some REITs shares are trading as low as $10 as I write this book (we have mentioned a few of them in chapter 9)

KEY TAKEAWAYS

⋄ Between 1972-2019, REITs grew at a faster rate than the overall stock market

⋄ The average REIT pays around 3x more dividends than a stock in the S&P 500

⋄ REITs also offer shareholders certain tax advantages

Chapter 5

THE 2 TYPES OF REITS

REITs are classed into two categories: equity REITs and mortgage REITs.

Equity REITs

Equity REITs raise money from investors to buy real estate properties. The properties are then rented out, and the REIT manages the properties like an individual real estate investor. These rentals income is then distributed to the investors in the form of a dividend. The majority of REITs in the United States are equity REITs.

Today, real estate is tied to nearly all the economic sectors and what we do. Equity REITs shoulder a wide variety of real estate properties, including storage facilities, shopping centers, hospitals and clinics, apartments, and offices.

Like all stocks, equity REITs are subject to the forces of demand and supply. You must understand the drivers behind the shifts in the balance between the supply and demand of equity REITs. Since you are investing for the long term, you don't have to worry much about the short-term volatility in the market. This book will guide you on how to pick REITs that are fundamentally strong so that you make good returns in the long term.

REITs are easy-to-understand instruments if you can differentiate one from the other. In light of that, let's carefully understand the different types of equity REITs.

Residential REITs

Residential REITs hold and operate a range of residential properties, renting out space to tenants. Apartment buildings, student housing, prefabricated houses, and single-family homes are all areas of expertise for residential REITs. Some residential REITs have additional niche geographic or property class interests inside those market segments. People require shelter in all types of economic circumstances, whether or not there is a recession, which is one of the key benefits of residential REITs. As a result, there is always a high demand for such properties, which results in high occupancy rates. This results in consistent revenue, which attracts investors to residential REITs. A staggering 145 million Americans reside in homes with REIT investments. They are an appealing addition and diversifier for the portfolios of many Americans due to their historically competitive total returns and relatively low correlation with other assets.

The FTSE Nareit US Real Estate Indexes list more than 20 residential REITs. Exchange-traded funds (ETFs) and mutual funds for REITs are popular ways for investors to purchase shares in these REITs. You can also invest directly in an office REIT with the aid of a broker.

Office REITs

Office REITs are companies that own, operate, and lease out office space to other people. Skyscrapers and office parks are examples of these types of properties. Office real estate investment trusts (REITs) specialize in office markets, including suburban or metropolitan cores. Some focus on specific categories of tenants, including governmental organizations or biotech companies. Renting offices makes property management and business operations hassle free. Additionally, some full-service leases are cheaper than commercial property ownership.

Office REITs take advantage of this and make office space available to businesses that opt to rent. As long as there's demand for office spaces, office REITs will consistently provide their shareholders with regular dividend income.

The FTSE Nareit US Real Estate Indexes currently list 19 office REITs. For instance, Amazon and Salesforce both utilize office buildings that are owned by publicly traded REITs. Institutional investors including pension funds, endowments, foundations, insurance firms and Bank departments also invest in Office REITs in addition to individuals who do so directly or through TSPs, 401(k), etc.

Industrial REITs

Industrial REITs build or purchase, own, and lease industrial buildings to a plethora of companies. Those industrial spaces could be used for manufacturing, production, or distribution of goods. The most common companies that industrial REITs lease commercial buildings to include warehouses, storage facilities, distribution centers, and e-commerce fulfillment centers. With the rise of U.S. retail e-commerce anticipated to hit $1.3 trillion by 2025, the demand for e-commerce fulfillment centers is expected to increase (Statista Research Department, 2022b). Companies such as Home Depot, Amazon, and Walmart rely on industrial REITs for their distribution facilities.

Industrial REITs offer a few advantages and benefits. They usually lease their real estate properties for long periods. It's not unusual for these leases to run for as long as 25 years. Most importantly, these leases could obligate the tenant to cover real estate taxes, maintenance, and building insurance. As a result, the REIT reduces its operational expenses and delivers higher profits. Another advantage of industrial REITs is that they tend to be recession-resistant. Thus, industrial REITs provide consistent income, which is attractive to income-focused investors.

Healthcare REITs

A healthcare REIT owns, manages, and collects rent from healthcare-related commercial buildings. This REIT may lease out facilities such as hospitals, senior housing, skilled nursing buildings, life science spaces or medical office buildings. The senior housing option is particularly attractive owing to the potential increase in the number of 65-year-olds or older in the United States. It's estimated that the number of older citizens would explode to 90 million by 2060. This is almost double the 2018 level (Reinberg, n.d.). An increase in the number of seniors will result in a need for more senior housing spaces, which is good for REITs that play in the senior housing place.

The population of the United States is aging. In the United States today, there are more than 46 million older adults aged 65 and older; by 2050, that figure is expected to rise to nearly 90 million. The number of older adults is expected to increase by nearly 18 million between 2020 and 2030, when the last of the baby boom cohorts reaches the age of 65. This means that by 2030, one in every five Americans will be 65 or older. These are people who need intensive personal care and medical help.

The growth of the U.S. pharmaceutical industry will increase demand for life sciences spaces. This industry is projected to hit $862 billion in market size by 2028, which is a 6.3% compound annual growth rate (CAGR) from 2021 (Fortune Business Insights, 2022). The biggest drivers of this rise include the aging population, an increase in the prevalence of diseases, and rising healthcare costs. We're also seeing an increase in the number of prescription drugs, which necessitates the founding of more pharmacies to distribute these drugs. Already facing a limited supply of laboratory space, the industry will need new buildings, which promise regular income for healthcare REITs.

Self-Storage REITs

Self-storage facilities have numerous use cases, including storage of vehicles, temporary storage of goods when renovating, storage of goods when relocating, and keeping valuables safe. Their customers are a mix of businesses and individuals, resulting in a large market base.

Self-storage REITs purchase or build, own, and manage these facilities. The rising demand means the REIT will keep increasing its revenue and pay more and more dividends to its shareholders. The United States has seen a jump in the construction of self-storage facilities by a massive 962% between 2012 and 2020. In fact, there are now almost as many self storage facilitates as there are fast food restaurants (Neighbor. com, 2022).

The nature of self-storage structures also plays in the hands of self-storage REITs in a couple of ways. For example, it's inexpensive to build and maintain them, which means a REIT can conserve operating expenses. This is crucial when considering which type of REIT to purchase because the fewer expenses it incurs, the more dividends its investors receive. Moreover, self-storage REITs often rent out their facilities month-to-month, which means they can adjust faster to changing market rates. When market rental rates increase, self-storage REITs can increase rental income quickly, resulting in more money going into the hands of investors.

Retail REITs

Retail REITs own, manage, and lease out space in retail facilities to tenants. Retail REITs focus on sizable regional malls, outlet centers, shopping centers with anchored grocery stores, and power centers with big box retailers. American multinational supermarket chains like Whole Foods and Krogers use retail space provided by retail REITs.

Before you invest in a retail REIT, it's crucial to understand the type of buildings that a retail REIT invests in. For instance, shopping mall REITs build or buy, own, and manage traditional shopping malls located in the suburbs of major cities. The success of shopping malls centers around a few anchor tenants in proximity to many retail tenants.

Unlike shopping mall REITs, freestanding retail REITs invest their capital in freestanding retail property. The entries to the shops in such retail real estate properties face the outside, and usually face a parking lot.

A retail REIT's performance depends on the presence of anchor tenants. Such a tenant is frequently well-known, and their fame serves as a magnet for customers and other tenants. By courting prominent anchor tenants, known for their ability to draw in consumers and tenants, retail REITs that acquire shopping malls hope to revitalize them.

While e-commerce is thriving, many still love to visit traditional brick-and-mortar retailers for shopping. Some such companies have to keep physical real estate because of the type of products they sell. Retail REITs continue to see strong demand for retail space, making them appealing to income-seeking investors.

Infrastructure REITs

Infrastructure REITs invest in, own, and manage real estate properties used for cellular and wireless communications. They collect rent from cellular and wireless communication providers that use such real estate. Tenants can use such real estate for infrastructures such as fiber cables, telecommunication towers, and wired and wireless infrastructure. The definition of infrastructure also includes any structure or network for moving goods, people, and energy. This means infrastructures like energy pipelines can be a part of an infrastructure REIT.

Infrastructure REITs dominate the FTSE Nareit ALL Equity REITs at nearly 15% of the index, making them one of the most popular in the REIT industry.

The benefits of infrastructure REITs include favorable lease structures and regulation and zoning. Leases are often long-term, ranging from five to ten years. Most importantly, leases have built-in rent increases allowing infrastructure REITs to maintain profits. As a result, investors can receive increasing dividends for long periods.

One of the major risks in the REIT industry is the oversupply of real estate properties. This can be risky for consistent generation of profit as prices could decline when there's more supply than demand. Such a risk is limited in infrastructure REITs due to tight zoning and regulations in the communication sector. As such, infrastructure REITs can keep customers longer and charge higher prices, which ensures consistent income for investors.

Timberland REITs

Timberland or timber REIT owns and manages timber real estate. A special rule ensures that timberland REITs must derive 50% or more of its real estate property through trade or production of timber (Wang, 2011). The timber industry is a significant economic sector in the United States. Commercial timberlands, which make up 206 million hectares of U.S. forestland, are estimated at $460 billion. Nearly 70% of timberlands belong to the private sector, and the balance is publicly owned.

Like all REITs, timberland REITs don't operate in isolation from other REITs. For example, about 50% of timberland REITs' wood products go toward home building. As a result, the performance of these REITs depends on the economic state of the home construction industry. As the home construction sector flourishes, timberland REITs perform well and vice-versa. Recent forecasts indicate that the U.S. real estate construction sector will grow by 3.4%–5.5% annually from 2022 to 2025 (Research and Markets, 2021). The growth percent is less formidable compared to other types of REITs. However, you can expect to receive consistent dividend.

223

Hospitality REITs

A hospitality REIT is a type of real estate investment trust that owns, manages, and leases out space in hotels, motels, luxury resorts, and business-class hotels. Hospitality REITs also prepare and serve meals, non-alcoholic and alcoholic beverages, and other services that would normally be provided in households but are unavailable to travelers and vacationers. Some hospitality REITs opt to develop real estate and hire third-party companies to manage the day-to-day operations. Other hospitality REITs choose to operate as third-party hotel and resort operators and share the revenue generated with owners.

There are numerous ways hospitality REITs generate income. These include selling meals and beverages, accommodation, conference venues, and parking space. These REITs also lease out portions of their properties to other businesses to generate extra income.

Hospitality REITs have a prominent advantage over other REITs. They can access information about hospitality real estate faster than many REITs. This helps them to acquire better real estate properties to beef up their portfolio.

Hospitality REITs are subject to economic conditions. They prosper when the economy thrives but during inevitable difficult financial periods, a hospitality REIT often suffer loses.

Data Center REITs

Data center REITs invest in real estate facilities that store data storage servers and related equipment. They purchase, own, and manage secure data storage facilities. These REITs may offer the following to their tenants:

◇ Reliable power sources

◇ High security

◇ Cooling equipment

◇ Cloud computing

Cyber security has become a major concern to all business corporations. This has served as a boost because the need for data centers has increased significantly. We expect this demand to keep increasing shortly, indicating market longevity and making the data center REIT sector an attractive investment. As recent as 2020, data center REITs have delivered the best performance of any type of REIT. This growth isn't expected to stop soon as we see the growth of areas such as self-driven cars, remote working, and cloud storage. You may take advantage of the potential growth by investing in data center REITs.

Diversified REITs

As you've discovered, there are numerous types of REITs. This makes it challenging to choose which to invest in. For example, you may like four to five types of REITs. It may become difficult to select and manage the best stocks. Fortunately, you can invest in a single REIT that offers the benefits of multiple REITs called a diversified REIT. Diversified REITs focus on diversifying their real estate investment by buying developing, owning, and managing various types of commercial structures. For example, such a REIT might invest in office buildings, data centers, residential buildings, and timber real estate properties.

The benefits of investing in a diversified REIT will depend mainly on the type of real estate properties in which it invests. However, numerous diversified REITs are known to pay out huge dividends, resulting in high dividend yields for their shareholders.

Specialty REITs

Other commercial real estate properties don't fall in any of the categories we discussed up to this point. Examples include, commercial structures designed for prisons, farmlands, cannabis facilities, and casinos etc. A type of REIT that focuses on any of these real estate properties is called a specialty REIT. Specialty REITs invest in newer and growing industries, offering potentially high gains and profits.

The vulnerability towards market condition is purely based on the industry the REIT invests in.

For instance, A specialty REIT that focuses on student housing can benefit from the popularity of such properties. During economic booms, many students enroll at colleges and other educational institutions. As a result, demand for student housing remains high. Additionally, as some colleges and universities increase enrollment, there's a need for more student housing. Whereas Prison REITs are unaffected by economic conditions like recession.

Specialty REIT lets the investors choose to invest in niche markets that may otherwise not be available.

In addition to equity REITs, there is another type of REIT you should be aware of. Mortgage REITs often get listed in lists of high yield stocks, but they are more complex than equity REITs and most investor should stay well clear of them. Here's why.

Mortgage REITs

The next class of REITs is mortgage REITs, often called mREITs, which are unique in that they don't purchase or own real estate. Instead, they generate income from originated or purchased mortgages and mortgage-backed securities (MBS). For instance, an mREIT lends money to a developer of apartments. They collect income in the form of interest paid on the money lent and is paid to the investors in the form of dividend. Here, an mREIT acts as a finance company for real estate developers.

Investing in mREITs means that you're two steps removed from the actual real estate. Neither you nor the mREIT that you've invested in is directly involved with the real estate. Instead of earning rental income, mREITs receive mortgage repayments from actual real estate owners.

Since mREITs don't deal directly with real estate, they are technically finance companies, not real estate businesses. As a result, you'll need to evaluate their stocks as if they were finance companies like banks and insurance businesses, and you get little to no exposure to real estate market. Here are the risks associated with mREITs you should be aware of.

Interest Rate Risk

Changes in interest rates can affect not only the net interest margin, which is the primary source of earnings for mREITs, but also the value of their mortgage assets, which affects corporate net worth.

Credit Risk

Commercial mREITs may be exposed to credit risk. The degree of credit risk for a particular security is determined by the credit performance of the underlying loans as well as the security's structure.

Prepayment

Changes in interest rates or home sales by borrowers influence the likelihood that some borrowers will refinance or repay their mortgages. When such a refinancing or repayment occurs, the investor who owns the mortgage or MBS must reinvest the proceeds in the current interest rate environment, which could be lower or higher. With borrowers refinancing at lower interest rates or paying off their mortgages earlier than the original schedule mREITs would receive fewer interest payments reducing investors' income.

Rollover

The assets of mREITs are primarily longer-term MBS and mortgages, while their liabilities may include a significant amount of short-term debt, particularly among residential mREITs. Because of this term mismatch, they must roll over their short-term debt before their assets mature. Their ability to do so is contingent on the liquidity and smooth operation of the short-term debt markets, which includes the repo market. With an estimated $2 trillion in outstanding and several hundred billion dollars in daily trading volume, the repo market is extremely liquid. This can be a double-edged sword for an investor.

Default in repayment

Their main risk are home loans, and other real estate borrowers might default. This is particularly prevalent during harsh economic conditions similar to what we saw during the COVID-19 pandemic. As people lose income due to businesses closing or closing temporarily, the number of mortgage defaulters could increase.

And wait... there's more!

Did I mention that mREITs are highly over-leveraged? Well, they are. Which makes them more reliant on the bond market.

The sum of these risks, as well as complicated business model means I'm not a fan of mortgage REITs.

Because our golden rule of investing is this: **Never invest in anything you don't understand**

So for the remainder of this book, we will focus purely on equity REITs.

KEY TAKEAWAYS:

◇ REITs can be broken down into Equity REITs and Mortgage REITs (mREITs)

◇ Equity REITs own real estate and derive the majority of their income from rental agreements. This can be a variety of sectors from residential to industrial. Mortgage REITs are both akin to banks than real estate companies and have their own set of risks to deal with

◇ For individual investors we prefer equity REITs

Chapter 6

THE ONE METRIC PROBLEM - THE BIGGEST MISTAKE INVESTORS MAKE WHEN BUYING REITS

The goal of investing is to generate the best possible return. It isn't just investing in stocks that have a high dividend yield. It is a mix of high and consistent income with capital appreciation and a sizable market cap. To create an investment strategy, you will require more than one metric.

Nevertheless, it is only natural for an income-oriented investor to fall prey to a high dividend yield. Well, it is not completely wrong to look for REITs with high dividend yield as it is an important metric for valuation.

Here, the real question to be addressed is: Should you go for REITs with the highest dividend yield at the expense of hidden risks? Now, let's look at the most common mistake every investor runs into while selecting REITs.

The Biggest Mistake: Only Focusing on Dividend Yield

If you are a relatively new investor entering the world of REITs, your default position may be to look for REITs with the highest yield.

If that's the case, don't worry, that's not your fault. After all, yield is a very easy equation to understand, and with any dividend stock, one of the first calculations you'll be making in your head is "How many shares do I need to own to get X amount per year in dividends?" Knowing a stock's dividend yield is the natural answer to this, therefore most people focus on yield above all else.

However, yield isn't the only factor to consider. In fact, a high dividend yield alone can be highly misleading.

Let me explain. A REIT by its legal structure is meant to pay out 90% of its net income to the shareholders. This means that most REITS will have a higher dividend yield than regular stocks.

With the above rule in mind let's look at certain scenarios where a high yield REIT may not be a good investment.

Excess Payout Ratio

What's the problem with a high payout ratio?

We know that REITs have high payout ratios by design, which is at least 90% of their taxable earnings. This taxable income is after deducting non-cash expenses such as depreciation (which is a large chunk of change for most real estate benefits). This gives REITs some room to pay out more than 90%. For example, the payout for top five high yield REITs ranges from 94.74%–112.15% (we'll explain why a payout ratio above 100% is acceptable in the next chapter).

However, some REITs can have payouts ratios above 200%, which is absurd. A payout ratio at this level is unsustainable, which only leaves the company with 2 options. Either borrow money to pay the dividend, or cut dividend payments. Neither of which benefit you as an investor.

Overleverage

Like regular real estate investors, most REITs use debt in order to purchase assets.

It's a simple model, they borrow funds with the hopes of buying assets, which will make more than they borrow, which is then reflected their revenue and profit numbers.

However, poorly managed REITs borrow too much money, or don't use that money to good effect. Which gives them unsustainable debt levels in relation to their payouts. To compensate all of this financial debt, a REIT is forced to take additional loan. This goes on as a loop until they liquidate their assets to payoff the debts.

Stock price decline

Bear markets often result in what's known in income investing circles as a "yield trap". This is where a company has an attractive yield on paper, but is likely to decline in share price. Because yield is calculated by dividend per share divided by share price, a declining share price results in a higher yield.

For example, a $20 stock which pays $1 per share yields 5%.

If that same stock declines to $10 a share, but still pays $1 per share, the yield is now 10%. You're still getting the same payout, but you've now lost half your investment principal because of a share price decline.

This is why we look for stocks which can provide a combination of steady payouts and share price growth. If the REIT cannot grow the revenue, it is a sign of no growth. Investing in a REIT with a declining revenue year-after-year is akin to betting on a horse you know will lose the race again and again.

Two Examples of Yield Traps

To drive home the point about considering multiple metrics, why don't we look at two REITs as examples: National Health Investors (NHI) and Brandywine Realty Trust BDN. We'll first evaluate National Health Investors.

National Health Investors

National Health Investors (NHI) is a Maryland-based REIT founded in 1991. It is a self-governing organization that invests in senior housing and medical facilities. NHI's real estate assets include entrance-free communities, senior living facilities, a specialty hospital, and assisted living facilities. NHI has a solid dividend yield of 5.71%, putting it in the top 25% of dividend payers in the US. Sounds good right? Let's have a look into the other factors:

◇ Its highest dividend per share was $4.41 in March 2021, which was then reduced to $3.60 per share in June.

◇ Earnings have declined by 2.9% in the past five years and 46.8% in the past 12 months.

◇ NHI's operating cash flow is insufficient to cover its debt. Furthermore, NHI has a high debt-to-equity ratio of nearly 82%.

◇ The share price has dipped almost 13% in the last year and 29% over the last 5 years. This means that you have lost almost $1/3^{rd}$ of your capital in just 5 years.

◇ If you have invested in NHI looking at the dividend yield, almost one-third of your investment has lost its value. On top of that, your REIT is not capable of paying of its debt, meaning you can be liable to additional dividend cuts in the future.

Brandywine Realty Trust

Brandywine Realty Trust, BDN on the New York Stock Exchange invests in and manages a portfolio of properties that include mixed-use, residential, life science, and office space. BDN pays out a solid dividend at 8.63%, which is higher than the industry average and is around the 90th percentile of dividend-payers. Every REIT investor looks for reliable income, and BDN doesn't disappoint them. However, let's find out what BDN has to reveal!

◇ It has a debt-to-equity ratio of almost 124% resulting in higher interest payments.

◇ They had a payout ratio of 1085% which is absurd for any REIT organization. A classic example of highly over leveraged REIT.

◇ The dividend per share have remained $0.760 for almost 5 years. The stock is 69.78% down all time and 46.88% down in the past 5 years. So if you had invested $10,000 at IPO, your principal would be worth just $3,022 today.

◇ The simple formula for dividend yield is dividend per share divided by share price. As you saw above, dividend per share remained static and the share price is continuously dropping. So the dividend yield increases, but you're still making less money!

Now that we've covered the **don'ts** of REIT investing, let's take a look at the metrics which do matter.

KEY TAKEAWAYS:

◇ The biggest mistake investors make with REITs (or any dividend paying stocks) is focused on dividend yield % above everything else

◇ Bear markets lead to more yield traps due to declining stock prices

◇ Falling in love with a company only using a single metric is a surefire way to buy a losing stock

---

Chapter 7

KEY METRICS
FOR INVESTING IN REITS

In this chapter, you will go over the main key terms that you will encounter when investing in REITs or the real estate market. I've provided an easy-to-use stock screener in the following chapter (don't worry – it's free), so you don't have to analyze each of these terms for each REIT you consider. It would be easy to separate the wheat (the right REITs) from the chaff (unwanted REITs) using this tool. Now that we are on the same page, let's get started learning the language of REITs.

Gross Lease and Net Lease

A lease is a contract detailing the terms that the renter of a real estate property agrees to in exchange for a regular payment. In the REIT industry, there are two major types of leases: gross lease and net lease. A gross lease obligates the renter to pay the real estate property owner a certain agreed fee for exclusive use of the structure. The rental fee only covers rent but not property ownership costs such as utilities, property taxes, and insurance. These expenses are the responsibility of the landlord, and is typical for single family apartment rental.

In contrast, a net lease obligates the tenant to pay rent and a portion, or all of the property ownership costs, including maintenance expenses. This is a much better deal for the landlord, and it surprisingly common

234

in the REIT business. The nature of the net lease determines whether the renter pays all or a portion of the ownership costs, as described further below in the section on net lease types.

◇ **Single net lease:** The tenant pays property taxes in addition to rent but assumes a minimum amount of risk. The landlord covers the cost of other ownership expenses like maintenance and repairs, insurance, and utilities. You can think of a single net lease as a pass-through lease. The main disadvantage of single net leases is that tenants may be less motivated to conserve energy because they will not be directly responsible for payments.

◇ **Double net lease:** This type of lease is also called a net-net (NN) lease. The renter pays the property taxes and insurance premiums rental amount in addition to the rent. A double net lease reduces risk to the landlord and may result in lower overall expenses. In this way, a double net lease is more advantageous to the property owner than a single net lease.

◇ **A triple net lease:** Unlike a double net lease, the tenant who signs a triple net lease agrees to pay all the costs associated with running a real estate property in addition to the rental fee. The tenant is generally motivated to take good care of the property and conserve water and energy because they pay for maintenance and repair costs as well as utilities.

It goes without saying that you should know what type of leases a given REIT employs. This helps in understanding the sources of revenue and the REITs operating expenses. Although most commercial real estate leases are triple net leases, you still want to confirm the type of lease your targeted REIT is involved in. You can locate this information in the REIT's 10-K form.

After you download the form, simply search for "net lease" using the "search and find option." An example below shows the type of lease for Innovative Industrial Properties (IIPR).

ITEM 1. *BUSINESS*

General

As used herein, the terms "we", "us", "our" or the "Company" refer to Innovative Industrial Properties, Inc., a Maryland corporation, and any of our subsidiaries, including IIP Operating Partnership, LP, a Delaware limited partnership (our "Operating Partnership").

We are an internally-managed REIT focused on the acquisition, ownership and management of specialized industrial properties leased to experienced, state-licensed operators for their regulated state-licensed cannabis facilities. We have acquired and intend to continue to acquire our properties through sale-leaseback transactions and third-party purchases. We have leased and expect to continue to lease our properties on a triple-net lease basis, where the tenant is responsible for all aspects of and costs related to the property and its operation during the lease term, including structural repairs, maintenance, real estate taxes and insurance.

Figure 1: *Excerpt from IIPR 10K-Form – Business Description (Source: Innovative Inⁱustrial Properties)*

Cash Available for Distribution (CAD)

Also known as funds available for distribution (FAD), cash available for distribution is a metric used to measure a REIT's ability to generate cash and pay out dividends to its shareholders. As such, CAD is the most meaningful metric to determine dividend safety. Generally, CAD is determined by subtracting recurring capital expenditures from the REIT's funds from operations (FFO). Recurring capital expenditures include expenses for repairing HVAC systems, resurfacing of parking lots, and replacing structure roofs.

Although there is no universal definition of CAD, understanding it is critical, or you risk investing in a dud—a REIT with an inconsistent dividend-paying record. To income-focused investors, CAD is a key benchmark to evaluate a REIT's strength. REITs can increase it in two general ways: organically or through real estate acquisitions. It's noteworthy to understand how each REIT sources its CAD to assure yourself of dividend safety.

Tip: There's no hard and fast rule about CAD and how it gets calculated. Each REIT may calculate it differently from many others, meaning that CAD is a non-GAAP measure and should be treated as Pro forma.

Fund From Operations (FFO)

The term "Funds from operations" was coined by REIT analysis website NAREIT. FFO informs you of the cash a REIT generated during a given accounting period. Some people confuse this term with cash flow. Remember that cash flow is money that comes in and goes out of a business. Unlike cash flow, FFO focuses only on money generated from the core operations of a REIT. Here's why there's a need for FFO instead of net income.

The majority of significant assets in most businesses are plants, machinery, and other items that depreciate over time. Net income for these businesses comes after depreciation. Accounting rules require assets to be depreciated yearly, which can result in undervalued assets on the balance sheet. However, land and buildings, the primary assets of REITs, do not always depreciate over time in the same way that machinery does. Instead, they may appreciate, which is why their values in the balance sheet may be understated.

For general stocks and companies, depreciation is an acceptable non-cash charge that allocates the cost of an investment made in a prior period. But real estate is completely different from most fixed-plant or equipment investments. Here the property loses value infrequently, and it often appreciates.

Net income - a measure which is reduced by depreciation - is, therefore, an inefficient gauge of performance. As a result, it makes sense to judge REITs by FFO, which excludes depreciation and amortization.

Although you'll not always need to calculate FFO as many REITs show it in the financial statements, it's valuable to understand how REITs determine it. Here's the process:

◇ Find the income statement of your targeted REIT on the SEC website.

◇ Locate the REIT's net income, which represents the company's earnings. You'll find it at the bottom of the income statement.

237

◇ Add back depreciation and amortization to the net income to find the actual revenue the REIT generated from its operations. Note that depreciation and amortization expenses are merely aimed at helping companies to spread out the costs of their plant and equipment, which results in reduced profits.

◇ Add any losses on the sale of assets, especially long-term assets. Since such losses are non-recurring, they shouldn't be included as they're not part of a REIT's normal operations.

◇ From the total figure above, subtract any gains from the sales of assets and interest income to get FFO for the given period.

Let's illustrate the above steps through an FFO calculation example. Suppose The Midwest Realty Company netted $10 million in income in 2021, a depreciation expense of $2.1 million, an amortization expense of $900,000, an interest income of $600,000, and a sales gain on assets sold of $1.5 million.

FFO = Net income + (Depreciation expense + Amortization expense + Losses on sale of assets) − (Gains on sale of assets + Interest income)

= $10 million + ($2.1 million + $0.9 million) − ($1.5 million + $0.6 million)

= $13 million − $2.1 million

= $10.9 million

The FFO figure for public REITs can be found in the footnotes of the income statements.

When analyzing an ordinary public company, you often look at earnings per share (EPS) and price to earnings (P/E) ratio. REITs are treated differently. We use FFO in the place of earnings. Here's how differently we use these metrics for a REIT and regular public company.

Regular Public Company	REIT
Earnings per share	FFO per share
Price to earnings ratio	Price to FFO ratio

At the time of print, the median price to FFO price for publicly traded REITs was 13.3.

Here are the price to FFO ratios for the 10 largest REITs at the time of print

◇ Prologis (PLD) – 20.41

◇ American Tower (AMT) – 15.73

◇ Crown Castle International (CCI) – 16.3

◇ Public Storage (PSA) – 20.05

◇ Equinix (EQIX) – 27.84

◇ Simon Property Group (SPG) – 8.54

◇ Realty Income (O) – 16.47

◇ Digital Realty (DLR) – 14.44

◇ SBA Communications (SBAC) – 25.26

◇ Mid-America Apartment Communities (MAA) – 19.32

Adjusted Fund from Operations (AFFO)

FFO is considered an adequate measure of the performance of a REIT. However, it has flaws, such as not accounting for recurring maintenance costs such as roof replacements and painting.

A better metric known as adjusted funds from operations (AFFO) aims to address these issues. Analysts now use AFFO to assess a REIT's earning power or potential.

There are two steps for determining AFFO: Once you've calculated a REIT's FFO (calculation demonstrated above) for a given period, subtract all capitalized and amortized recurring expenses. Recurring capital expenditures may include costs for painting, tenant improvements, roof replacements, and carpet replacement. The second step is to straight-line rents, which means distributing rents evenly over the lease's term.

Let's make the AFFO calculation clear by using an example. Suppose The Midwest Realty Company mentioned in the previous example reported $200,000 in recurring capital expenditures and straight-lined rents of $120,000. It incurred recurring capital expenses when replacing carpets, HVAC, and fixing roofs.

As you'll recall from the previous example, The Midwest Realty Company's FFO was $10.9 million. The next step is to deduct recurring capital expenditures and straight-lined rents from its FFO to obtain AFFO.

AFFO = FFO – Capital Expenditures – Straight-line Rent Adjustments

= $10.9 million – $0.2million – $0.12 million

= $10.68 million

FFO Payout Ratio

Similar to how dividend stocks have a payout ratio calculated as net income divided by dividend payouts, with REITs we can calculate the same payouts by using FFO.

We've already discussed why FFO is a superior metric than net income for REITs. So by using the same logic, FFO payout ratio is superior to using payout ratio from net income.

The lower the FFO payout ratio, the more sustainable a REIT's dividend payouts are.

The sector median FFO payout ratio for REITs is 65%.

Net Operating Income (NOI)

Net operating income is one of the important terms you should understand regarding investing in REITs and commercial real estate. NOI - net operating income measures the income from an income-producing real estate property after deducting operating expenses and vacancy losses. Investors primarily use it to establish the profitability of a property. The NOI calculation excludes capital expenditures, taxes, depreciation, and amortization.

You calculate NOI from this formula: NOI = (Gross operating income + other income) - Operating costs, where gross operating income includes rent and vacancy losses.

Real estate investors use NOI to determine a property's capitalization rate, a figure necessary to calculate the value of a property. Here's an example on how to determine NOI for a potential real estate investment.

Let's say you're evaluating whether to invest in a small, four-unit apartment in a central business district. You can rent out each unit for $1,500 monthly, meaning that your potential rental income is $72,000 ($1,500 x 4 x 12 = $72,000) annually. The property boasts a laundry in the basement, and you can generate $1,000 yearly from it.

We wish you could make the whole $72,000 annually but can't because occupancy is rarely 100%. You're likely to lose potential income due to vacancy. Let's assume vacancy in this area for similar properties is 10%, which means you'll lose $7,200 (10% of $72,000 = $7,200) in potential rental income. The current owner's records show that operating expenses are $15,000 annually.

NOI = Gross income + other income - operating costs

= $64,800 + $1,000 - $15,000

= $50,800

The property nets $50,800 annually. Using this figure, you might establish if the property earns enough to service loans, work out the property's value and determine what to offer, or compare the property with others.

Capitalization Rate

REITs evaluate the attractiveness of a building by using the capitalization rate (also known as Cap rate). Cap rate is the ratio of net operating income to current fair market value of a real estate property. The higher it is for a given property, the better.

You can use cap rate as a proxy for Return on Investment. A cap rate of 10% means that a REIT's investment in a building will yield the REIT roughly 10% per year and take 10 years to return principal. A cap rate of 5% means that it would take 20 years to return principal.

To calculate a REIT's cap rate the formula would be

Cap rate = (Current Year NOI – Last Year NOI) / (Current Year Real Estate Asset Value – Last Year Real Estate Asset Value)

The majority of REITs will disclose their NOI in their 10K and 10Q forms

Same-Store (Organic) Revenues

The term "same-store" is derived from the retail industry where it's used to analyze retail businesses. It refers to either revenue, NOI, or operating expenses generated from real estate properties that operate over the same fiscal period. Evaluating a REIT using the same-store concept allows you to gauge the effectiveness of management in operations of existing properties.

The NOI of a REIT might increase due to either internal growth or external growth. When same-store NOI increases, the growth is called internal or organic growth. In contrast, if the rise stemmed from recently acquired or newly built properties, the increase in NOI is termed external growth. Generally, a REIT adds a real estate property it owned for at least 12 months into its same-store portfolio.

You'll often find same-store details in form 10-Q or 10-K of the REIT you're analyzing.

For example, you found that IIPR (one of our suggestions in this book) increased its same-store revenue by $20.7 million from March 2020 to March 2021. The screenshot below provides further details about this. You can see that the $20.7 million increase contributes nearly 98% of the rise in revenue, which suggests management and their teams did well in collecting rents during the period.

Investments in Real Estate

See Note 6 in the notes to the condensed consolidated financial statements for information regarding our investments in real estate activity and property portfolio activity during the three months ended March 31, 2022.

Comparison of the Three Months Ended March 31, 2022 and 2021

The following table sets forth the results of our operations (in thousands):

	For the Three Months Ended March 31,	
	2022	2021
Revenues:		
Rental (including tenant reimbursements)	$ 64,114	$ 42,885
Other revenue	390	—
Total revenues	64,504	42,885
Expenses:		
Property expenses	1,982	770
General and administrative expense	8,777	5,600
Depreciation and amortization expense	13,868	8,839
Total expenses	24,627	15,209
Income from operations	39,877	27,676
Interest and other income	57	124
Interest expense	(4,766)	(1,873)
Loss on exchange of Exchangeable Senior Notes	(118)	—
Net income	35,050	25,927
Preferred stock dividends	(338)	(338)
Net income attributable to common stockholders	$ 34,712	$ 25,589

Revenues.

Rental revenues for the three months ended March 31, 2022 increased by approximately $21.2 million, or 50%, to approximately $64.1 million, compared to approximately $42.9 million for the three months ended March 31, 2021. Approximately $532,000 of the increase in rental revenues was generated by the properties acquired during the three months ended March 31, 2022. The remaining approximately $20.7 million increase in rental revenues was generated by properties we acquired in prior periods, including contractual rent escalations and amendments to leases for additional improvement allowances and construction funding at existing properties that resulted in adjustments to rent. Rental revenues for the three months ended March 31, 2022 and 2021 included approximately $1.9 million and $727,000, respectively, of tenant reimbursements for property insurance premiums and property taxes.

Other revenue for the three months ended March 31, 2022 consists of interest revenue from property acquisitions that did not satisfy the requirements for sale-leaseback accounting.

Figure 2: *Excerpt from IIPR 10K Form – Revenue*
(source: Innovative Industrial Properties)

INVESTING FOR PASSIVE INCOME

Gearing Ratio

Debt is a vital part of the successful operation of a REIT. It is because REITs are required to distribute at least 90% of their earnings to their shareholders as dividends that the remaining amount might not be sufficient for acquiring new real estate properties, forcing it to apply for credit. If debt is used wisely it will result in increased investor returns. However, if a REIT uses too much debt, it can go down on its knees during unfavored economic times.

It's helpful to gauge how much debt leverage a REIT has so that you can establish the stability of receiving dividends. A gearing ratio is a tool designed to measure the level of financial leverage of a REIT.

The gearing ratio is measured using a variety of formulas. For the REIT's overall gearing ratio, the most common formula is:

Gearing ratio = total debt/total assets x 100.

When total debt exceeds total assets, a REIT can't pay off its debt even if it declares bankruptcy. The lower the gearing ratio, the stronger the business is. They can easily weather the storms when they surface. Most importantly, such REITs can keep paying dividends, which is what we want.

Although the gearing ratio is helpful, it's more meaningful when compared to those of similar businesses and the industry average. Having said that, the total debt of a REIT should be about a third or 66% of its total assets. In a standard scenario, this gearing ratio is the same as a debt-to-equity ratio of two (2).

Debt-to-EBITDA Ratio

EBITDA is short for earnings before interest, taxes, depreciation, and amortization. This metric allows you to compare companies without the influence of non-cash expenses such as depreciation and amortization. Debt-to-EBITDA ratio measures the amount of income produced which could be used to pay down debt before allocation to depreciation, taxes, amortization, and interest.

Since debt-to-EBITDA helps check a company's ability to pay its debt, when EBITDA is high, the company may struggle to meet its debt repayment obligations. Preferably, you want this ratio to be as low as possible. As such, the debt-to-EBITDA ratio is another way of determining financial leverage. You can find debt-to-EBITDA ratios in stock screeners. Also, you will find it on the income statement and debt in the balance sheet.

Interest Coverage Ratio (ICR)

Companies, like individuals, pay interest on the debt they owe. A REIT's ability to cover interest payments is crucial. You calculate the ICR by dividing earnings before interest and taxes (EBIT) by its interest expense during a particular accounting period. In formula form:

ICR = EBIT/Interest expense

A variation of the above definition of ICR uses EBITDA instead of EBIT, which results in this formula:

ICR = EBITDA/Interest expense

As the above formulas show, a high ratio suggests that a company would battle to cover the interests on its debt. That's why it's preferable to have an ICR that's as low as possible.

Here's an example of how to calculate ICR. Imagine that a particular REIT has reported an operating profit (EBIT) of $94 million and $68 million in interest expense. Its ICR is:

EBIT/Interest expense = $94 million / $68 million

= 1.38

You cannot tell whether this ICR is good or bad unless you compare it with those of similar businesses and the industry. An ICR of less than one gives hope that the company can meet its interest payment obligation. You can find both EBIT and EBITDA and interest expenses from income statements.

KEY TAKEAWAY : CHEATSHEET FOR ALL METRICS

◇ **FFO per share** – higher is better

◇ **FFO payout ratio** – lower is better, aim for less than 65%

◇ **Price to FFO ratio** – lower is better, the sector median for publicly traded REITS is 13.3

◇ **Capitalization rate** – typical cap rates will be between 4 and 10%

◇ **Same store organic revenues** – positive trend is better

◇ **Gearing ratio** – lower is better, aim for less than 40%

◇ **Debt to EBITDA ratio** – higher is better, aim for more than 3.5

◇ **Interest coverage ratio** – higher is better, aim for more than 3

◇ Armed with the above terminology, you'll find analyzing REITs much easier. Let's move forward to REIT analysis.

Chapter 8

HOW TO PICK GREAT REITS

N ow that you have understood the common mistakes that an investor could run into. Let's look at the analysis of REITs.

Since REITs are income-generating stocks, you always analyze them like dividend-paying regular stocks. The main distinctions are in some metrics specific to accounting for commercial real estate properties. Now that I have given enough introduction, let's get down to business.

What to Look for When Analyzing a REIT

Like the traditional dividend-paying regular stocks, REITs also follow the same rule. The more information you have, the better your analysis will be. In that aspect, your primary focus is to consider only public REITs for investment. The public REITs are SEC regulated and provides you with easily accessible public information like quarterly and annual reports. Public REITs also file quarterly Form 10-Q and annual Form 10-K reports with the SEC.

On top of providing summary of the most recent financial performance, the reports also cover qualitative aspects of business. These reports offer 100% transparency on the company's activities. However, analyzing one can often be hard as there is no standard reporting – each company reports slightly different. For instance, some REITs will spell out clearly how they determine the AFFO (adjusted funds from operations) while others may choose to not show this calculation.

Despite the slight differences, Form 10 Q and Form 10 K are crucial for analyzing a REIT and its operations. These reports include the type of real estate assets the REIT invests in, its internal and external risks, and tenant concentration. Does it sound a bit too nerdy for you? Let me illustrate how to find all the *critical* REIT information from these forms.

For this example, we'll use Innovative Industrial Properties (IIPR), a Maryland-incorporated REIT that operates in the cannabis industry. You can access both its Form 1o-Q and Form 10-K on the investor relation page of its website. To make it easy to follow with us throughout this example, we suggest you download both forms and open them.

The first thing is to learn what this business is about. Form 10-K is ideal for this purpose as it has a section or item called 'Business': as shown below.

Table of Contents

INNOVATIVE INDUSTRIAL PROPERTIES, INC.

FORM 10-K – ANNUAL REPORT
DECEMBER 31, 2021
TABLE OF CONTENTS

PART I

Figure 3: IIPR 10K Form – Table of Contents (Source: Innovative Industrial Properties)

The **business** section is arguably the most important as it covers pertinent details about the company. Once you read the 2021 Form 10-K, you'll quickly understand that IIPR is a self-managed UPREIT (An UPREIT is a unique REIT structure that allows property owners to exchange their property for share ownership in the UPREIT) that rents out its real estate assets to state-licensed cannabis operators. Renters enter a triple-net lease with IIPR, which means they are responsible for all maintenance and operational costs of the properties they rent. One quality to look out for when investing in a REIT is its competitive advantage—what Warren Buffett calls an economic moat.

The business section of Form 10-K includes what sets IIPR apart from its competitors. For example, IIPR cites its management team's expertise, relationships built in the cannabis and real estate industries, and long lease periods averaging 16.6 months combined with contractual rental increases as competitive advantages. (Innovative Industrial Properties, 2022). You don't have to take IIPR's word for it when it comes to what its moat is, as there are numbers to back up their claims. You could, for example, compare IIPR's average leases to those of its competitors.

The next critical section to go through is "**Risk Factors**". Here, you get a summary of the main risks IIPR faces and the details about each risk. This is crucial for REIT investing as you want to know if you'll consistently receive dividends throughout your investing period.

We must make a critical point about Form 10-Q and Form 10-K. Public companies try to ensure that they don't make statements that could land them in trouble in the future. When making these filings, the company will try to be as defensive as possible.

For example, one of the risk factors you'll pay in IIPR's 10K form is as follows.

"IIPR cannot assure shareholder that they will generate sufficient cash to keep distributing dividends"

At face value, this is a scary thought. A REIT being unable to pay dividends would spell disaster for us as investors. However this is typical language that you'll find in a 10K form. Companies will do anything they can to manage investor expectations.

Despite IIPR not wanting to commit to paying dividends regularly, financial statements can tell a different story as IIPR has never interrupted dividend payments. That is why, before deciding whether to invest in a REIT, it is critical to consider its qualitative and quantitative characteristics. Then evaluate the risk and determine if this is acceptable enough for you to invest your money

There are a couple more sections that you should read in both Form 10-Q and Form 10-K. What we covered above are the major highlights. The other sections you should go through are **legal proceedings** to see if the company is involved in any current lawsuits. You should also look at **Management's discussion and analysis** which is where you'll find the most up to date commentary on business activities.

The above are a few examples of how to study a REIT before investing in it. Form 10-K and Form 10-Q are your go-to sources for learning as much as you can about a company, both qualitatively and quantitatively.

Information Sources for Researching REITs

The SEC filings (10 Q and 10 K) mentioned above help you take a deep dive into a REIT. Even though the information provided by SEC filings are useful, the analysis does not stop there. The next step is to analyze the sector in which your potential REIT belongs to.

For this, one of the best resources is the National Association of Real Estate Investment Trusts (NAREIT). NAREIT is a Washington, D.C.-based trade organization that represents the interests of the REITs and other real estate companies interests in U.S. real estate.

For investors, NAREIT produces rigorous REIT research and sponsors research on REIT investments which is published on their website – www.reit.com With the aid of the FTSE Nareit U.S. Real Estate Index Series, individual investors can gauge the performance of the REIT sector against other industries and the market as a whole.

Other sources for researching and analyzing REITs, albeit not as comprehensive, include financial websites such as Yahoo! Finance, Google Finance, VettaFi (formerly ETF Database), and GuruFocus. However, there is another resource we prefer to all of the above.

A Quick Free Method of Finding Quality REITs

How do you select the best REITs from the more than 200 available? The answer is that you need to have selection criteria. Armed with that criterion, you may use a stock screener to quickly find the gems you're looking for.

Here, I will spell out the selection criteria I've used to pick the seven best REIT described in Chapter 8. I will also show you how to use a stock screener to quickly filter for the best REITs.

The quickest way of finding equity REITs is by using a stock screener. I have used the stock screener from the website www.stockanalysis. com. There's no need pay for fancy screeners that cost you hundreds of dollars per month in subscription fees. Stockanalysis is a free website (there is a paid tier for $99/year if you want to save your searches and download data) and has all the necessary information needed for picking the best REITs.

First go to https://stockanalysis.com/screener/stock Then click or tap on the blue button named 'Filter.' You'll immediately be provided with a list of metrics to use for selecting stocks. You can filter them by the following metrics:

◇ **Industry = Equity REIT**

One cool feature on stockanalysis.com is the ability to only show Equity REITs in the stock screener tab. Use this as your first filter

◇ **Market cap > $300 million:**

Market capitalization tells you the size of a stock or the value of a company as perceived by the market. Selecting stocks with market caps above $300 million means you'll include only stocks with relatively long track records and high liquidity. Most importantly, you'll avoid investing in penny stocks.

◇ **Dividend growth > 0%:**

Most importantly, it's crucial that the dividend grows over time to aid in beating the increasing inflation. To achieve this objective,

251

select REITs that grow dividends annually.

◇ **Debt-to-equity ratio < 2.5:**

REITs extensively use financial leverage to acquire real estate assets. The lower the debt a REIT has relative to equity, the better. I recommend investing in a REIT that have less than twice the investor equity in debt. The lower this ratio, the better the REIT. The REIT is more likely to cover debt repayments.

◇ **Dividend yield > 3%:**

As stated elsewhere, investing in high-yield REITs is paramount. The higher the dividend yield, the better the dividends you receive, thereby boosting your income faster. That's why we want to invest in these assets in the first place.

◇ **Net income growth > 5%:**

Although net income isn't as important for our purpose, it helps as a proxy to FFO in selecting REITs. The higher the growth of a REIT's net income, the higher the FFO should be. Once you've plugged the above criteria in the Stock Analysis screener, this is how the screen will look:

Figure 4: Filtere Stock Screener snapshot (source: stockanalysis.com)

You can further filter the results by industry so that you can easily spot equity REITs. Note that changing the net income growth from year-on-year to 3-year or 5-year will change the number of results you get.

How to Value REITs

Now that you have filtered the REITs according to the metrics, it's time to do the valuation to determine if they're fit to add to your portfolio. We'll arrive at an intrinsic value and compare it with the current share price to find if it's undervalued or overvalued. According to our golden law, you will always buy the REIT if it is undervalued since they are more likely to provide capital appreciation along with regular dividends.

When valuing REITs, we should remember that they're similar to dividend stocks, and therefore we'll use the dividend discount model.

There are other valuation models like NAV. However, those valuations require complex calculations and a fair number of estimates, assumptions, and projections. For instance, the NAV model suggested by gurus require you to calculate fair market value of the properties held by the REIT which is impossible.

It's better to stick with a simple model that anyone with basic math and common sense can do.

The Dividend Discount Model

The valuation of REITs using the dividend discount model is similar to valuing dividend stocks.

The intrinsic value of a REIT is calculated as follows: Dividend per share / (discounting rate - dividend growth rate), where the discount rate is the minimum return you expect to receive for investing in a REIT.

We can determine the discount rate by using a combination of how much we expect the inflation rate to be in the medium term, along with the average return we would get by holding a broad index of dividend stocks.

While many examples for income investing use 5% as a discount rate, I prefer to be a little more conservative and use an 8% discount rate.

With the help of three metrics, you can find the fair value of a REIT. But there's one problem. This figure might be overstated because we make a couple of assumptions, such as the average market return, which might be inaccurate. To avoid burning our fingers, we apply a margin of safety.

Applying the margin of safety means that we reduce the fair value calculated above by a certain percentage. If the resulting value is lower than the prevailing share price of a REIT, we say it is undervalued. The percentage you apply varies based on how confident you are about your estimates and the REIT you're analyzing. If you're very confident, you might apply a small margin of safety, such as 10%. Otherwise, use higher margins of safety, such as 20% or 30%.

Let's say that you calculate the fair value of a REIT and find it to be $60 while its share price is $56.56.

Additionally, let's assume you're fairly confident in your assumptions. Applying a 20% margin safety results in the fair value of the REIT being $48 ($60 - ($60 x 0.20) = $48).

At this point, that we have checked all qualitative aspects of the REIT while analyzing the REIT, used stock screener to filter out the quantitative parameters and found it to be undervalued. In such a scenario, I strongly suggest buying and hold.

To make it easier, we've created a ready-to-use Google sheet for valuing REITs. The valuations for the seven REITs suggested in the next chapter is also punched in it. You can also do the valuation for different REITs. All it takes to use the sheet is punching in desired metrics. It will automatically perform the necessary calculations using built-in formulas.

You can access the sheet by going to freemanpublications.com/reitsheet

KEY TAKEAWAYS:

◇ A company 10-K form is the best place to get impartial information on a REIT's prospects

◇ Using the screener criteria above can help you easily filter for quality REITs

◇ Use the dividend discount model to value REITs

Chapter 9

7 BEST REITS TO BUY TODAY

1. Innovative Industrial Properties: Expect a New High

We shall, by an• by, want a worl• of hemp more for our own consumption.
— **John Adams**

Innovative Industrial Properties (IIPR) is focused on buying, owning, and managing properties that are leased to state-licensed and regulated cannabis facility operators. Cannabis regulations are changing at a rapid pace in the U.S., and IIPR is staring at a bright future. The REIT's price has gained a whopping 193% in the last 3 years and a humongous 978% in the last 5 years. Plus, its forward dividend yield is a healthy 3.75% – the price gain and dividend yield make IIPR a portfolio pick for the long term, and here is why we are convinced that IIPR is a high-quality story.

Cannabis Usage Prospects in the U.S.

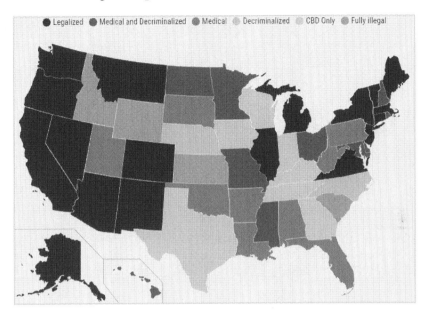

Figure 5: *Cannabis usage in the US*
*(source: https://*isa.com/*map-of-marijuana-legality-by-state)*

As of February 15, 2022, cannabis usage in the USA is:

a. Considered fully illegal ONLY in four states (Idaho, Wyoming, Kansas, and South Carolina)

b. Allowed only in CBD (Cannabidiol) oil form in seven states (Texas, Iowa, Wisconsin, Indiana, Kentucky, Tennessee, and Georgia)

In the rest of the 39 states, cannabis is legalized, decriminalized, and/or allowed for medical use.

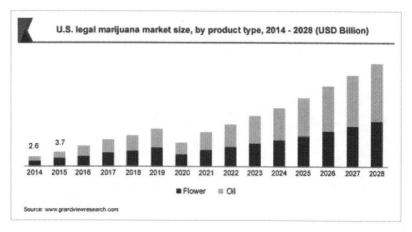

Figure 6: US legal marijuana market size by type (Source: Gran◆ View Research)

Cannabis growers have recovered after COVID-19 hit their logistics in 2020 and are now chugging along nicely. The global cannabis market is estimated to grow at a CAGR of 26.7% between 2021 and 2028. The main reasons are the growing demand for medical marijuana and the growing number of countries that are legalizing it. A CAGR of 26.7% represents phenomenal growth, and therefore, the first takeaway in our thesis is that IIPR will keep growing its business going forward and that it makes for a solid growth REIT.

What's Working in Favor of IIPR

◇ IIPR has the first-mover advantage and is expanding at a rapid clip. As of February 2022, the REIT owned 100 properties in 19 states, and from the data reflected in Figure 5, 39 states that allow marijuana for medical or recreational consumption. The opportunity to expand in 20 untapped states and grow in the 19 states where it is present is too huge to ignore.

◇ In May 2021, IIPR obtained an investment-grade corporate credit rating. The rating enables IIPR to borrow funds easily at a low interest rate. This liquidity will help IIPR expand and stay a step ahead of the competition. In February 2022, IIPR launched a public offering of $300M in senior notes due 2027. The REIT will use these funds for expansion.

258

◇ Senate Majority Leader Chuck Schumer, along with his colleagues, is on a mission to reform America's creaky marijuana laws. He has recently asked lawmakers to opine on a bill that federally legalizes marijuana. If the bill passes, the industry's estimated CAGR of 26.7% is expected to increase drastically. Even if it doesn't, the marijuana industry will continue to grow at the estimated rate, which is good enough.

Forward Dividend Yield

Dividend Payout History

Download to Spreadsheet

Year	Declare Date	Ex-Div Date	Record Date	Pay Date	Frequency	Amou
2022						
	9/15/2022	9/29/2022	9/30/2022	10/14/2022	Quarterly	1.8000
	6/15/2022	6/29/2022	6/30/2022	7/15/2022	Quarterly	1.7500
	3/14/2022	3/30/2022	3/31/2022	4/14/2022	Quarterly	1.7500
2021						
	12/15/2021	12/30/2021	12/31/2021	1/14/2022	Quarterly	1.5000
	9/15/2021	9/29/2021	9/30/2021	10/15/2021	Quarterly	1.5000
	6/15/2021	6/29/2021	6/30/2021	7/15/2021	Quarterly	1.4000
	3/15/2021	3/30/2021	3/31/2021	4/15/2021	Quarterly	1.3200

Figure 7: IIPR total distribution per share (source: https://seekingalpha.com)

IIPR distributed $1.2 as dividend in 2018, $2.83 in 2019, $4.25 in 2020. Then IIPR's total dividend distribution per share in 2021 was $5.72, while the dividends in 2022 have increased further from there.

Given its booming prospects, and considering the 26.7% CAGR for this sector, we estimate that IIPR will announce a total distribution of about $7.25 as dividend in 2022 ($5.72 total distribution in 2021, plus 26.7%), which gives it a healthy forward dividend yield of 7.61% based on its current price of $95.33 as of October 24, 2022.

This dividend yield on top of the phenomenal price growth that IIPR has delivered has the potential to take the REIT's shareholders to a new high.

Financials

Income Statement (Annual)

Financials in millions USD. Fiscal year is January - December.

Year		2021	2020	2019	2018
Revenue		204.55	116.9	44.67	14.79
Revenue Growth (YoY)		74.98%	161.71%	202.07%	130.33%
Cost of Revenue		4.44	4.95	1.32	0.45
Gross Profit		200.11	111.94	43.35	14.34
Selling, General & Admin		22.96	14.18	9.82	6.38
Other Operating Expenses		41.78	28.03	8.6	2.63
Operating Expenses		64.74	42.21	18.42	9
Operating Income		135.37	69.74	24.94	5.34
Interest Expense / Income		18.09	7.43	6.31	0
Other Expense / Income		3.3	-3.42	-4.85	-1.65
Pretax Income		113.99	65.73	23.48	6.99
Net Income		113.99	65.73	23.48	6.99
Preferred Dividends		1.35	1.35	1.35	1.35
Net Income Common		112.64	64.38	22.12	5.63
Net Income Growth		74.96%	191.00%	292.74%	-

Figure 8: IIPR revenue an• operating profits (Source: stockanalysis.com)

IIPR's revenues and operating profits are witnessing a quantum leap every quarter when compared on a year-over-year (YOY) basis. Imagine this: From Q4 2019 to Q3 2020, IIPR's revenues grew between 197% and 243% per quarter on a YOY basis. From Q4 2020 to Q2 2021, the REIT's revenues grew between 101% and 110% per quarter on a YOY basis. This is a solidly massive base, and despite its massiveness, IIPR's revenues registered a growth of 57% in Q3 2021 on a YOY basis.

In Q3 2021, IIPR reported a solid 78% bump in its operating income on a YOY basis. The profit growth is likely to trend up because of the nature of the cannabis industry and the first-mover advantage that IIPR has.

Cash Flow Statement (Annual)

Financials in millions USD. Fiscal year is January - December.

Year		2021	2020	2019	2018
Net Income	🕮	113.99	65.73	23.48	6.99
Depreciation & Amortization	🕮	41.78	28.03	8.6	2.63
Share-Based Compensation	🕮	8.62	3.33	2.5	1.47
Other Operating Activities	🕮	24.37	13.73	10.37	4.61
Operating Cash Flow	🕮	**188.75**	**110.81**	**44.93**	**15.69**

Figure 9: IIPR cash from operations (Source:stockanalysis.com)

IIPR's operating cash flows are growing at a rapid pace. In 2019, the REIT generated $44.93 million in operating cash flows, on which it distributed $8.87 million, i.e., 45% of its operating cash flows, as dividend. In 2021, IIPR generated $188.75 million worth of operating cash flows, more than 4 times what it generated in 2019.

IIPR's growth in generating revenues and operating cash flows goes way beyond the 26.7% CAGR estimated by analysts. The percentage of payouts, too, is increasing. We estimate that the company's revenues, operating cash flows, and net income will keep increasing over time.

Summing Up

Data and market conditions suggest that:

◇ The marijuana market is estimated to grow at a CAGR of 26.7% – BUT IIPRs growth is on a different level altogether. Its operating cash flows have grown by an enormous 260% between Q4 2019 and Q3 2021. Its revenues have grown by 57% in Q3 2021, on a YOY basis, and that too on a massive base.

◇ The REIT's price has gained a humongous 978% in the last 5 years. Given the favorable market conditions and the political inclination to federally legalize marijuana consumption, IIPR's growth prospects seem solidly bright.

◇ IIPR's dividend payout as a percentage of its operating cash flows has been growing. The operating cash flows are growing at a healthy rate as well. This implies that its dividend payouts are slated to increase. Its estimated forward dividend yield of 7.61% makes it investable even by pure income investors.

◇ IIPR has the first-mover advantage, it now owns an investment-grade rating, and is easily the pick from all the cannabis REITs out there.

Given these favorable tailwinds, we are extremely bullish on IIPR as a long-term growth and income-generating pick.

2. Care Trust REIT: A Long-Term Value Pick

Love, care an• treasure the el•erly people in the society. - **Lailah Gifty Akita**, Pearls of Wisdom: Great mind

CareTrust REIT (CTRE) is in the business of owning, acquiring, and leasing senior housing and healthcare real estate. As of Q4 2021, CTRE had invested $1.9B in 224 properties spread across 27 states. Currently, 71% of its funds are invested in Skilled Nursing Facilities (SNF), 17% in Assisted Living Facilities (ALF), and 11% in campuses (blend of SNF and ALF).

Past price and dividend data straightaway suggest that CTRE is a value pick for long-term income investors. In the last 5 years, CTRE's price has gained 17% while its dividend payout has increased by 43%. This steady REIT, with a current dividend yield that works up to a solid 5.90%, helps investors generate a healthy income on their investment year over year, hedge against inflation, and earn interest that is way beyond the estimated post-hike Fed interest rate.

But we think there is much more to CTRE than what the data above indicate. We opine that CTRE is a blend of dividend and growth. Here is our analysis of CTRE's prospects.

The Senior Housing Market

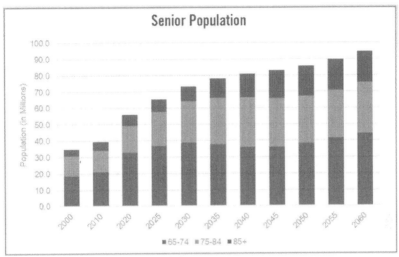

Source: U.S. Census Bureau, 2017 Population Estimates

Figure 10: *US senior population projection (source: https://www.naiop.org/Research-and-Publications/Magazine/2021/Fall-2021/Business-Trends/The-Senior-Living-Sector-is-Poised-for-Growth)*

The National Association of Industrial and Office Properties (NAIOP) estimates that by 2034 the number of people over 65 years of age will outnumber the population of children. It also estimates that by 2060 25% of our population will be aged 65 and above. According to NAIOP, as of now, senior housing is the most appealing sector for real estate investors. The organization's estimates also reveal that with growing life expectancy rates, America will be home to about 79 million seniors (65 years and over) by 2035. In 2020, America was home to about 55 million seniors.

As of 2021, about 810,000 senior Americans, or about 1.47% of the seniors' population in America as of 2020, live in assisted living facilities.

With growing life expectancy rates, and with professionally managed REITs like CTRE leasing out their properties to trusted and experienced care providers and nursing facilities, we see no reason why CTRE will not deliver spectacular growth numbers going forward.

New Developments at CTRE

◇ CTRE's COVID-19-related rent collection hassles ended in Q4 2021 as it was able to collect 100% of contractual rents during the quarter as well as receive the full repayment of the deferral of rent that it had granted its tenants in 2020. This proves that the CTRE's tenants and properties are of very high quality.

◇ The company has identified a few operators with a high risk of default, and with them, it is ending its contractual relationships. The company is also restructuring and optimizing its operations by either selling or repurposing 32 of its properties into behavioral health facilities. It intends to reinvest the sale proceeds in assets that are likely to generate profitable returns in the post-COVID-19 world. The good news is that because of the growing demand, CTRE finds itself in a sellers' market and it will face no difficulties in selling its assets at a profit. This restructuring exercise will take the company anywhere between 18 and 32 months to complete.

Forward Dividend Yield

Year	Declare Date	Ex-Div Date	Record Date	Pay Date	Frequency	Amount
2022						
	9/15/2022	9/29/2022	9/30/2022	10/14/2022	Quarterly	0.2750
	6/17/2022	6/29/2022	6/30/2022	7/15/2022	Quarterly	0.2750
	3/15/2022	3/30/2022	3/31/2022	4/15/2022	Quarterly	0.2750
2021						
	12/15/2021	12/30/2021	12/31/2021	1/15/2022	Quarterly	0.2650
	9/15/2021	9/29/2021	9/30/2021	10/15/2021	Quarterly	0.2650
	6/16/2021	6/29/2021	6/30/2021	7/15/2021	Quarterly	0.2650
	3/15/2021	3/30/2021	3/31/2021	4/15/2021	Quarterly	0.2650

Dividend Payout History — Download to Spreadsheet

Figure 11: CTRE distribution schedule history (source: seekingalpha.com)

CTRE came into existence in 2014 and has been paying dividends consistently since. What is even better is that its dividend payouts have been growing year over year. The REIT paid $0.82 as dividend in 2018, $0.90 in 2019, $1 in 2020, and $1.06 in 2021.

Given the prospects of the senior housing sector, we are assuming that CTRE's dividend payouts in 2022 will grow by at least 6% over its 2021 payout. Therefore, we estimate that it will end up paying at least $1.09 in 2022, which gives it a forward dividend yield of 6.3% based on its current price of $17.37 (as of October 24, 2022).

Financials

Cash Flow Statement (Annual)

Financials in millions USD. Fiscal year is January - December.

Year		2021	2020	2019	2018
Net Income	⌀	71.98	80.87	46.36	57.92
Depreciation & Amortization	⌀	55.39	52.82	51.87	45.78
Share-Based Compensation	⌀	10.83	3.79	4.1	3.85
Other Operating Activities	⌀	18.66	8.26	23.97	-8.2
Operating Cash Flow	⌀	156.87	145.74	126.3	99.36
Operating Cash Flow Growth	⌀	7.64%	15.39%	27.11%	11.89%

Figure 12: CTRE cash from operations (source: stockanalysis.com)

CTRE's cash flows are increasing year over year. The REIT's operating cash flows have registered a solid jump from $40.24 million in 2015 to $145.7 million in 2020. The healthy operating cash flow generation proves that the REIT is expanding and is efficiently managed.

CTRE's total dividends are currently around 72% of its FFO. Which is slightly highly than we'd like. However going by the favorable market conditions, CTRE's forthcoming business optimization/sale of its 32 properties, and its focus on expansion, we estimate that cash from operations will increase at a steady clip and investors will be rewarded with higher dividend payouts.

CTRE's revenues and operating income have been growing year after year on a TTM basis. That implies that the company is witnessing an improvement in its revenues and operating income in every quarter.

CTRE has a robust balance sheet. It owns assets worth $1.644 billion and has liabilities worth $726.05 million. Moreover, it is operating in a sellers' market, which implies that its properties are most likely valued way higher than what the books say. Aside from its growing profitability and increasing dividend payouts, the increasing market value of its assets makes the stock a bargain hunter's pick.

Summing Up

Current conditions suggest that the skilled nursing facilities and assisted living facilities markets have barely scratched the surface. As life expectancy increases, the population of people over 65 years of age is estimated to grow rapidly and put pressure on our overloaded healthcare systems.

Over time, seniors will prefer enrolling in housing that is managed by trusted and experienced providers. As CTRE is focused on signing up such high-quality tenants, we reckon that it will gradually become a sought-after REIT by investors.

A forward dividend yield of 6.3%, a steady price appreciation in the last 5 years, and a market that is all set to witness exponential growth – all these factors combine to make CTRE an irresistible stock.

Long-term income investors, value investors, and growth investors who are interested in adding to their portfolio a quality REIT that faces tremendous growth prospects and favorable tailwinds can consider investing in CTRE.

3. Digital Realty Trust (DLR): On Cloud 9

People outsource, their memories to ,ata centers an, basic skills to tabs. —
David Mitchell

The Digital Realty Trust (DLR) REIT buys and operates data centers
all over the world – currently, it owns and operates 290+ data centers
in 26 countries. The data center market is growing at a rapid pace and
though DLR is in a sweet spot business-wise, its stock price has taken a
severe beating recently which seems contrary to its fundamentals.

DLR's chart below makes for an extremely interesting analysis:

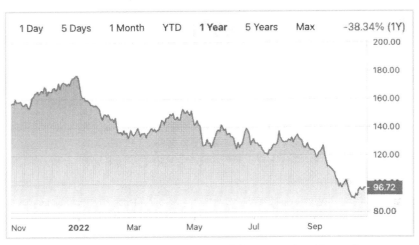

Figure 13: *DLR price, ,ivi,en, an, cash from operations history chart
(source: stockanalysis.com)*

DLR's price has slipped from a high of about $178 in January 2022 to
about $96 as of October 24, 2022. The drawdown is because of a mix of
global (Russia–Ukraine) and domestic (the forthcoming Fed rate hike).
Though its price has slipped in 2022, its dividend payout has increased
by about 7% and its cash from operations has increased by about 13%
in the last 3 years.

Improving fundamentals coupled with a fall in price make DLR a value
pick at a time when the global data center market is witnessing a boom
in business.

The Data Center Market

In 2020, the global data center market was valued at $187.35 billion and was estimated to touch $517.17 billion before 2030. However, COVID-19 has accelerated its growth rate. The current size of just the global data center co-location market is $54 billion, and it too is growing at a furious pace. DLR is among the top 15 global players.

Analysts opine that while top data center markets have peaked, the boom in global connectivity is still raging because the number of people coming online is increasing by the day and businesses are aggressively shifting to the cloud. The new capacities that are being added are spread out as follows:

◇ 38% in the Asia Pacific

◇ 30% in North America

◇ 27% in Europe, Middle East and Africa region

◇ 5% in Latin America

New data centers like Indonesia, Japan, and India are witnessing intensified activity, and there is little doubt that the sector is booming. We estimate that the market will witness a CAGR that is much higher than estimated earlier.

The Latest Developments at DLR Validate the Increasing Growth Rate

◇ In Q4 2021, DLR received $156 million in new bookings. That was a significant increase because the average bookings per quarter in 2021 were about $115 million. The new business kind of proves that, though DLR's price is falling, the demand for its infrastructure is increasing.

◇ In Q4 2021, DLR successfully launched Digital Core REIT's IPO on the Singapore Stock Exchange. It generated $950 million from the IPO and retained a 35% stake in the newly listed REIT. This move gives DLR adequate dry powder to expand into the rapidly growing Asian markets.

◇ DLR has entered into a definitive agreement to acquire a 55% stake in Teraco, Africa's top co-location provider. The acquisition makes DRL a leading data center provider in the African continent.

◇ In Q4 2021, DLR spent $580 million on capital expenditure. The REIT has 44 work-in-progress projects. Moreover, 46% of the space under development was presold as of December 2021.

Here is an estimation of its forward dividend yield and a summary of its financials:

Forward Dividend Yield

DLR has been paying dividends consecutively for the last 16 years, and what's more, its payouts are steadily growing.

Dividend Payout History						Download to Spreadsheet
Year	Declare Date	Ex-Div Date	Record Date	Pay Date	Frequency	Amou < >
2022						
	8/17/2022	9/14/2022	9/15/2022	9/30/2022	Quarterly	1.2200
	5/24/2022	6/14/2022	6/15/2022	6/30/2022	Quarterly	1.2200
	3/3/2022	3/14/2022	3/15/2022	3/31/2022	Quarterly	1.2200
2021						
	11/18/2021	12/14/2021	12/15/2021	1/14/2022	Quarterly	1.1600
	8/11/2021	9/14/2021	9/15/2021	9/30/2021	Quarterly	1.1600
	5/10/2021	6/14/2021	6/15/2021	6/30/2021	Quarterly	1.1600
	2/25/2021	3/12/2021	3/15/2021	3/31/2021	Quarterly	1.1600

Figure 14: DLR ◦ivi◦en◦ ◦istribution sche◦ule history (source: seekingalpha.com)

DLR paid $4.04 as dividend in 2018, $3.47 in 2019, $4.37 in 2020, and $4.64 in 2021. Based on its dividend growth record in the last 2 years, and taking into account the increasingly bright prospects for the data center business, we estimate that DLR will end up paying about $4.88 (a 6% rise over its 2021 payout) in 2022.

The estimated payout gives DLR a forward dividend yield of around 5% based on its market price of $96.88 as of October 24, 2022. That is quite a solid yield, given DLR's solid growth prospects.

Financials

Income Statement (Annual)

Financials in millions USD. Fiscal year is January - December.

Year		2021	2020	2019	2018
Revenue	📊	4,427.88	3,903.61	3,209.24	3,046.48
Revenue Growth (YoY)	📊	13.43%	21.64%	5.34%	23.95%
Cost of Revenue	📊	1,570.51	1,331.49	1,020.58	957.07
Gross Profit	📊	2,857.38	2,572.12	2,188.66	2,089.41
Selling, General & Admin	📊	400.65	351.37	211.1	163.67
Other Operating Expenses	📊	1,762.71	1,663.22	1,383.35	1,375.96
Operating Expenses	📊	2,163.37	2,014.59	1,594.45	1,539.63
Operating Income	📊	694.01	557.53	594.22	549.79
Interest Expense / Income	📊	293.85	333.02	353.06	321.53
Other Expense / Income	📊	-1,381.9	-169.94	-350.6	-105.07
Pretax Income	📊	1,782.06	394.45	591.76	333.33
Income Tax	📊	72.8	38.05	12	2.08
Net Income	📊	1,709.26	356.4	579.76	331.25
Preferred Dividends	📊	27.76	93.06	86.75	81.32
Net Income Common	📊	1,681.5	263.34	493.01	249.93
Net Income Growth	📊	538.52%	-46.59%	97.26%	44.34%

Figure 15: DLR revenue history (source: stockanalysis.com)

DLR's revenues are increasing at a steady pace quarter over quarter. The REIT reported revenues of $3.9 billion in 2020 and $4.4 billion in 2021. Thus, in a space of seven quarters, DLR reported an increase of about 35% in its revenues. It has achieved this whilst its total operating expenses have remained relatively static. Currently, the company owns and operates 260 data centers, and it is adding 44 more properties.

Data based on DLR's 2021 cash flow statements 2021 reveal that DLR generated an average of $417 million worth of operating cash per quarter. In Q2 and Q3 2021, DLR paid about $347 million as dividend per quarter, implying that the REIT distributes 83% of its operating cash flows to its shareholders. This is a generous payout that has room to increase going forward.

In a balance sheet of $36.37 billion, DLR owns long-term assets worth $35.56 billion. Its paid-in capital is $21.068 billion. In other words, the book value of DLR's properties is 1.75 times its paid-in equity capital, implying that DLR is an extremely well-managed REIT. Given the booming market, there is little doubt that the market value of DLR's properties and intangibles will be way higher than their book value.

Summing Up

We believe that DLR is a value pick for both income investors and growth investors because:

◇ The REIT's price has corrected from about $178 to $95.88, amounting to a substantial drop of 38% - despite improving fundamentals

◇ The fundamentals of this efficiently managed REIT are extremely strong and its business is all set to grow at a rapid rate. This reality is not reflected in its price.

◇ It boasts a healthy forward dividend yield of 5%. Plus, DLR has paid dividends consecutively for 16 years. That makes DLR a very attractive play for flexible income investors who prefer to invest in quality instruments that offer both growth and income.

◇ DLR has a very robust balance sheet. The market value of its long-term assets is way higher than its paid-in capital.

With new bookings picking up quarter over quarter, DLR is literally floating on cloud 9. We reiterate our bullish view on this stock for long-term investors.

4. Four Corners Property Trust: Just REIT for Income Investors

It is better to have a permanent income than to be fascinating. – **Oscar Wilde**

The Four Corners Property Trust (FCPT) REIT has two business segments, real estate operations and restaurant operations:

◇ The real estate segment earns rental revenues from investing in and then leasing restaurant and retail properties. This division is the main revenue earner for the REIT.

◇ The restaurant operations segment is operated by FCPT's subsidiary, which runs restaurants on FCPT properties rather than leasing them to a third party. It earns revenues from restaurant sales and bears all the business expenses.

The restaurant business has recently extracted itself from the COVID-19 disruption, which had hit the sector hard. FCPT has yet to recover fully from the impact that COVID-19 had on the restaurant and retail sectors. But it is getting there slowly and steadily. The REIT's revenues have been rising steadily despite the COVID-19 impact. In the last 5 years, its revenues have grown by around 11% per year.

On top of this. cash flows had been rising steadily but were understandably hit by the pandemic. In the last 5 years, they grew by 16%. Now that things are returning to normal, we estimate that FCPT's operating cash flows will keep rising.

FCPT's Current Status (as of Q2 2022)

◇ FCPT has recorded an occupancy rate of 99.9% and has collected 99.7% of its rent.

◇ The revenues of its restaurant operations segment have now exceeded pre-pandemic levels. According to its CEO, the REIT's tenanted quick service restaurants operated at 118%, and casual dining operated at 100% of pre-pandemic levels

◇ In Q4 2021 the REIT acquired 33 low-rent, high-quality-tenant properties for $70.5 million. The properties are home to high-quality tenants and have a cash yield of 6.4%. In the whole of 2021, FCPT acquired a total of 122 properties.

◇ FCPT has decided to diversify into other sectors. Thus far in 2022, the REIT has invested just 25% in restaurants – 37% of its investments went into auto service facilities and 28% in medical retail. The diversification augurs well for the REIT because the disruption wrought about by the pandemic has boosted the fortunes of many sectors that were otherwise sulking.

Financials

FCPT is an efficiently managed REIT that generates positive operating cash flows even in adverse times. After COVID-19 landed on our shores and locked down our economy, FCPT optimized its operations and generated positive operating cash flows even during this mega disruption.

Cash Flow Statement (Annual)

Financials in millions USD. Fiscal year is January - December.

Year		2021	2020	2019	2018
Net Income		85.58	77.33	72.62	82.4
Depreciation & Amortization		34.83	29.43	26.31	23.88
Share-Based Compensation		3.95	3.38	3.6	3.97
Other Operating Activities		-1.94	-18.68	2.14	-29.37
Operating Cash Flow		122.42	91.46	104.67	80.88
Operating Cash Flow Growth		33.85%	-12.63%	29.41%	2.46%

Figure 16: FCPT operating cash flow (Source: stockanalysis.com)

In 2020, a COVID-impacted year, FCPT generated $91.5 million in operating cash flows. In 2021, the REIT generated $122.4 million in operating cash flows, registering an increase of about 34% year on year. What is remarkable about this growth is that this happened even though 2021 too was impacted by COVID-19 (Delta and Omicron). The inference is that once things fully normalize, FCPT's prospects along with its revenues, profits, and cash flows will increase, especially because it is adding new properties and diversifying into sunrise sectors.

Cash Flow Statement (Annual)

Financials in millions USD. Fiscal year is January - December.

Year		2021	2020	2019	2018
Net Income		85.58	77.33	72.62	82.4
Depreciation & Amortization		34.83	29.43	26.31	23.88
Share-Based Compensation		3.95	3.38	3.6	3.97
Other Operating Activities		-1.94	-18.68	2.14	-29.37
Operating Cash Flow		122.42	91.46	104.67	80.88
Operating Cash Flow Growth		33.85%	-12.63%	29.41%	2.46%
Capital Expenditures		-268.26	-229.07	-207.35	-268.19
Other Investing Activities		3.34	0	0	21.14
Investing Cash Flow		-264.92	-229.07	-207.35	-247.05
Dividends Paid		-96.9	-86.33	-78.49	-69.49

Figure 17: FCPT operating cash flow (Source: stockanalysis.com)

In 2020, FCPT distributed $86.3 million, or 94% of its operating cash flows, as dividend. In 2021, it paid $96.9 million, or 79% of its operating cash flows, as dividend. Things are expected to get better going forward because the REIT is efficiently managed, the economy is recovering, and FCPT is acquiring more and more properties and diversifying its business.

As of December 2021, FCPT owns land and buildings worth $1.7 billion and owes $878 million worth of long-term debt. This is an important metric because FCPT is operating in a sellers' market and long-term debt makes up only 49% of its long-term assets. As it operates in a sellers' market, the market value of its properties will be considerably higher than their book value.

Forward Dividend Yield

FCPT has been paying dividends consistently since its inception in December 2015.

Year	Declare Date	Ex-Div Date	Record Date	Pay Date	Frequency	Amou...
2022						
	9/16/2022	9/29/2022	9/30/2022	10/14/2022	Quarterly	0.3325
	6/16/2022	6/29/2022	6/30/2022	7/15/2022	Quarterly	0.3325
	3/8/2022	3/30/2022	3/31/2022	4/14/2022	Quarterly	0.3325
2021						
	11/29/2021	12/31/2021	1/3/2022	1/14/2022	Quarterly	0.3325
	9/27/2021	10/6/2021	10/7/2021	10/15/2021	Quarterly	0.3175
	6/14/2021	6/29/2021	6/30/2021	7/15/2021	Quarterly	0.3175
	3/8/2021	3/30/2021	3/31/2021	4/15/2021	Quarterly	0.3175

Dividend Payout History — Download to Spreadsheet

Figure 18: FCPT dividend payments (source: seekingalpha.com)

It paid a dividend of $1.285 in 2021. Based on its Q4 2021 payout of $0.3325, we estimate that the REIT will pay $1.33 as dividend in 2022. This translates to a forward dividend yield of 5.6% based on its current market price of $23.88 as of October 24, 2022.

This is a healthy forward dividend yield that is much higher than the estimated post-hike Fed interest rate.

Summing Up

We believe that FCPT makes the cut for long-term income investors because:

◇ It is a consistent dividend payer and going forward its payouts are likely to be higher than its 2021 payouts.

◇ FCPT's forward dividend yield of 5.6% helps income investors beat inflation to a large extent and protect the purchasing power of their money.

The REIT has started making sense also for long-term growth investors because it is diversifying and moving into sectors that have been positively impacted by the pandemic. The diversification will pay off going forward, and though we cannot estimate its value addition, it

275

does seem that the REIT's price will gain and its dividend payouts will increase as the years roll by.

To wrap up, FCPT definitely makes the cut for long-term income investors. Plus, it has started looking attractive for growth investors too.

5. Office Properties Income Trust: Quality REIT at a Bargain Price

Bargain... anything a customer thinks a store is losing money on. – **Kin Hubbard**

The Office Properties Income Trust (OPI) REIT owns, invests in, operates, and leases office buildings mainly to high-quality single tenants such as large corporations who have been in business for many years and have an established market presence, multinational companies, and government agencies/entities. Large companies and government entities are geared up to face major market disruptions, be they due to pandemics or wars. The implication of this is quite evident – that OPI has a wide and formidable economic moat.

However, a look at its price chart suggests that investors have largely ignored the REIT's solid business model and economic moat and have instead likened it with other REITs that lease out their properties to small and medium businesses. An analysis of OPI's chart confirms that its market price is highly undervalued and divergent when benchmarked against its fundamentals.

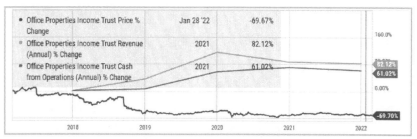

Figure 19: OPI price, revenue and cash from operations history chart (source: YCharts)

In the last 5 years, OPI's price has fallen by a massive 70% while its revenues have increased by 82% and its cash flows from operations have increased by 61%. This divergence is too significant to ignore.

So, on the face of it, OPI's valuations seem attractive. And, to confirm our thesis, here is a deep dive into why this REIT makes sense for income investors:

New Developments at OPI as of Q2 2022

◇ To stay self-reliant and reduce dependence on Chinese manufacturers, the White House administration plans to bring back manufacturing to America and strengthen domestic supply chains. If manufacturing activity increases, it is a no-brainer that offices will be back in demand. Moreover, as of this writing the full impact of the sanctions on Russia is not fully known – all that analysts can estimate is that investments will flow out of Russia and get parked in developed and developing nations. This factor too can cause a spurt in the demand for office space by multinationals. But the jury is still out on this one.

◇ OPI leased 2.5 million square feet of office space as of Q4 2021, at an average lease term of 9.5 years and a rent increase of 6.5% in 2020. Of the total area leased, 846,000 square feet represents new leasing, which amounts to 3× the area leased in 2020 and 2× the area leased in 2019 (pre-pandemic). This is a clear indication that office space demand from large companies and government entities is strong and increasing.

◇ The company ended Q2 2022 with a consolidated occupancy rate of 89.4%. About 63% of OPI's revenues are generated from tenants rated as investment-grade. The REIT expects to end 2022 with an occupancy rate of 90%, along with a 5% increase in rent.

◇ OPI also restricted and optimized its operations in 2021 by selling 9 properties (2.9 million square feet) for $250 million. The company plans to sell $400–500 million worth of properties in 2022 and use the proceeds to deleverage its balance sheet.

◇ OPI's latest leasing pipeline covers more than 3.4 million square feet, of which 1.5 million square feet pertain to new leasing.

Financials

Cash Flow Statement (Annual)

Financials in millions USD. Fiscal year is January - December.

Year		2021	2020	2019	2018
Net Income		-8.18	6.68	30.34	-21.88
Depreciation & Amortization		92.27	83.83	89.4	66.69
Share-Based Compensation		0	0	0	0
Other Operating Activities		137.41	143.12	95.59	100.12
Operating Cash Flow		221.49	233.63	215.33	144.92
Operating Cash Flow Growth		-5.20%	8.50%	48.59%	5.35%

Figure 20: OPI cash from operations (source: stockanalysis.com)

In 2021, OPI generated operating cash of $221.50 million, which is higher than the $215.30 million it generated in 2019, a pre-COVID-19 year. As the company is optimizing its business operations and registering an increase in leasing activity, we reckon that its operating cash flows will increase going forward. In 2021, OPI distributed 48% of its operating cash flows as dividend. As the business activity increases going forward, its cash flows from operations are obviously going to increase, and so will dividend payouts.

Balance Sheet (Annual)

Financials in millions USD. Fiscal year is January - December.

Year		2021	2020	2019	2018
Cash & Equivalents		84.52	56.86	100.7	38.94
Cash & Cash Equivalents		84.52	56.86	100.7	38.94
Cash Growth		48.65%	-43.54%	158.57%	97.88%
Receivables		112.89	101.77	83.56	72.05
Property, Plant & Equipment		3,441.77	3,145.41	3,176.45	3,822.99
Total Assets		4,241.68	3,946.44	4,193.14	5,238.58
Accounts Payable		149.4	122.59	132.19	180.42
Total Liabilities		2,744.97	2,337.04	2,487.38	3,459.62

Figure 21: *OPI balance sheet (source: stockanalysis.com)*

In a balance sheet of $4.24 billion, OPI owes $2.58 billion, or about 61% of the total balance sheet, in long-term debt, which it has planned to deleverage in 2022. The deleveraging will help the REIT save on interest costs and bump up its net cash flows. OPI's real estate assets are about 64% higher than its long-term debt, which indicates that the REIT is prudently and efficiently managed. All in all, OPI has a robust balance sheet.

Forward Dividend Yield

OPI was founded in 2009, and since then it has been paying dividends consistently.

Year	Declare Date	Ex-Div Date	Record Date	Pay Date	Frequency	Amou < >
2022						
	10/13/2022	10/21/2022	10/24/2022	11/17/2022	Quarterly	0.5500
	7/14/2022	7/22/2022	7/25/2022	8/18/2022	Quarterly	0.5500
	4/14/2022	4/22/2022	4/25/2022	5/19/2022	Quarterly	0.5500
	1/13/2022	1/21/2022	1/24/2022	2/17/2022	Quarterly	0.5500
2021						
	10/14/2021	10/22/2021	10/25/2021	11/18/2021	Quarterly	0.5500
	7/15/2021	7/23/2021	7/26/2021	8/19/2021	Quarterly	0.5500
	4/15/2021	4/23/2021	4/26/2021	5/20/2021	Quarterly	0.5500
	1/14/2021	1/22/2021	1/25/2021	2/18/2021	Quarterly	0.5500

Figure 22: *OPI dividend distribution history (source: Seeking Alpha)*

Based on OPI's track record of paying $0.55 as dividend per quarter since 2019, we estimate that it will end up paying a minimum of $2.2 as dividend in 2022. This estimated payout tags OPI with a forward dividend yield of 15.28% based on its market price of $14.40 as of October 25, 2022.

This is a spectacular forward dividend yield coming from a high-quality REIT that has consistently paid dividends since its inception.

Summing Up

We believe that OPI makes the cut as a long-term investment for income investors because:

◇ The REIT's price has fallen by a whopping 70% in the last 5 years, while its revenues have increased by 82% and its cash flows from operations have increased by 61% in the same period. The data imply that OPI's current market price is unjustified and undervalued because of its improving fundamentals. It is a value pick in our opinion.

◇ OPI is a consistent dividend payer and its forward dividend yield of 15.28% looks irresistible, mainly because of its efficient management and improving prospects. The yield helps income investors beat inflation and generate a healthy income.

◇ OPI leases out properties to single tenants with an average lease term of at least 7 years. Such companies and government entities do not fold up even when a severe disruption hits the market. Therefore, OPI is likely to report higher revenues and higher cash flows going forward as the economy shrugs away the pandemic and the "Make in America" program of the Biden administration gathers pace.

6. SL Green Realty Corp.: Manhattan Undervalued

*Lan*lor*s grow rich in their sleep without working, risking, or economizing.*
– John Stuart Mill

It's one thing to own stock in a hedge fund or high flying tech company, it's another to be their landlord. Well that's precisely what SL Green Realty Corp (SLG) does. This Manhattan based REIT focuses on investing in commercial properties and leasing them out. It rewards its shareholders by paying a healthy dividend every year. As of December 31, 2021, SLG owns 26.9 million square feet in 73 buildings and 7.1 million square feet worth of property in secured debt and equity investments.

We are past the COVID-19 stage and are entering into a new phase of growth. Employment numbers are rising month over month and the White House is aggressively pushing a "Make in America" program. This is great news for business in general and even more so for the commercial property leasing business. The current market conditions are in favor of REITs like SLG.

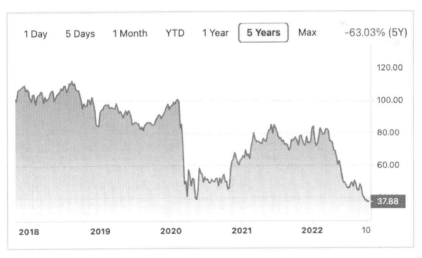

Figure 23: SLG price an *ilute* EPS history chart (source: stockanalysis.com)*

Moreover, SLG's price chart suggests that it is an undervalued REIT. In the last 5 years, SLG's price has fallen by about 33% while its EPS has risen by about 62%. The price damage occurred because of the COVID-19 disruption.

Now that COVID-19 is on the verge of becoming endemic and we have learned how to live with it, we believe that SLG is all set to witness boom times. In our opinion, therefore, SLG can definitely make the cut as a long-term income investment.

Here are our reasons why:

Developments at SLG in Q4 2021

◇ SLG's recently completed project at Dey Street saw rental demand for more than 100 units at an average rent that was just a notch below $100 per square foot. This is adequate proof that Manhattan commercial realty demand is picking up.

◇ The REIT is confident about achieving its FY 2022 leasing goals of realizing and maintaining 94% occupancy. This confidence stems from the fact that within a short span after its Investor Conference, held on December 6, 2021, SLG was able to lease out 250,000 square feet of office space. In 2021 the REIT signed on leases for a total of 1.9 million square feet, and this year it is targeting a minimum of 2 million square feet.

◇ A new trend emerging in the office leasing market post-Covid-19 is the strategy of flight-to-quality (strong, reputed, and stable) landlords. SLG happens to be one of the best REITs in the business. Currently, Manhattan's office market has a vacancy rate of about 17%, but SLG's vacancy rate is less than 8%. This proves that tenants are flocking to quality and established landlords.

Financials

Like all office landlords, SLG was badly hit by the COVID-19 disruption. But that is past now and financial data suggest that the company is all set to reclaim its past glory:

Cash Flow Statement (Quarterly)

Financials in millions USD. Fiscal year is January - December.

Quarter Ended		2022-06-30	2022-03-31	2021-12-31	2021-09-30	2021-06-30	2021-03-31	2020-12-31	2020
Net Income		-40.14	11.49	-47.53	391.94	109.07	-3.73	174.74	
Depreciation & Amortization		54.87	54.97	54.82	55.75	64.81	70.16	62.66	
Share-Based Compensation		0	0	0	0	0	0	0	
Other Operating Activities		86.3	14.94	57.68	-359.95	-89.22	-47.82	-11.11	
Operating Cash Flow		101.03	81.4	64.97	87.75	84.66	18.6	226.29	
Operating Cash Flow Growth		19.34%	337.60%	-71.29%	-16.33%	-53.55%	-55.74%	193.73%	

Figure 24: SLG cash from operations (source: stockanalysis.com)

In Q4 2021, SLG generated about $65 million in operating cash flows, which is lower than the operating cash flows of $88 million and $85 million that the REIT generated in Q3 and Q2 2021, respectively. The flows were lesser in Q4 2021 because of working capital adjustments worth $18 million. However, since then the company has increased operating cash flow in the subsequent two quarters.

In FY 2021, SLG generated total operating cash flows of about $344 million as compared to $554 million in FY 2020. We believe that the COVID-19 damage will not repeat unless there is another pandemic and that the REIT's operating cash flows will edge up substantially from 2022 onwards because tenants are preferring high-quality landlords and the demand for office space is picking up nicely. SLG may even report operating cash flows that are higher than the 2020 numbers because it estimates that its 2022 vacancies will be just 7%.

Balance Sheet	
Total Assets (Quarterly)	.11.07B
Total Liabilities (Quarterly)	5.748B
Shareholders Equity (Quarterly)	4.765B
Cash and Short Term Investments (Quarterly)	286.17M
Total Long Term Assets (Quarterly)	10.23B
Total Long Term Debt (Quarterly)	4.017B
Book Value (Quarterly)	4.543B

Figure 25: SLG balance sheet (source: YCharts)

SLG's balance sheet is extremely robust. The REIT owns long-term assets with a book value of $10.23 billion and carries long-term debt of $4.02 billion. Its shareholders' equity is $4.77 billion. So, after rewarding shareholders with healthy dividend payouts year after year, the book value of the REIT's long-term assets exceeds its liabilities and shareholders' equity by about 16%. The market value will be much higher as the REIT has been investing in properties since 1997. These numbers imply that SLG is efficiently managed.

Forward Dividend Yield

SLG has been paying dividends consistently since its inception in 1997. It hasn't paused even when the market was hit by extremities like the dotcom bust (2001), subprime/global financial crisis (2008), Greece's default (2015), and COVID-19 (2020). It has sailed through each crisis with ease.

Dividend Payout History						Download to Spreadsheet
Year	Declare Date	Ex-Div Date	Record Date	Pay Date	Frequency	Amou ⟨ ⟩
2022						
	10/19/2022	10/28/2022	10/31/2022	11/15/2022	Monthly	0.3108
	9/19/2022	9/29/2022	9/30/2022	10/17/2022	Monthly	0.3108
	8/16/2022	8/30/2022	8/31/2022	9/15/2022	Monthly	0.3108
	7/19/2022	7/28/2022	7/29/2022	8/15/2022	Monthly	0.3108
	6/14/2022	6/29/2022	6/30/2022	7/15/2022	Monthly	0.3108
	5/18/2022	5/27/2022	5/31/2022	6/15/2022	Monthly	0.3108
	4/22/2022	4/28/2022	4/29/2022	5/16/2022	Monthly	0.3108
		3/30/2022	3/31/2022	4/18/2022	Monthly	0.3108
	2/22/2022	2/25/2022	2/28/2022	3/15/2022	Monthly	0.3108
	1/21/2022	1/28/2022	1/31/2022	2/15/2022	Monthly	0.3108

Figure 26: SLG dividend distribution 2021/22 (source: Seeking Alpha)

In 2020, the REIT switched from paying dividends quarterly, to a monthly payout schedule. 2022's monthly dividend is set at $0.3108 per share per month to give an annualized payout of $3.73 in 2022. This payout tags SLG with a forward dividend yield of 9.88% based on its market price of $37.88 as of October 25, 2022.

This kind of dividend yield can help income investors beat the core inflation rate to a large extent.

Summing Up

The four facts that emerge from this analysis are:

◇ SLG's EPS has risen in the last 5 years, but its price has tanked by about 60% in the same period.

◇ The REIT's business has recovered from the COVID-19 disruption and seems all set to take off.

◇ The Manhattan office leasing market is rebounding quickly back to pre-COVID-19 levels.

◇ SLG's forward dividend yield is a healthy 9.88%.

So if you are a long-term income investor who wants to protect the purchasing power of your money and earn a healthy dividend yield, go for SLG.

7. Alpine Income Property Trust: An Undervalued Income Generator

Alpine Income Property Trust (PINE) invests in high-quality net lease properties to generate income. In a net lease property, in addition to the rent, the lessee agrees to bear the entire or share a part of the property expenses that are normally borne by the owner, in exchange for a reduction in rent. Property expenses shared or borne entirely by the lessee may include taxes, insurance, and operating costs required to maintain and manage the property. Such leases are usually taken on by high-quality tenants who are in for the long haul. The tenants get the advantage of lower rent along with greater control over the property. For PINE, this business model offers an advantage in that it ensures that the company can enjoy passive income, and focus on expanding its business without bothering about day-to-day management and expenses of its properties.

As of October 2022, PINE owns 143 properties (3.3 million square feet) that are leased to quality companies such as Dollar General, Walgreens, 7-Eleven, and others. The properties have 100% occupancy rate and an average remaining lease term (average) of 7.8 years.

PINE launched its IPO in 2019 at $19/share, and since then its price has fallen by 6%. However, its cash from operations has jumped by 83%, revenue by 57%, and dividend payouts by 35% in the same period. Straightaway, the data suggest that the REIT is doing great on the business front, but investors are ignoring its fundamentals.

Given PINE's growing revenues and cash flows, and its strong business model, we are bullish on the REIT as a long-term income generator. Here are the facts that substantiate our opinion.

Latest Developments at PINE

◇ In Q4 2021, PINE acquired 26 properties spread across 11 different states, which were leased to high-quality tenants. The investment will doubtless help the REIT boost its revenues and cash flows going forward.

◇ In 2021, PINE acquired 68 net lease retail properties for about $260 million. These fresh additions to its portfolio had a remaining lease term of 8.1 years (at the time of acquisition). New tenants included marquee names like Bose, Academy Sports, Burlington, Camping World, and more.

◇ As of October 2022, all of PINE's 143 properties were occupied and had an average remaining lease term of 7.8 years.

◇ Comments from the REIT's management suggest that it is a nimble and agile team that takes full advantage of market conditions to maximize shareholder value. In 2021, PINE sold its Hilton Grand Vacations properties at a book value gain of more than $9 million. It is also in discussions to hive off its Wells Fargo property in Hillsboro, Oregon. PINE intends to deploy the funds towards more profitable acquisitions.

Financials

Income Statement (Annual)

Financials in millions USD. Fiscal year is January - December.

Year		2021	2020	2019	2018
Revenue		30.13	19.25	11.84	11.72
Revenue Growth (YoY)		56.53%	62.61%	1.00%	38.62%
Cost of Revenue		3.67	2.32	1.66	1.62
Gross Profit		26.46	16.93	10.17	10.1
Selling, General & Admin		5.03	4.66	1.68	1.18
Other Operating Expenses		6.26	9.66	4.86	4.9
Operating Expenses		11.29	14.32	6.54	6.09
Operating Income		15.16	2.61	3.63	4.02
Interest Expense / Income		3.7	1.46	0	0
Other Expense / Income		1.5	0.16	0	0
Pretax Income		9.96	0.99	3.63	4.02
Net Income		9.96	0.99	3.63	4.02
Net Income Common		9.96	0.99	3.63	4.02
Net Income Growth		911.57%	-72.87%	-9.56%	42.74%

Figure 27: PINE cash from operations (source: stockanalysis.com)

In Q4 2021, PINE's revenues grew by 76% on a year-over-year (YOY) basis and its operating income zoomed by 159%, also on a YOY basis. In 2021, its increase in operating income averaged 160% per quarter, on a YOY basis. PINE is a young company that has acquired 68 properties with high-quality tenants in 2021. This implies that in 2021 alone the REIT picked up 60% of its property portfolio. We expect the revenues and operating profits to snowball from here on as the unemployment numbers are down and our economy is booming. Sure enough, the Russia–Ukraine war will impact most stocks in the near term, but in the long run, PINE is moving on a solid growth path.

In Q4 2021, PINE reported operating cash flows of $4.14 million on which it paid $3.53 million, or 85% of the operating cash flow, as dividend. We estimate that PINE will reach an inflection point somewhere in 2022–23, after which its revenues and operating cash flows will experience phenomenal growth. We believe that PINE will reward investors substantially with dividends and price gains in the long term.

Balance Sheet	
Total Assets (Quarterly)	505.51M
Total Liabilities (Quarterly)	277.61M
Shareholders Equity (Quarterly)	196.52M
Cash and Short Term Investments (Quarterly)	8.851M
Total Long Term Assets (Quarterly)	492.21M
Total Long Term Debt (Quarterly)	267.74M
Book Value (Quarterly)	196.52M

Figure 28: PINE balance sheet (source: YCharts)

Though PINE was listed quite recently (in 2019), it has a robust balance sheet. Of its total long-term assets with a book value of $492 million, the REIT owes just $268 million in long-term debt. Likewise, we believe that its dynamic and agile management team will keep flipping low-yield properties at a profit in favor of high-yield ones that have a lot of scope for price appreciation. The future looks bright for the REIT.

Forward Dividend Yield

Dividend History			Export ⌄
Ex-Dividend Date	**Cash Amount**	**Record Date**	**Pay Date**
Sep 9, 2022	$0.275	Sep 12, 2022	Sep 30, 2022
Jun 8, 2022	$0.270	Jun 9, 2022	Jun 30, 2022
Mar 9, 2022	$0.270	Mar 10, 2022	Mar 31, 2022
Dec 8, 2021	$0.270	Dec 9, 2021	Dec 30, 2021
Sep 8, 2021	$0.255	Sep 9, 2021	Sep 30, 2021
Jun 18, 2021	$0.250	Jun 21, 2021	Jun 30, 2021
Mar 19, 2021	$0.240	Mar 22, 2021	Mar 31, 2021
Dec 14, 2020	$0.220	Dec 15, 2020	Dec 31, 2020
Sep 14, 2020	$0.200	Sep 15, 2020	Sep 30, 2020
Jun 12, 2020	$0.200	Jun 15, 2020	Jun 30, 2020
Mar 19, 2020	$0.200	Mar 20, 2020	Mar 31, 2020

Figure 29: PINE dividend distribution history (source: stockanalysis.com)

PINE paid a dividend of $1.015 in 2021 and has paid $0.815 so far through 2022. Based on its 2022 payouts and its improving business prospects, we estimate that the REIT will end up paying a minimum of $1.09 as dividend in 2022. This payout tags PINE with a forward dividend yield of 6.1% based on its market price of $17.79 as of March 4, 2022.

PINE's forward dividend yield of 6.1% is good enough to beat the core inflation rate to a large extent and generate a healthy income for long-term income investors.

Summing Up

PINE makes the cut for both long-term growth and income investors. However, since its price has remained static since its listing in 2019, we are recommending it only for income investors – though we believe that growth investors too will benefit in the long run.

To sum up, here are the reasons why PINE makes for a compelling investment:

◇ A handsome forward dividend yield of 6.1% helps investors beat the core inflation rate to a large extent.

◇ A rock-solid business model with very low risk and clarity of revenues for the next 7.8 years. Note that this clarity is for its current portfolio. The REIT adds property every year and flips low-yielding ones – therefore, as PINE grows, its average remaining lease term will keep ticking up and its revenues and operating cash flows will keep increasing.

◇ PINE has a nimble and sharp management team that stays up to speed with the available opportunities.

◇ The US economy is doing well, and there is a lot of bipartisan support in the move to boost manufacturing in America and become self-reliant. Over time, we estimate the American economy to do well, unemployment to go down, and disposable incomes to increase.

Therefore, serious long-term income investors should consider parking a part of their funds in PINE, an undervalued income generator.

Chapter 10

REIT ETFS VS INDIVIDUAL REITS

An exchange-traded fund (ETF) is a type of pooled investment security that operates much like a mutual fund. Typically, ETFs will track a particular index, sector, commodity, or other assets.

REIT ETFs track the performance of certain REIT indexes. The first REIT ETF launched was the iShares Dow Jones Real Estate Index Fund which debuted in 2000. Since then, more than 20 REIT ETFs have been created (Nareit, n.d.-a).

Should I invest in a REIT or REIT ETF?

Well, that's a tricky question. Let's look into the major factors affecting that decision.

REITs invest in various properties but within the same property sector, such as residential or office properties. REIT ETFs purchase shares in REITs spanning all the property sectors from residential, office, self-storage, and data center REITs to healthcare REITs.

REIT ETFs are, therefore, more diversified than single REITs which is a good thing if you are looking to get a broader exposure of real estate market.

Individual REITs give you exposure to the real estate industry but there's a catch. Your exposure will be focused on the industry that your

REIT deals in. On the other side, if it's a diversified ETF, you will gain exposure to the real estate industry. However, your returns will be the average of the industry – the profit from booming sectors might be eaten up by the non-performing sectors.

Expense ratio is the next big factor. Every fund, whether a mutual fund or ETF, charges fees to run the fund. These fees make up the expense ratio of the fund's operating expenses to the size of its assets.

A reasonable expense ratio for an actively managed portfolio is about **0.5% to 0.75%**. For passive or index funds, the typical ratio is about **0.2%**.

In conclusion, if you are looking for passive investment and willing to pay around 0.2-0.5% for your return, or an overall exposure in the real estate industry, then REIT ETFs are a better option for you.

Best 3 REIT ETFs

Here is my best 3 best ETF suggestion to you if you would like to consider investing in ETFs.

The Vanguard Real Estate ETF (VNQ) and the Schwab US REIT ETF (SCHH) are the 2 largest REITs. Then we have the GlobalX Super Dividend REIT ETF which pays out monthly. Let's briefly look at each of these REIT ETFs to provide an insight into what's achievable.

The Vanguard REIT ETF (VNQ)

Probably the most well-known REIT ETF, The Vanguard REIT ETF began trading in 2004. It is the largest REIT ETF with over $30 billion in Assets Under Management (AUM).

Before 2018, it tracked the MSCI US REIT Index. Then they changed to include selected specialized REITs and real estate management and development businesses. It now tracks the performance of the MSCI US Investable Market Real Estate 25/50 Index and aims to achieve a high income and moderate long-term capital growth rate.

VNQ had $41.5 billion in assets under management, 171 stocks, an expense ratio of 0.12%. Its last dividend yield stood at 2.96%. The fund has returned 21.67% and 45.97% in the previous three and five years, respectively (VettaFi, 2022c).

Its top five holdings are

◇ Vanguard Real Estate II Index Fund Institutional Plus Shares (11.61%),

◇ American Tower Corporation (7.53%)

◇ Prologis (5.63%)

◇ Crown Castle International Corp (4.70%)

◇ Equinix (3.85%)

The top ten holdings accounting for 45.93% of its assets (VettaFi, 2022c).

The Schwab US REIT ETF (SCHH)

The Schwab US REIT ETF began trading in September 2004, and like similar ETFs, it offers investor exposure to the U.S. equity REIT market. SCHH tries to mimic the performance of the Dow Jones U.S. Select REIT Index. This benchmark index caps the holding of each stock at 10% of the index size.

With an expense ratio of 0.07%, SCHH is arguably the cheapest REIT ETF. This means that the bulk of your investment would go toward buying its shares rather than covering operating costs.

Boasting an AUM of $6.28 billion, this ETF is one of the largest. Compared to VNQ, SCHH delivers a low dividend at 1.91% and weaker performances for both the 3-year and 5-year periods at 8.89% and 29.19%, respectively (VettaFi, 2022b).

As of August 14, SCHH held 138 stocks. The top five holdings of SCHH are:

◇ American Tower Corporation (9.12%)

◇ Prologis (7.03%)

◇ Crown Castle (5.56%)

◇ Equinix (4.56%)

◇ Public Storage (3.73%)

The top 10 stocks in the ETF makeup 43.74% of the fund's assets.

GlobalX Super Dividend REIT ETF (SRET)

GlobalX is one of the newer fund houses, but has carved out a position for itself with unique strategy ETFs and monthly dividend payers. If you're looking for a more consistent income stream, then SRET is a solid option.

It's significantly smaller than the first 2 ETFs we mentioned, with an AUM of just $275 million. The expense ratio is also higher at 0.58%.

However, the fund has just 28 holdings, which are concentrated in the highest yielding REITs. Therefore, it pays the highest dividend of the 3 ETFs mentioned, with a trailing 12 month yield of 9.16%.

The top five holdings of SRET are:

◇ Gaming and Leisure (5%)

◇ Getty Realty (4.62%)

◇ W.P. Carey (4.56%)

◇ Suntec (4.17%)

◇ Mapletree Pan Asia (4.16%)

If you have more time to focus on your investments, then individual REITs provide higher upside potential. However, if you're looking for a more passive approach, ETFs can provide diversification while lowering volatility.

KEY TAKEAWAYS:

◇ If you want a more passive approach to REIT investing, then REIT ETFs are a good choice

◇ The key things to note with any ETF are expense ratio and the concentration of holdings

Chapter 11

PRIVATE REITS - YAY OR NAY

What Are they?

Private REITs, sometimes called private placement REITs, are offerings that are exempt from SEC registration under Regulation D of the Securities Act of 1933 and whose shares intentionally do not trade on a national securities exchange.

For a long time, private REITs could only be sold to institutional investors, such as large pension funds, and/or to "Accredited Investors" generally defined as individuals with a net worth of at least $1 million (excluding primary residence) or with income exceeding $200,000 over two prior two years.

However, in the past decade, new private REITs with low minimum investment thresholds have gained prominence. These have exploded in popularity in the past 3-4 years through social media and influencer marketing.

The Pros of Private REITs

Although private REITs aren't for every REIT investor, they offer certain advantages, including the following:

⋄ They aren't subjected to the stock market valuations, making them immune to emotionally charged buying and selling. Additionally, private REITs calculate their share prices quarterly. As a result, their prices aren't as volatile as their counterparts.

⋄ Stronger dividend yields. On average, private REITs have historically generated 7%–8% in dividend yield, which is a percentage or two points above the average for public REITs (Frankel, 2022).

The Cons of Private REITs

The benefits listed above may have enticed you to believe that private REITs are your best option. Before making such an important decision, consider their disadvantages as potential investments.

⋄ **Lack of Transparency.**

We looked at 10-K and 10Q forms in the analysis section. No such information is publicly available for private REITs. Only investors who have invested in private REITs can get performance information from internal sources. And there is a chance that this information can be biased or manipulated.

⋄ **Lower liquidity**

When you purchase shares in a private REIT, you may have your holdings locked in for up to two years. Following that period, you may need to participate in a share redemption program, which may be limited, non-existent, or subject to change. Each company has its own rules when it comes to redemption of shares, and these can be very restrictive

Your hard-earned money will be locked in a non-performing REIT and might not be recovered.

◇ **High commissions and other fees:**

Private REITs are often sold by financial advisers or stockbrokers, which is why they tend to have high upfront fees. It's not unusual to pay between 9%–10% in sales commissions and other upfront fees before you buy the shares (Investor.gov, n.d). Adding management fees, costs for onboarding new investors, and administrative and marketing fees can push costs to 15% of your investment (Funes, 2022).

Investing in such private REITs is like making investment losses of 15% before you even begin investing. Not all private REITs have this type of commission structure, but it's worth noting that costs eat on the amount of your investment money.

◇ **Conflicts of interest and more fees:**

Many private REITs hire external managers to operate them instead of their staff. It's common for managers to be paid based on the size of AUM, which can lead to a conflict of interest. For example, the manager may acquire non-performing real estate properties to pump up AUM instead of driving shareholder value.

A note about Fundrise

Fundrise is one of the more popular private REITs, and one that has defied the conventional norms of the private REIT industry.

Investors can start with a little as $10, and management fees are a flat 0.85%.

What really impressed me though is how the fund's returns have performed in the most recent downturn. The YTD performance as of October 1st 2022 has been +5.4% compared to an average of -28.4% for US publicly traded REITs. That being said, the fund underperformed the REIT index average during 2021.

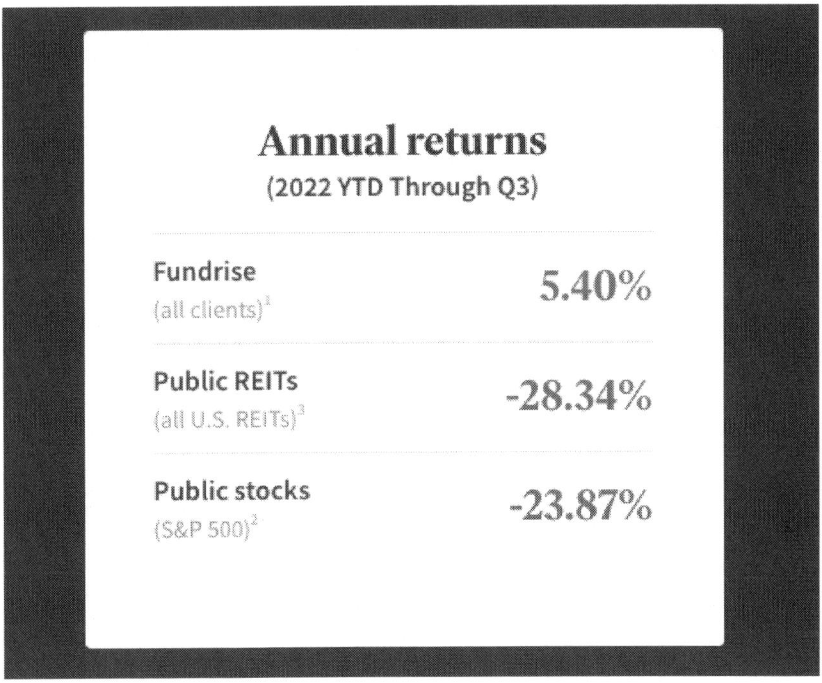

Annual returns
(2022 YTD Through Q3)

Fundrise (all clients)[1]	**5.40%**
Public REITs (all U.S. REITs)[1]	**-28.34%**
Public stocks (S&P 500)[2]	**-23.87%**

Figure 30: Fundrise annual returns (source: fundrise.com)

While Fundrise has only been around since 2016, it might be worth looking into if you're looking for downside protection for your portfolio.

KEY TAKEAWAYS:

◇ New private REITs have now allowed individual investors to access this asset class

◇ While there is data that they outperform public REITs, private REITs have lower liquidity than public REITs and may often have higher commissions

◇ Fundrise has outperformed the public REIT market this year, but underperformed public REITs in 2021

Chapter 12

HOW REIT TAXATION WORKS

Tax for regular stock investors is straightforward. The company you invest in pays corporate tax, and you pay tax on your dividends. The amount of tax paid on a dividend depends on whether it's qualified or non-qualified. Investors are taxed either 0%, 15%, or 20% if they have received qualified dividends. The tax rate for non-qualified dividends is equivalent to the income tax rate (Parys & Orem, 2022).

Taxation is different when it comes to REITs. They are exempt from paying corporate income tax if they pay at least 90% of their taxable income to shareholders. Income tax on REIT dividends is a bit complicated. It's even possible to defer dividend taxes if you know how, which you'll discover below.

REIT Taxation on Dividends

Think of REITs as a form of pass-through entity when it comes to taxes. Instead of being taxed at the corporate level, they pass on the responsibility of paying taxes to their shareholders. These shareholders might pay taxes on the dividends and capital gains they receive. It doesn't sound fair. Does it? You'll be glad to know that this is fair, but before we show you why, let's dig deeper to understand how REIT taxes on dividends work.

Taxes on REIT dividends consist of three components: ordinary income, long-term capital gains, and return of capital. Each of these distributions is subject to different tax treatment The type of distribution you receive will be listed on Form 1099-DIV, Dividends and Distributions, which you will receive annually from each public REIT in which you invest.

Taxes on Dividends as Ordinary Income

Most of the distributions REITs make to their shareholders are in the form of ordinary income. Since this sort of income isn't a qualified dividend, REIT investors get taxed at their marginal rates, also known as a tax bracket. Here's an extreme example to demonstrate the point.

If you were single and earned more than $523,600 in taxable income in 2021, your marginal rate was 37% (Internal Revenue Service, 2022a).

However, there is one advantage to this, if you qualify. The Tax Cuts and Jobs Act created a tax deduction called the qualified business income deduction, or QBI. Often referred to as the pass-through deduction, this allows taxpayers to deduct as much as 20% of their income that comes from pass-through sources. The good news is that ordinary income distributions from REITs qualify for this.

Let's look at an example to summarize what we've covered about dividends as ordinary income. Suppose that you're in the 37% marginal tax rate and you own 200 shares of DEF Realty Company, a qualified REIT. You receive a $1.95 per share dividend classed as ordinary income in 2021, meaning that your total dividend as ordinary income is $384 ($200 x $1.95 = $384).

Assuming that you qualify for the 20% QBI, you would reduce your taxable dividend as ordinary income to $307.20 ($384 x 0.20 = $76.80, $384 - $76.80 = $307.20). As a result, you'd reduce your taxes on ordinary dividends from $142.08 ($384 x 0.37 = $142.08) without QBI to $113.66 ($307.20 x 0.37) with it.

If you factor in the 20% deduction, the highest *effective* tax rate on Qualified REIT Dividends is typically 29.6%.

Taxes on Long-Term Capital Gains or Losses

The bulk of REIT dividends come as ordinary income, but often you'll receive long-term capital gains. During a given year, a REIT might sell a real estate asset it owned for at least a year and pass on the income to its shareholders. This isn't much different from owning a physical real estate property. The difference is that in a REIT, instead of owning the entire property, you are a unit holder.

Selling a real estate property owned for more than a year attracts long-term capital gains instead of short-term gains. Long-term capital gains are taxed at a lower rate than ordinary income and short-term gains. In the U.S., long-term capital gains tax rates are 0%, 15%, or 20%, based on your taxable income and filing status. For example, if filing jointly with a spouse and earning from $80,800 up to $501,600, you'd be taxed at 15% on your capital gains in 2022 (Internal Revenue Service, 2022b).

Taxes on Return of Capital

The last component of REIT distribution is called the return of capital, which is not taxable. Instead, it drops the amount you paid to purchase an asset. In this case, it would lower the capital paid for the shares you bought in a REIT. For instance, if you paid $63 for a share in each REIT and receive $1 from that REIT as a non-taxable return of capital, your cost basis drops to $62. As you can note, reducing your cost basis for buying REIT shares could result in higher capital gains when you sell them.

A non-taxable return can occur when a REIT distributes more cash than its earnings, such as when it realizes large depreciation expenses. The return of capital isn't applied in the year in which the REIT pays it but later when you liquidate your REIT holdings.

It's now time to look at whether it's fair for REIT investors to pay tax on their dividends instead of the REIT paying corporate income tax on the dividends. It's far better to illustrate this by using an example.

302

Suppose that a REIT pays out dividends categorized as follows: 70% as ordinary income, 15% as capital gains, and the remaining 15% as the return of capital. The proportions of distributions vary by REIT.

Let's take an example of a company & REIT which earns $100 pre-tax and channels 100% to its investors. Will the typical company's shareholders be better off than the REIT's investors? The table below summarizes the outcome.

Typical Corporation		REIT	
Pre-tax income	$100.00	Distributable cash	$100.00
Corporate income tax @21%	-$21.00	After-tax funds from operations	$100.00
After-tax income	$79.00	Ordinary income tax @37%	-$25.90
Qualified dividend tax @20%	-$15.80	Capital gains tax @20%	-$3.00
After-tax dividend	$63.20	Return of capital cost basis reduction @20%	-$3.00
		After-tax distribution	$68.10

Which account should you hold REITs in?

From the above example, REIT's shareholders take home more even if they pay dividend tax at the highest marginal tax rate. The primary reason for this is that REITs are not taxed at the corporate level.

There are two main varieties of IRAs – pre tax and post tax.

A traditional or simple IRA is a **tax-deferred retirement account**. Any dollars you contribute to these are not taxed immediately and will lower your taxable income for the current year. However, when you withdraw your money from a traditional IRA, it will be considered as taxable income.

On the other hand, a Roth IRA is an **after-tax retirement account**. So when you contribute money to a Roth IRA, you'll get no immediate tax deduction.

Then because you didn't get a tax break at the time of your contributions, qualified withdrawals from a Roth IRA are 100% tax-free. As of the time of writing, you must hold your money in a Roth IRA for a minimum of 5 years to meet the tax-free withdrawal requirement.

When it comes to REIT taxation, it's often preferable to hold your REITs in a Roth IRA – here's why.

In a Roth IRA, your REIT dividends won't be taxed at an individual level – and this also saves you the headache of calculating REIT taxes in tax season. Plus, because Roth IRA withdrawals are tax-free, you won't have to pay capital gains taxes either. Over time, this really adds up.

As always, you must follow account rules to avoid penalties. More importantly, please consult your tax adviser to evaluate what is best for your personal situation.

Chapter 13

EVEN A FOREIGN INVESTOR CAN INVEST IN U.S. REITS

As around 80% of our readers are from the US, this chapter may appear to be redundant. However, for our non-US readers, this chapter will answer a burning question you may have.

In the 1970s, Congress pushed for legislation to prevent non-U.S. investors from buying U.S. real estate. It became so urgent that in 1980, it passed the Foreign Investment in Real Property Act (FIRPTA) aimed at discouraging foreigners from gobbling up U.S. real estate. FIRPTA delivered desired results through a combination of barriers, especially high tax rates and inconvenient withholding requirements.

As the world changed, Congress saw the need to make changes to FIRPTA to encourage foreign investment. In 2015, it passed the Protecting Americans from Tax Hikes Act (PATH Act), leading to changes in the FIRPTA rules. In particular, the PATH Act resulted in FIRPTA allowing foreign investment through publicly traded REITs making investments much more convenient. As a result, more foreign money crossed the U.S. borders to invest in the real estate industry, meaning that a non-U.S. investor will be able to invest in public REITs.

How a Foreign Investor Can Invest in U.S. Public REITs

Public REITs, as you already know, are similar to regular stocks. Non-U.S. citizens can invest in them the same way they do regular stocks. The process for doing so might not be as easy as when investing locally or a U.S. citizen investing in U.S. stocks. The major requirement for investing in U.S. stocks is a stockbroker account that allows you to invest in U.S. stocks. Furthermore, you might have to jump a few hoops before you're allowed to invest in U.S. stocks.

These requirements shouldn't concern many foreign investors interested in generating clean money. The easiest way of ensuring you comply with all the requirements is by opening an international stockbroker account. We recommended to shopping around for a reputable international stockbroker with reasonable fees. In case you struggle to find the right broker, try international financial institutions, as some give access to the U.S. stock exchanges.

U.S. REITs Taxation for Non-U.S. Investors

When it comes to investing in U.S. REITs, the major challenge is taxes. Not only are you subject to U.S. tax laws, but also the tax laws of your country of residence. Any tax treaties between the United States and your country of residence will impact your taxes. To make it easier to prepare for investing in U.S. REITs as a foreigner, we've gathered relevant information and put it together below. It's crucial that you understand this information before investing in U.S. REITs.

*Please note: We are not legal or accounting a*visors an* the tax laws an* treaties vary from country to country. So please consult your local tax a*visor an* attorney before making REIT investment *ecisions.*

With that disclaimer out of the way, let's get to the meat of the matter. But before we look at REIT taxation for foreign investors, let's first clarify what it means to be a U.S. non-resident.

What Is a Non-U.S. Resident

U.S. tax law applies differently to U.S. citizens and non-citizens. How do you tell if you're a U.S. citizen or not for tax purposes? You take and pass one of two tests: the green card test or the substantial presence test (Internal Revenue Service, 2022d).

◇ **The green card test:** For federal tax purposes, you are considered a U.S. person if you are a lawful permanent resident of the United States during a calendar year. Someone who permanently resides in the United States by virtue of immigration laws is also a U.S. resident. Proof that you're a permanent U.S. resident is having a Permanent Resident Card, Form I-551, which is commonly called a green card. As long as you keep this status with the U.S. Citizenship and Immigration Services (USCIS), you'll stay a permanent U.S. resident.

◇ **The substantial presence test:** You can also be considered a U.S. resident if you pass the substantial presence test for a given calendar year. This test checks if you physically spend 31 days in the United States during the calendar year and you should have been physically present in the United States for 183 days during the three-year period from the current year going back two years. You must count all of the days you spent physically in the United States in the current year, one-third of the days in the previous year, and one-sixth of the days in the second year before the current one.

An example of the substantial presence test will help clarify what we mean by it. Suppose that you were present in the United States for 130 days in each of 2019, 2020, and 2021. To apply the substantial presence test, you count all the days in 2021, 43.33 (⅓ of 130 = 43.33) days in 2020, and 21.66 (⅙ of 130 = 21.66) days in 2021. Since the sum of the days in these three years is 195, you qualify as a U.S. resident for tax purposes.

If you're a non-U.S. resident then the discussion below applies to you.

How a Non-U.S. Resident Can Be Taxed If They Own U.S. REITs

Foreign companies, organizations such as trusts, and individuals, collectively called international investors, pay U.S. income tax on two types of income: Effectively Connected Income (ECI) and U.S. source income. The IRS defines ECI as income you receive from a U.S. source that generates income through trade or business (Investor.gov, 2022c). This definition applies irrespective of whether there's a direct connection between that income and the trade that takes place. For this reason, dividends and interest sourced from a U.S. company qualify as U.S. source income.

Remember, REITs pay dividends categorized as ordinary income, capital gains or return of capital. The tax rate on dividends paid by a REIT is determined by the applicable US withholding rules imposed on US corporations. Distributions made as ordinary incomes are subject to a 30% statutory withholding tax rate. If the dividend is in the form of capital gains, the withholding tax rate for individual investors is 35% (Deloitte, 2015). The aforementioned tax rates don't apply to foreign investors from countries that entered an income tax treaty with the United States.

In this case, the income tax treaty between the United States and a specific foreign country limits the amount of income tax that either country can charge permanent residents of the other country. For example, if the withholding tax rate on dividends in the United States is 30%, a UK investor may be charged a lower rate of income tax or be tax-exempt based on the two countries' agreement. The income tax treaty between the United States and selected countries helps thwart tax evasion and double taxation.

Some of the countries that the United States has income tax treaties with include Australia, China, Egypt, Canada, Germany, India, Japan, South Africa, and the UK. An income tax treaty usually overrides U.S. statutory law. In most cases, the entity paying out the dividends is responsible for withholding income tax and passing it on to the IRS on behalf of the non-U.S. resident. The REIT paying out dividends might be the withholding agent to collect the withholding tax for the IRS. Many online stockbrokers handle the necessary forms, such as form W-8BEN, on your behalf, making the process simple.

When investing in stocks, you don't only receive dividend income. There are times when you'll dispose of shares in a REIT. How do the proceeds from such a sale get taxed? Like short-term capital gains distributions, capital gains from the sale of U.S. shares don't attract tax (Villamena, 2021). Keep in mind that you'll likely pay tax in the country of your residence, meaning that you should declare it.

The sale of shares of a U.S. REIT that is foreign controlled, defined as a REIT in which non-U.S. stockholders own 50% or more, is taxed differently in the United States. In such a situation, the REIT stock is considered a U.S. real property interest (USRPI) and is subject to tax. As a result, the withholding agent must charge you a withholding tax. In contrast, if a foreign investor owned or owns a five percent or less interest in a publicly traded, foreign-controlled REIT, they don't pay tax. The same goes if a foreign investor disposes of their shares in a 50% domestically controlled REIT.

To add clarity to the withholding rules, imagine a resident of Australia earns $12,000 USD in ordinary dividends from a U.S. public REIT in the current tax year. According to the IRS, Australia and the United States have an income tax treaty that allows Australian residents to reduce the typical withholding rate from 30% to 15% (Internal Revenue Service, 2019). We'll assume that all the other requirements for the convention to apply are met.

The reduction in the withholding tax results in a dividend tax amount of $1,800 ($12,000 x 0.15 = $1,800). If the investor is from a non-treaty country, the tax amount on the dividend would be $3,600 ($12,000 x 0.30 = $3,600).

Income treaty tax rates on dividend income from U.S. companies range from 0% to 15% or higher, as provided by the Tax Code. Generally, the reduced dividend withholding tax rates are restricted in the case of dividends paid by REITs. Under some treaties, dividends from REITs to treaty-resident shareholders generally are not eligible for tax rates below 15%. To be eligible for any treaty benefits, one of three following requirements must be met (Internal Revenue Service, 2019):

◇ The beneficial owner is an individual or pension fund that owns less than 10% of the REIT.

◇ The stock of the REIT is publicly traded, and the owner holds an interest of less than 5%.

◇ A beneficial owner is a person (individual, estate, trust, or company) holding an interest of less than 10% and the REIT is diversified.

By now, we have covered the basics needed for a non-US person. Most stockbrokers who provide access to US REITs will give basic guidance from their side. Also, it's always better to get consultation from attorneys/tax consultants from your country as your country laws might vary.

Chapter 14

PORTFOLIO CONSTRUCTION WITH REITS

Conventional wisdom suggests there's a perfect investment portfolio. When you are retired or about to retire, you may be advised to invest a significant portion of your retirement savings in bonds, such as 70%, and the remainder in stocks.

Another common wisdom suggests you subtract your age from 100 to determine the makeup of stocks in your portfolio. For example, if you're 40, you'd put 60% of your money into stocks. The goal of this portfolio is to minimize risk while maximizing returns.

This begs important questions: Are all 40-year-olds or people about to retire the same? What if a person is retiring or about to retire without sufficient savings? Will a portfolio structured this way help them meet their financial goals? The answers to these questions instantly make us realize that no investment portfolio fits everyone. An investment portfolio is constructed to suit the needs of an individual.

The financial world has changed significantly since many of these asset allocation strategies came into vogue. For example, newer assets are now available, including cryptocurrency. Additionally, the economy has become global rather than localized, which means businesses' risk profiles are different.

With all that said, how do you construct an investment portfolio that suits your needs? What assets do you include in it and why? Most importantly, what's your investment goal?

Do This Before Constructing an Investment Portfolio

Your portfolio should outperform the market as a whole, limit risk, and withstand the storm of high inflation. The portfolio should appreciate over time while generating dividend or interest income. The typical assets to include in your portfolio are regular stocks, bonds, investment funds like ETFs, REITs, and cash equivalents. Which of these assets should you include, and in what proportions?

The first step is to determine your reason for investing. Reasons for investing vary, but for many people, retirement and perhaps college education for children might be their goals. In the final analysis, you want to determine if income generation or capital appreciation is more important. This step is crucial because it informs the next one.

The second step before even thinking about asset allocation is to establish the level of risk, you're comfortable with. Your biggest risk is to lose capital, which automatically kills off any chance of reaching your financial goals. It's great to have a large investment portfolio, but it can be devastating if you lose it all in a matter of days, as Bill Hwang of the defunct Archegos Capital Management did. Hwang had built his net worth to around $20 billion and lost all of it in just two days (Schatzker *et al.*, 2021). The main reason for Hwang's downfall was using leverage to make money, which is why you're not going to borrow money to invest. Furthermore, we build a portfolio using assets we understand, and no asset class makes up 100% of our portfolio.

Once you've worked out the level of risk you can stomach, it's time to decide on the assets to include in your portfolio. Whatever portfolio you have, stocks will play a big part in its performance. The reason is that stocks, as measured by the S&P 500, have returned 14.83% from 2012 to 2021. For a 30-year-period from 1992 to 2021, the S&P generated annualized returns of 9.89% (Lake, 2021). For our desired time frame of 10 years, stocks deliver far better returns than over a 30-year investment horizon. When compared to the performance of bonds, bond yields, as measured by the long-term government bond, have barely reached 5% since August 2001. (Organization for Economic Co-operation and Development, 2022).

The next thing to consider is having a mix of investment accounts. For example, you could have tax-advantaged retirement accounts like the 401(k) or IRA and a taxable brokerage account. The benefit of having a taxable brokerage account is that you can withdraw your money early without incurring a penalty. This combination of tax-advantaged and taxable brokerage accounts helps save taxes now and when you retire or reach your long-term goal.

Contribution of REITs to Your Portfolio

REITs are a special breed of dividend stocks and we should treat them like dividend stocks for portfolio construction purposes. The goal of income producing stocks is to allow you to live of the dividends/distributions without necessarily needing to touch your principle. However there comes a trade-off between income and potential capital upside if dividends are not being reinvested.

Therefore when constructing a portfolio, you'll need to factor in your investment goals and your tolerance for both volatility and risk. We should note at this time that volatility and risk are not the same thing. In fact, when most investors say they are looking to decrease risk, what they actually mean is they would like decrease volatility in their portfolio. In investing, we can measure risk using Beta – which benchmarks how volatile an investment against the S&P 500. For example, the REIT focused VNQ ETF has a beta of 1.04 (around the same volatility as the S&P 500), whereas a growth focused ETF like ARKK has a beta of 1.56.

Now that we've covered your goals, we'll look at two sample portfolio construction strategies based on your situation and risk profile.

1. For an investor close to retirement or currently retired

This portfolio suits you if you're close to retirement or already retired and want more income more than capital appreciation. Therefore we have roughly 45% of the portfolio in income producing stocks like REITs. We also have an additional 25% in bonds in the form of government bonds and TIPS. Then the remaining 30% is more upside and non-correlation focused with smaller cap positions and alternative assets. With a 70/30 split towards income focus – this should provide steady cash flow while minimizing volatility. The reason that we still suggest owning some capital gains focused positions is that potential for outsized reward vs. risk. A single smaller cap position (note: this generally refers to stocks with a market cap of $500m-$10bn, we aren't talking about penny stocks with zero revenue) that has the potential to grow at 20% per year can lead to significant outperformance.

Here's a summary of the makeup of an income-focused portfolio:

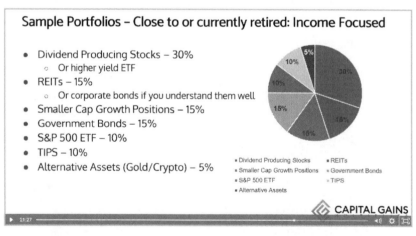

Figure 31: Sample retirement portfolio (source: Freeman Publications)

2. For an investor at least 20 years away from retirement

If you're in your 20s and 30s, immediate income isn't necessary as you should be receiving a steady income from a job or business that you own. Therefore the aim of your portfolio can be to grow your investments over a longer time period. That's why you notice that dividend stocks and REITs make up only five percent of the portfolio. Small-cap growth positions shoot up to 45%. The reason is that a long-term-focused investor can have a higher tolerance for volatility to stomach the ups and downs of the market and still recover.

Here are the contributions of all the positions in this type of portfolio:

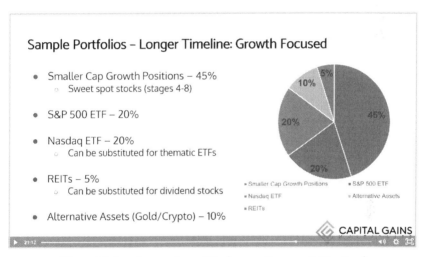

Figure 32: Sample growth portfolio (source: Freeman Publications)

The portfolios presented above belong to two extremes: income-focused on one hand and growth-focused on the other. If your risk profile is different, feel free to adjust these portfolios to suit your needs and risk profile. Portfolio construction is always a personal preference.

KEY TAKEAWAYS:

◇ Portfolio construction should be first and foremost based on your individual needs

◇ Volatility and risk are not the same thing. Most investors are more concerned with volatility

◇ The closer you are to retirement, the more it makes sense to focus on income from your portfolio

CONCLUSION

If you're looking for income from your investments, then REITs are a fantastic addition to your portfolio.

By concentrating on stability, dividend growth and avoiding yield chasing, you'll avoid most of the REIT investing traps out there. In 2022, the decline in stock prices has created many dividend and yield traps, so watch out for these stocks. Don't automatically assume a high yield is a good thing. Remember to stay focused on minimizing risk as much as possible, and this won't be an issue for you.

Remember that capital gains are just as crucial as dividends are. Without steady capital gains, you'll end up losing your investment principal, and your dividend income will inevitably decline because of it, if the company slashes its payouts.

What truly matters is a REIT's payout ratio (using FFO payout ratio) and a history of growing dividend payments. But as long as the dividend payment is growing and the payout ratio remains stable, you'll end up earning more income as time goes by.

This is the essence of income investing, and it's what you should aim for. Don't chase monthly dividend payments for their own sake. A monthly payment that yields five percent is no different from a semi-yearly payment that yields the same amount.

Feel free to use our recommended stocks such as OPI, IIPR and CTRE as a starting point for more research or as parts of your portfolio. For further research, we recommend examining the latest 10-K reports from each company, as well as checking key financial metrics using our Company Valuation 101 criteria, which you can access for free at https://freemanpublications.com/bonus

Investing for income is critical as you grow older, but it doesn't have to be complicated. Make it a point to refer to this book whenever you have any doubts.

Alternatively, you can email us at admin@freemanpublications.com if you would like something clarified. We answer every single reader's email.

2022 was a chaotic year, so as we move into 2023, we wish you the best of luck with your investing!

One final word from us. If this book has helped you in any way, we'd appreciate it if you left a review on Amazon.

Reviews are the lifeblood of our business. We read every single one and incorporate your feedback into our future book projects.

To leave an Amazon review, go to https://freemanpublications.com/leaveareview

OTHER BOOKS BY
FREEMAN PUBLICATIONS
(AVAILABLE ON AMAZON & AUDIBLE)

 The 8-Step Beginner's Guide to Value Investing: Featuring 20 for 20 - The 20 Best Stocks & ETFs to Buy and Hold for The Next 20 Years

 Bear Market Investing Strategies: 37 Recession-Proof Ideas to Grow Your Wealth - Including Inverse ETFs, Put Options, Gold & Cryptocurrency

 Iron Condor Options for Beginners: A Smart, Safe Method to Generate an Extra 25% Per Year with Just 2 Trades Per Month

 Covered Calls for Beginners: A Risk-Free Way to Collect "Rental Income" Every Single Month on Stocks You Already Own

 Credit Spread Options for Beginners: Turn Your Most Boring Stocks into Reliable Monthly Paychecks using Call, Put & Iron Butterfly Spreads - Even If The Market is Doing Nothing

*"The most successful people in life are the ones who ask questions.
They're always learning. They're always growing.
They're always pushing."*

Robert Kiyosaki

CONTINUING YOUR JOURNEY

Like Robert Kiyosaki said on the previous page, "The most successful people in life are always learning, growing, and asking questions."

Which is why we created our investing community, aptly named *How To NOT Lose Money in the Stock Market,* so that like-minded individuals could get together to share ideas and learn from each other.

We regularly run giveaways, share wins from our readers, and you'll be the first to know when our new books are released.

It's 100% free, and there are no requirements to join, except for the willingness to learn.

You can join us by going to

http://freemanpublications.com/community

ACKNOWLEDGMENTS

This book is a team effort, and while I get to be the face of the business and receive all the kind messages from readers, I can't ignore the people who helped make this book what it was.

Thank you first to our content team for their writing, editing, and proofreading efforts and dealing with my persistent questions about why specific changes needed to be made.

Thank you to Mark Greenberg, our superstar narrator, who has really become "the voice" of Freeman Publications over the past year.

Thank you to Ed Fahy over at UBF for always being there every time I needed to make a minor update to the book interior.

Thank you to all 52 Freeman readers who participated in our advanced reader program for this book. Your notes and feedback were invaluable in going from the final draft to the finished product. I'd particularly like to highlight the efforts of Jakub Wierzba, Stevie Christie and Yacoob Kathrada.

A special mention must go to David Buck for his incredibly detailed feedback ranging from things we didn't clarify well enough to points we outright missed. Without your input, this book simply would not have been as good as it is today, so for that David, I thank you.

Thank you to everyone who picked up the phone when I called to ask if they were free for 5 minutes, only to spend an hour discussing the merits of one company versus another. You know who you are.

Thank you to our hundreds of readers on social media for your words of encouragement throughout this project.

Finally, thank you to my family, whose initial uncertainty of "are you still doing that book thing" has blossomed into full support for my vision here at Freeman Publications. This means more than you will ever know.

Oliver

London, England

January, 2021

REFERENCES

AAA Gas Prices. (2022). *National average gas prices.* AAA Gas Prices. https://gasprices.aaa.com/

Alpert, G. (2020, September 11). *Government stimulus efforts to fight the COVID-19 crisis.* Investopedia. https://www.investopedia.com/government-stimulus-efforts-to-fight-the-covid-19-crisis-4799723

Bengen, W. (1994). *Determining withdrawal rates using historical data* (pp. 171–180). Journal of Financial Planning.

Bove, T. (2022, June 11). *Used and new car prices are surging again, and it's bad news for inflation.* Fortune. https://fortune.com/2022/06/11/used-cars-new-prices-inflation-market/

Cox, J. (2021, July 19). *It's official: The Covid recession lasted just two months, the shortest in U.S. history.* CNBC. https://www.cnbc.com/2021/07/19/its-official-the-covid-recession-lasted-just-two-months-the-shortest-in-us-history.html

Federal Reserve. (2022, March 16). *Federal Reserve issues FOMC statement.* Federal Reserve. https://www.federalreserve.gov/newsevents/pressreleases/monetary20220316a.htm

Finch, P. (2018, November 29). *The myth of steady retirement spending, and why reality may cost less.* The New York Times. https://s3.amazonaws.com/static.contentres.com/media/documents/394af83f-a65a-48ca-9e7e-23a3c471045e.pdf

FTSE Russell. (2016). *Insights Understanding the benefits of REITs in the US market The FTSE NAREIT US Real Estate Index Series What are REITs?* FTSE Russell. https://content.ftserussell.com/sites/default/files/research/understanding_the_benefits_of_reits_final.pdf

Green, J. M. (2021, October 24). *How do stock and bond performance compare over time?* The Balance. https://www.thebalance.com/stocks-vs-bonds-the-long-term-performance-data-416861

Mutikani, L. (2022, June 10). U.S. annual inflation posts largest gain in nearly 41 years as food, gasoline prices soar. *Reuters.* https://www.reuters.com/article/usa-economy-inflation-cpi-idCAKBN2NR0ZS

Navin, J. (2022, June 16). *5 REITs with massive dividend yields.* Yahoo! Finance. https://finance.yahoo.com/news/5-reits-massive-dividend-yields-155532745.html

Paraskova, T. (2022, July 5). *Are U.S. gasoline refiners running out of steam?* OilPrice.com. https://oilprice.com/Energy/Crude-Oil/Are-US-Gasoline-Refiners-Running-Out-Of-Steam.html

Reuters. (2022, May 13). Why are food prices going up? Key questions answered. *Reuters.* https://www.reuters.com/business/retail-consumer/why-are-food-prices-going-up-key-questions-answered-2022-05-10/

Subin, S., & Imbert, F. (2022, June 12). *S&P 500 tumbles nearly 4% to new low for the year, closes in bear market territory.* CNBC. https://www.cnbc.com/2022/06/12/stock-market-news-open-to-close.html

U.S. Bureau of Labor Statistics. (2022). *Consumer Price Index - May 2022.* U.S. Bureau of Labor Statistics. https://www.bls.gov/news.release/pdf/cpi.pdf

Yahoo! Finance. (n.d.). *Amazon.com, Inc. (AMZN).* Yahoo! Finance. https://finance.yahoo.com/quote/AMZN/

Adams, J. (2021, December 16). *How do REITs make money?* Realized. https://www.realized1031.com/blog/how-do-reits-make-money

Askola, J. (2020, May 30). *The dark side of REITs: Challenged sectors, overleveraged and conflicted management.* Seeking Alpha. https://seekingalpha.com/article/4349591-dark-side-of-reits-challenged-sectors-overleveraged-and-conflicted-management

Ciura, B. (2022, April 18). *10 Super high dividend REITs with yields up to 17.6%*. Sure Dividend. https://www.suredividend.com/high-dividend-reits/

Coltongardner. (2022, August 15). Self Storage Industry Statistics (2022). Neighbor Blog. Retrieved October 21, 2022, from https://www.neighbor.com/storage-blog/self-storage- industry-statistics/

Deloitte. (2015, July). *Introduction to the taxation of foreign investment in US real estate*. Deloitte. https://www2.deloitte.com/content/dam/Deloitte/us/Documents/Tax/us-tax-introduction-to-the-taxation-of-foreign-investment-in-us-real-estate.pdf

FNRP Editor. (2022, January 10). *10 Commercial real estate investing statistics*. First National Realty Partners. https://fnrpusa.com/blog/commercial-investing-statistics/

Fortune Business Insights. (2022, January). *U.S. pharmacy market size*. Fortune Business Insights. https://www.fortunebusinessinsights.com/u-s-pharmacy-market-106306

Frankel, M. (2022, June 10). *A beginner's guide to private REITs*. The Motley Fool. https://www.fool.com/investing/stock-market/market-sectors/real-estate-investing/reit/private-reits/

Funes, D. (2022, February 4). *Private REIT fee structure: What You Need to Know*. Realized. https://www.realized1031.com/blog/private-reit-fee-structure-what-you-need-to-know

Guggenheim Investments. (n.d.). *Asset class correlation map*. Guggenheim Investments. https://www.guggenheiminvestments.com/mutual-funds/resources/interactive-tools/asset-class-correlation-map

GuruFocus.com. (2020, February 6). *Warren Buffett explains his moat principle*. Yahoo! Finance. https://finance.yahoo.com/news/warren-buffett-explains-moat-principle-164442359.html

Innovative Industrial Properties. (2022). *Form 10-K: Innovative Industrial Properties*. Innovative Industrial Properties. https://

otp.tools.investis.com/clients/us/iip_inc/SEC/sec-show. aspx?FilingId=15599639&Cik=0001677576&Type=PDF&hasPdf=1

Internal Revenue Service. (2019, February). *Table 1. Tax rates on income other than personal service income uner Chapter 3, Internal Revenue Coe, an Income Tax Treaties (Rev. Feb 2019)*. Internal Revenue Service. https://www.irs.gov/pub/irs-utl/Tax_Treaty_Table_1_2019_Feb.pdf

Internal Revenue Service. (2022a, March 28). *IRS provies tax inflation ajustments for tax year 2021*. Internal Revenue Service. https://www. irs.gov/newsroom/irs-provides-tax-inflation-adjustments-for-tax-year-2021

Internal Revenue Service. (2022b, May 19). *Topic No. 409 capital gains an losses*. Internal Revenue Service. https://www.irs.gov/taxtopics/ tc409

Internal Revenue Service. (2022c, July 27). *Effectively connecte income (ECI)*. Internal Revenue Service. https://www.irs.gov/individuals/ international-taxpayers/effectively-connected-income-eci

Internal Revenue Service. (2022d, August 3). *Determining an iniviual's tax resiency status*. Internal Revenue Service. https://www.irs.gov/ individuals/international-taxpayers/determining-an-individuals-tax-residency-status

Investor.gov. (n.d.). *Real estate investment trusts (REITs)*. Investor.gov. https://www.investor.gov/introduction-investing/investing-basics/ investment-products/real-estate-investment-trusts-reits

Lake, R. (2021, October 11). *What is the average stock market return?* SoFi. https://www.sofi.com/learn/content/average-stock-market-return/

MarketBeat. (n.d.). *High ivien REITs*. MarketBeat. https://www. marketbeat.com/dividends/high-dividend-reits/

Mordor Intelligence. (n.d.). *Unite States self-storage market - Growth, trens, COVID-19 impact, an forecast (2022 - 2027)*. Mordor Intelligence.

https://www.mordorintelligence.com/industry-reports/united-states-self-storage-market

Nareit. (n.d.-a). *Exchange-traᵗeᵗ funᵗs*. Nareit. https://www.reit.com/investing/investing-reits/list-reit-funds/exchange-traded-funds

Nareit. (n.d.-b). *Guiᵗe to equity REITs*. Nareit. https://www.reit.com/what-reit/types-reits/guide-equity-reits

Nareit. (n.d.-c). *Guiᵗe to private REIT investing*. Www.reit.com. https://www.reit.com/what-reit/types-reits/guide-private-reits

Nareit. (n.d.-d). *What's a REIT (Real Estate Investment Trust)?* Nareit. https://www.reit.com/what-reit

National Health Investors. (2022, February 22). *Form 10-K: National Health Investors*. National Health Investors. https://d18rn0p25nwr6d.cloudfront.net/CIK-0000877860/145cf542-18d8-4651-8733-dfd368e1742d.html

Organization for Economic Co-operation and Development. (2022, August 14). *Long-term government bonᵗ yielᵗs-10-year: Main (incluᵗing benchmark) for the Uniteᵗ States*. Federal Reserve Bank of St. Louis. https://fred.stlouisfed.org/series/IRLTLT01USM156N

Parys, S., & Orem, T. (2022, June 13). *Diviᵗenᵗ tax rate 2021-2022: Finᵗ out what you'll owe*. NerdWallet. https://www.nerdwallet.com/article/taxes/dividend-tax-rate

Reinberg, B. (n.d.). *Why this is the best time to invest in healthcare REITS*. Alliance Group Companies. https://alliancecgc.com/education/time-to-invest-in-healthcare-reits/

Research and Markets. (2021, December). *Construction in the Uniteᵗ States of America (USA) - Key trenᵗs anᵗ opportunities to 2025 (Q4 2021)*. Research and Markets. https://www.researchandmarkets.com/reports/5546599/construction-in-the-united-states-of-america

Schatzker, E., Natarajan, S., & Katherine, B. (2021, April 8). Bill Hwang had $20 Billion, then lost it all in two days. *Bloomberg*. https://www.

bloomberg.com/news/features/2021-04-08/how-bill-hwang-of-archegos-capital-lost-20-billion-in-two-days

Simply Wall St. (n.d.-a). *Brandywine Realty Trust.* Simply Wall St. https://simplywall.st/stocks/us/real-estate/nyse-bdn/brandywine-realty-trust#about

Simply Wall St. (n.d.-b). *National Health Investors stock report.* Simply Wall St. https://simplywall.st/stocks/us/real-estate/nyse-nhi/national-health-investors#past

Statista Research Department. (2022a, April 1). *Value of U.S. commercial construction put in place from 2002 to 2021(in billion U.S. dollars).* Statista. https://www.statista.com/statistics/245029/value-of-us-commercial-construction

Statista Research Department. (2022b, July 27). *Retail e-commerce revenue in the United States from 2017 to 2025(in billion U.S. dollars).* Statista. https://www.statista.com/statistics/272391/us-retail-e-commerce-sales-forecast/

Steiner, K. (2020, June 24). *Historical returns of corporate bonds.* Mindfully Investing. https://www.mindfullyinvesting.com/historical-returns-of-corporate-bonds/

U.S. Bureau of Labor Statistics. (2022, October 13). *Consumer price index summary - 2022 M09 results.* U.S. Bureau of Labor Statistics. Retrieved October 15, 2022, from https://www.bls.gov/news.release/cpi.nr0.htm

Vandenboss, K. (2022, June 10). *3 High-dividend REITs to buy now.* The Motley Fool. https://www.fool.com/investing/stock-market/market-sectors/real-estate-investing/reit/high-dividend-reits/

VettaFi. (2022a, August 12). *Real Estate Select Sector SPDR Fund.* VettaFi. https://etfdb.com/etf/XLRE/#etf-ticker-profile

VettaFi. (2022b, August 12). *Schwab US REIT ETF.* ETF Database. https://etfdb.com/etf/SCHH/#holdings

VettaFi. (2022c, August 12). *Vanguard Real Estate ETF*. VettaFi. https://etfdb.com/etf/VNQ/#performance

Villamena, V. (2021, March 1). *Foreign investment in the U.S. – Great opportunities but with U.S. tax implications.* Online Taxman. https://onlinetaxman.com/foreign-investment-in-us-tax/

Wang, L. (2011, August). *Timber REITs and taxation: A briefing of key issues.* USDA Forest Service. https://www.fs.fed.us/spf/coop/library/timber_reits_briefing.pdf

Yahoo! Finance. (n.d.-a). *Brandywine Realty Trust interactive stock chart.* Yahoo! Finance. https://finance.yahoo.com/quote/BDN/chart

Yahoo! Finance. (n.d.-b). *National Health Investors interactive stock chart.* Yahoo! Finance. https://finance.yahoo.com/quote/NHI/chart

Yosifova, A. (2022, May 24). *What percentage of American households make over $200k a year?* (D. Pilkova, Ed.). Web Tribunal. https://webtribunal.net/blog/american-households-that-make-over-200k/#gref

Made in the USA
Las Vegas, NV
04 October 2024